IMMIGRATION AND INTEGRATION IN POST-INDUSTRIAL SOCIETIES

MIGRATION, MINORITIES AND CITIZENSHIP

General Editors: Zig Layton-Henry, *Professor of Politics and Head of the Centre for Research in Ethnic Relations, University of Warwick*; and Danièle Joly, *Lecturer in Politics, Centre for Research in Ethnic Relations, University of Warwick*

This series has been developed to promote books on a wide range of topics concerned with migration and settlement, immigration policy, refugees, the integration and engagement of minorities, dimensions of social exclusion, racism and xenophobia, ethnic mobilisation, ethnicity and nationalism. The focus of the series is multidisciplinary and international. The series will publish both theoretical and empirical works based on original research. Priority will be given to single-authored books but edited books of high quality will be considered.

Titles include:

Naomi Carmon (*editor*)
IMMIGRATION AND INTEGRATION IN POST-INDUSTRIAL SOCIETIES
Theoretical Analysis and Policy-Related Research

Danièle Joly
HAVEN OR HELL?
Asylum Policies and Refugees in Europe

John Rex
ETHNIC MINORITIES IN THE MODERN NATION STATE
Working Papers in the Theory of Multiculturalism and Political Integration

Immigration and Integration in Post-Industrial Societies

Theoretical Analysis and Policy-Related Research

Edited by

Naomi Carmon
Division of Urban and Regional Planning
Faculty of Architecture and Town Planning
Technion-Israel Institute of Technology
Haifa, Israel

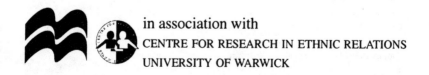

in association with
CENTRE FOR RESEARCH IN ETHNIC RELATIONS
UNIVERSITY OF WARWICK

First published in Great Britain 1996 by
MACMILLAN PRESS LTD
Houndmills, Basingstoke, Hampshire RG21 6XS
and London
Companies and representatives
throughout the world

A catalogue record for this book is available
from the British Library.

ISBN 0–333–65113–8 hardcover
ISBN 0–333–65114–6 paperback

 First published in the United States of America 1996 by
ST. MARTIN'S PRESS, INC.,
Scholarly and Reference Division,
175 Fifth Avenue,
New York, N.Y. 10010

ISBN 0–312–15962–5

Library of Congress Cataloging-in-Publication Data
Immigration and integration in post-industrial societies : theoretical
analysis and policy-related research / edited by Naomi Carmon.
  p. cm.
Includes bibliographical references and index.
ISBN 0–312–15962–5
1. Assimilation (Sociology)—Congresses. 2. Emigration and
immigration—Psychological aspects—Congresses. I. Carmon, Naomi.
JV6342.I47 1996
303.48'2—dc20   96–7686
                                                                               CIP

Editorial matter and selection © Naomi Carmon 1996
Text © Macmillan Press Ltd 1996

All rights reserved. No reproduction, copy or transmission of
this publication may be made without written permission.

No paragraph of this publication may be reproduced, copied or
transmitted save with written permission or in accordance with
the provisions of the Copyright, Designs and Patents Act 1988,
or under the terms of any licence permitting limited copying
issued by the Copyright Licensing Agency, 90 Tottenham Court
Road, London W1P 9HE.

Any person who does any unauthorised act in relation to this
publication may be liable to criminal prosecution and civil
claims for damages.

10 9 8 7 6 5 4 3 2 1
05 04 03 02 01 00 99 98 97 96

Printed and bound in Great Britain by
Antony Rowe Ltd, Chippenham, Wiltshire

To my parents

who immigrated and integrated

and to my eldest son

who is considering migration and integration

Contents

Acknowledgements   ix
Notes on the Contributors   xi

    Introduction   1
    Naomi Carmon

PART I   IMMIGRATION AND INTEGRATION IN A CHANGING WORLD

1   Immigration and Integration in Post-Industrial Societies: Quantitative and Qualitative Analyses   13
    Naomi Carmon

2   Of Walls and Immigrant Enclaves   30
    Peter Marcuse

3   Determinants of Immigrant Integration: An International Comparative Analysis   46
    Myron Weiner

PART II   NEW IMMIGRANTS IN NEW CIRCUMSTANCES: USA EXPERIENCE

4   Second-Generation Decline: Scenarios for the Economic and Ethnic Futures of the Post-1965 American Immigrants   65
    Herbert J. Gans

5   Immigration and Integration: Lessons from Southern California   86
    William A.V. Clark

PART III   COPING WITH MASS IMMIGRATION OF EDUCATED PEOPLE: THE ISRAELI EXPERIENCE

6   Short-run Absorption of the Ex-USSR Immigrants in Israel's Labor Market   107
    Karnit Flug and Nitsa Kasir (Kaliner)

7   Social Values and Health Policy:
    Immigrant Physicians in the Israeli Health-Care System   127
    Judith T. Shuval and Judith Bernstein

8   Urban Restructuring and the Absorption of Immigrants:
    A Case Study in Tel-Aviv   144
    Gila Menahem

9   From International Immigration to Internal Migration:
    The Settlement Process of Immigrants
    from the Former Soviet Union in Israel   166
    Shlomo Hasson

PART IV   IMMIGRANT INTEGRATION:
          USA, AUSTRALIA, BRITAIN AND FRANCE

10 Earlier Immigration to the United States:
    Historical Clues for Current Issues of Integration   187
    Stanley Lieberson

11 Immigration and Settlement in Australia:
    An Overview and Critique of Multiculturalism   206
    Laksiri Jayasuriya

12 The Theory and Practice of Immigration
    and 'Race-Relations' Policy:
    Some Thoughts on British and French Experience   227
    John Crowley

Index   249

Acknowledgements

The chapters in this volume are the work of individual authors, but the sum total is the product of extensive collaboration. The project was conceived at the Center for Urban and Regional Studies at the Technion – Israel Institute of Technology in Haifa, following the public and academic debates regarding the large wave of immigrants from the former USSR to Israel in the early 1990s. International experts were invited to submit their contributions and to discuss them face to face. A group of Israelis and some 30 highly experienced analysts of migration processes from universities in the US, the UK, France, the Netherlands and Australia participated in the project. Most of them came to the workshop in Haifa and enjoyed its pleasant and highly fruitful three days of discussions. Resubmission on the basis of what was learnt in the workshop and a formal process of anonymous peer review followed. The essays that survived all these stages are presented in this collection. I deeply thank the many colleagues who took part in the review process.

The workshop and this volume have been made possible by the generous support of the following institutions and persons: the *Estate of Ladislas and Vilma Segoe,* whose managers kindly provided the majority of the funds for the workshop; the *American Technion Society,* and especially Mr Melvin Bloom and Mr Stanley J. Abrams, whose support enabled us to initiate the project; the *Ministry of Science and Technology* of Israel and the *Cultural Center of the American Embassy in Israel,* which provided a necessary additional support.

The *S. Neaman Institute for Advanced Studies in Science and Technology* at the Technion, its director, Professor Daniel Weihs, and its administrative assistant, Ms Ruth Rivkind, gave us vital and efficient assistance, especially in the stages that followed the workshop, and are completed by the publication of this book. The *Klutznick Center for Urban and Regional Studies* at the Faculty of Architecture and Town Planning at the Technion served as the home-base of this enterprise; its coordinator – Mr Amnon Frenkel, its secretary, Ms Nurit Krengel, and the workshop secretary – Ms Tamar Eres, took care of the many administrative details. My deep thanks go to all of them. Professor William A.V. Clark from UCLA deserves special appreciation for his involvement in the first stage of completing this book.

Acknowledgements

The authors have my special gratitude for the diligence and good grace with which they responded to my many requests.

Mt Carmel, Haifa, Israel   NAOMI CARMON

Notes on the Contributors

Judith Bernstein was born in the United States and immigrated to Israel in 1971. She studied at Elmira College (BA) University of California at Los Angeles (MA) and Cornell University (PhD). She was founding member of the Sociology of Health Unit in the Medical School of the Ben-Gurion University of the Negev in Beer Sheva. Since 1990, she has been dividing her time between Beer Sheva and Jerusalem, where she is a lecturer in the Programme in the Sociology of Health at the School of Public Health, Hebrew University. She is the author of 'The Integration of Ethnic Groups in Israel', *Jewish Journal of Sociology*, 23, 1981, and a series of publications based on a longitudinal study of medical school stressors.

Naomi Carmon heads the Graduate Program of Urban and Regional Planning at the Faculty of Architecture and Town Planning, Technion – Israel Institute of Technology. She is a sociologist and urban planner who gained her degrees from the Hebrew University of Jerusalem, the Technion in Haifa and MIT, Cambridge MA. Dr Carmon has taught, served as consultant and directed research in Israel and the US. She has written extensively on social aspects of urban planning, on planning and evaluation of social policy and programs, issues of migration and integration, housing and neighborhood regeneration. Her former book is *Neighborhood Policy and Programs – Past and Present* (editor), Macmillan and St Martin's Press, 1990.

William A.V. Clark is Professor of Geography at UCLA where he has taught since 1970. He was born in New Zealand and graduated with BA and MA degrees in Geography from the University of New Zealand. He completed a PhD in Geography at the University of Illinois. In 1992 he received an Honorary Doctorate from the University of Utrecht in part for his research on population migration and housing choice. He has taught in New Zealand and The Netherlands and is currently a Fellow at the Netherlands Institute for Advanced Studies in the Humanities and Social Sciences. He is author or coeditor of *Residential Mobility and Public Policy; Human Migration: An Introduction to Population Movement;* and *Modelling Housing Market Research.*

John Crowley was born in the UK but has been a resident in France for over fifteen years. Dr Crowley is a Research Fellow at the Centre d'Etudes et des Recherches Internationales of the Fondation Nationale des Sciences Politiques, Paris, France, and lectures in Politics at the Institute d'Etudes Politiques de Paris and at the University of Paris-Dauphine. His research currently focuses on the theoretical implications of democracy in complex societies, with particular reference to the issues deriving from immigration and minority status. Recent publications include 'Paradoxes in the politicization of race: A comparison of the UK and France', *New Community*, 19(4), 1993; 'Integration in theory and practice: a comparison of France and Britain', *West European Politics*, 17(2), 1994 (with Patrick Weil); 'Social complexity and strong democracy', *Innovation – European Journal of the Social Sciences*, 7(3), 1994.

Karnit Flug is senior economist at the Bank of Israel Research Department. She acquired her PhD degree at Columbia University. She was previously an economist with the International Monetary Fund. Her fields of interest include labor economics, stabilization policies, international trade and the Israeli economy. Her publications include: 'Immigrant absorption in the labor market' (with N. Kasir), *Economic Quarterly*, 1993; 'Labor costs in Israeli industry' (with N. Kasir), *Bank of Israel Review*, 1992; 'The absorption of Soviet immigrants into the labor market from 1990 and onwards: aspects of occupational substitution and retention' (with N. Kasir and G. Ofer), *Economic Quarterly* (Hebrew), 1991; 'Minimum wage in a general equilibrium model of international trade and human capital' (with O. Galor), *International Economics Review*, 1986.

Herbert J. Gans is the Robert S. Lynd Professor of Sociology at Columbia University and a former President of the American Sociological Association. He immigrated to the US at the age of 13. He received his MA in social science from the University of Chicago and his PhD in city planning from the University of Pennsylvania. His fields of interests include issues of equality, poverty and antipoverty policy, social planning and social policy, urban studies, ethnicity, the news media, mass media and popular culture. His most recent books include *Middle American Individualism*, 1991; *People, Plans and Policies*, 1991; and *The War Against the Poor*, 1995.

Shlomo Hasson is Associate Professor and former chairman of the Department of Geography at the Hebrew University of Jerusalem. He is a senior researcher at the Jerusalem Institute for Israel Studies and editor of the Hebrew scientific and professional journal *Ir veEzor (City and Region)*. Among his recent publications are: *Neighborhood Self Administration in Jerusalem: A New Experiment in Urban Politics*, 1989 (Hebrew), *Public Housing in Israel – Immigrant Absorption and Territorial Control* (accepted for publication), and *Urban Social Movements in Jerusalem* (1993).

Laksiri Jayasuriya is Emeritus Professor of the University of Western Australia, Perth, and has held appointments in Sri Lanka, Australia, England and the United States. He obtained his first-class BA (Hons) degree from the University of Sydney, and his PhD from the London School of Economics and Political Science (LSE), University of London in 1959. He has recently taken early retirement from the University of Western Australia (UWA), where he held the Foundation Chair of Social Work and Social Administration. He was also the Director of the Center for Asian Studies at the University of Western Australia. Professor Jayasuriya is a Fellow of the British Psychological Association and also a member of several academic and professional bodies in Australia and overseas. He has held a variety of public appointments in Australia and Sri Lanka where he was Dean of Social Sciences before coming to Australia in 1971.

Nitsa Kasir (Kaliner) is an economist in the Bank of Israel Research Department. She received her degrees from the Hebrew University of Jerusalem. Her fields of interest are labor economics, industry and the Israeli economics. Her publications include 'The absorption of Soviet immigrants into the labor market from 1990 and onwards: aspects of occupational substitution and retention' (with K. Flug and G. Ofer), *Economic Quarterly* (Hebrew), 1991; 'Labor costs in Israeli industry' (with K. Flug), *Bank of Israel Review*, 1992; 'Immigrant absorption in the labor market' (with K. Flug), *Economic Quarterly* (Hebrew), 1993.

Stanley Lieberson is the Abbott Lawrence Lowell Professor of Sociology at Harvard University. He was born in Montreal, Quebec and grew up in Brooklyn, New York. He received his MA and PhD from the University of Chicago, with Colver–Rosenberger Prize for the best dissertation in Sociology in the preceding three years – an award which came just in time to pay for a honeymoon. Lieberson is a former President of the Sociological Research Association, the American Sociological Association, and the Pacific Sociological Association. He is a Fellow of the American Academy of Arts and Sciences, and a member of the National Academy of Sciences. He is author or co-author of: *Making it Count; Language*

Diversity and Language Contact; A Piece of the Pie (winner of the Sorokin Award); *Language and Ethnic Relations in Canada; Explorations in Sociolinguistics; Ethnic Patterns in American Cities; From Many Strands; Metropolis and Region in Transition*; and *Metropolis and Region*.

Peter Marcuse is Professor of Urban Planning at Columbia University in New York City. He received his undergraduate degree from Harvard University, an MA from Columbia, a JD from Yale, and a PhD from the University of California at Berkeley. Marcuse was in private practice of law in Waterbury, Connecticut for 20 years, where he also served as Majority Leader of the Board of Alderman and member of its City Planning Commission. When he entered teaching, at the school of Architecture and Urban Planning at the University of California, Los Angeles, he was also elected Chairman of its City Planning Commission. In New York City, he has been chair of the Housing Committee of Community Board #9 in Manhattan. Marcuse's publications include *The Myth of the Benevolent State*; *Divide and Siphon: New York City's Housing Policy*; *Dual City: Muddy Metaphor for a Quartered City*, and, most recently *Missing Marx: The Personal and Political Journal of a Year in East Germany, 1989–98*.

Gila Menahem teaches sociology and public policy analysis in the graduate Public Policy Program and in the Department of Sociology at Tel-Aviv University, where she received her PhD in 1985. She has published articles on political and social cleavages, public policy formulation, urban policy, resident participation and first and second generation of holocaust survivors in Israel. Dr Menahem recently received a grant from the National Academy of Sciences for a research project on urban economic restructuring and its implications on immigrant absorption in Israel.

Judith T. Shuval was born and educated in the United States and holds an MA and PhD in Sociology from Harvard University. She immigrated to Israel after completing graduate school and has spent all of her professional life in Israel. She is the Louis and Pearl Rose Professor of Sociology at the Hebrew University in Jerusalem where she holds a joint appointment in the Department of Sociology and in the School of Public Health. She is Director of the Programme in the Sociology of Health. Her major fields of interest are immigration and the sociology of health. She is a former Chair of the Israel Sociological Association and was awarded the Israel Prize for the Social Sciences for her first book *Immigrants on the Threshold*, a sociological analysis of the mass immigration to Israel during the 1950s. Her other books are: *Social Functions of Medical Practice; Entering Medicine: A Seven Year Study of Medical Education in Israel; Newcomers and Colleagues: Soviet Immigrant Physicians in Israel; Social Dimensions of Health: The Israeli Experience.*

Myron Weiner is Ford International Professor of Political Science at the Massachusetts Institute of Technology, Cambridge, Massachusetts. He received his degrees from the City College of New York and Princeton University. He taught at Princeton University and the University of Chicago before coming to MIT in 1961. From 1987 to 1992 he was director of the MIT Center for International Studies. He has held visiting appointments at Balliol College, Oxford, Harvard University, the Hebrew University, the University of Paris, and Delhi University. His recent writings on ethnicity and migration include *The Global Migration Crisis, Challenge to States and to Human Rights*, 1995, *Threatened Peoples, Threatened Borders: World Migration and US Policy* (editor, with Michael S. Teitelbaum), 1995, and *International Migration and Security* (editor), 1993.

Introduction
Naomi Carmon

What are the carriers of development in the post-industrial world? Many believe that science and technology are the carriers, because they generate the rapid changes experienced by people in the highly developed countries. Scientific discoveries and technological innovations have had an enormous impact on national economy and particularly on the structure of the labor force, but their influence on family and community life and on the political order have been less marked. But what about the future? Can the accelerated rate of technological and economic change continue, without parallel social and political change? The answer to this question seems to depend in large part on migration, which may turn out to be the carrier of development in the next century.

Human history is replete with examples of migration movements that changed the course of history. The widespread invasions and settlement of Goths and Vandals from central Europe and Hun invasions from Central Asia gradually destroyed the Roman empire in the fifth century. Immigration of Norsemen from Scandinavia to the British Isles, France and Russia reshaped the political and social structure of Europe in the eighth and ninth centuries. Much later, European countries became the largest exporters, rather than importers, of migrants. Migration from Europe was especially high between the mid-nineteenth century and the mid-twentieth century (c. 1930), the same years which witnessed the worldwide revolutionary process of Westernization (von Laue, 1988).

Among other things, the Europeans spread the concept of the nation-state, which gradually became the leading player on the world stage. In the past half-century, almost all of the world's population has been sorted and organized – not always neatly – according to the principles of territoriality and citizenship which characterize the nation-state (Alonso, 1987). In spite of specific disturbances, it seems that the nation-state has been accepted as a focus of identity in almost all of the developed and many of the developing countries.

Most of the essays in this collection consider the response of developed countries to streams of immigrants, who are frequently thought of as an intolerable burden on the economies of the receiving societies, and are always viewed as a potential threat to the identity and social cohesiveness of the host nation-states. The essays are briefly presented below. Following the presentation, I shall return to the issue of immigration and the future of nation-states in our world.

The chapters in this book are organized into four parts, the first of which sets the framework by pointing out crucial questions and variables. In the opening chapter, I try to characterize the new post-industrial era by identifying its five megatrends: global orientation, economic restructuring, demographic changes, legitimized diversification of life styles (not only between but also within countries), and a growing disparity between the haves and the have-nots, as evinced by the socioeconomic characteristics of groups of population within each country, as well as by comparisons among countries.

The chapter examines the relationship between the characteristics of the post-industrial era and the number and types of immigrants to the countries that have entered this age. It finds that the current numbers of immigrants in the various countries, at least in Europe, are still quite modest. However, the popularity of anti-immigration policies is increasing in all of the rich countries, in spite of the clear evidence regarding net economic gains to the receiving countries, which increase with time. Because many of the new immigrants are ethnically very different from the majority of the existing populations, because economic benefits are seldom felt (at least in the short run) by the localities that receive most of the immigrants, and especially because the numbers are expected to grow immensely in the coming years, all of the highly developed countries are trying to limit legal immigration sharply and are doing their utmost to prevent the entry of illegal immigrants. It is yet unclear whether they can succeed, at a time when the conditions of improving communication tools and growing disparity between nations continue to exist. If they do not, the chances of highly increased social diversification and major political changes will be very high.

In Chapter 2, Peter Marcuse touches upon the issue of the ideal society and the questions regarding desirable patterns of immigrant integration in a democratic society. He does this by using his extensive observation of social behavior in the urban settings of several countries as a basis for an essay on the different meanings of walls which separate people. Walls of the type he describes can be tangible or intangible, physical, social or economic, official or customary. They draw distinctions between the 'dominating city', the 'gentrified city', the 'suburban city', the 'tenement city' and the 'abandoned city'. New immigrants tend to settle in 'tenement cities', places that are typically occupied by lower-paid, blue and white collar workers, and generally (although not in the US) include substantial social housing. These places are walled-in socially, if not physically, and defined either as 'enclaves', which are perceived as having positive value, or as 'ghettos', a designation with clearly pejorative connotations. Marcuse suggests that, even though for the blacks in the US the real meaning of spatial segregation has been the formation of ghettos, separation of apparently the same kind has worked differently for most other non-white groups and for most new immigrants; for them, living in separate communities defined by their national origin has resulted in vital mutual support and an orientation toward the new land. Most of the immigrant communities have been voluntary and transitional, and have assisted their members in joining the mainstream. Marcuse's conclusion is that certain kinds of walls between people may be desirable, as long as they separate cultures of equal status; walls that increase social and political inequality are always undesirable. Hence, he advocates abandoning not only the melting pot idea but also multiculturalism (in which, according to Marcuse, equal treatment often results in bland egalitarianism, where the essence of differences is played down or ignored), in favor of a mosaic formulation, in which differences are highlighted but presumptively seen as parts of a larger pattern that makes sense in its totality.

Myron Weiner is also interested in the study of immigrant integration. He does not try to define the desirable patterns of integration, but focuses on ways of achieving it, assuming that each country knows its special meaning of the term. He has studied immigration and integration in many countries and has been able to bring to his analysis illustrations from the US, the UK, France, Germany, the Netherlands, Israel and other countries. He suggests several plausible hypotheses regarding the determinants of immigrant integration, dividing them into three categories. First is the willingness of a society to absorb immigrants, as expressed by its social contract with the newcomers, that is, the specification of the conditions under which the immigrants may enter the country (including what is expected of them and what in turn is promised to them by the government, especially regarding conditions for obtaining citizenship). Second, is the level of commitment of the immigrants to their new society. Third, and often most important, is the combination of objective circumstances at the time of entry. Most salient among these is the condition of the economy and whether or not it provides opportunities for mobility to people with the kind of drive, education and capabilities that the immigrants bring; also important is whether the stream of immigrants is sufficiently diversified, or the numbers from one source are not large enough to enable the immigrants to build permanent, self-contained enclaves. Weiner argues that many of these factors, though by no means all, can be affected by state policies; yet, due to conflicting political attitudes and the difficulty of fine-tuning these policies, especially in slow growth economies, the integration of immigrants in most countries remains problematic and conflictive.

Part II, New Immigrants in New Circumstances, opens with Herbert Gans' analysis of 'the myth of nearly automatic immigrant success' in America, against the background of changes in the economy that are typical of a post-industrial society. Gans focuses on the children, 'the second generation' of poor immigrants, especially dark-skinned ones. According to his analysis, they will not be willing or even able to take low-wage, long-hour 'immigrant' jobs as their parents did. Hence, his scenario for the future is that they, and the young men among them in particular, may join Blacks and Hispanics among those already excluded, apparently permanently, from the mainstream economy. The paper also deals with the relations between ethnicity and economic conditions in the US, and with the continued relevance of old theories of assimilation and acculturation under the new circumstances. His second scenario is that in the future, acculturation of immigrants will be more partial or segmented than in the past. All the issues raised by Gans in his analysis of the US society seem to be relevant to other post-industrial societies experiencing immigration of poor people, because all of them are living through the turbulent transitional period between the industrial age and a new era. As mentioned in the opening chapter of the book, this period is characterized by a shrinking number of jobs in the mainstream economy, an attribute which may support Gans' first scenario, and also by legitimized diversification of life styles which may corroborate the second one.

Even though many of the immigrants to North America in the last decade have been legal, skilled and highly-skilled workers, it is the growing numbers of illegal, unskilled immigrants that generate public debate as well as scholarly publications. William Clark is among those who are worried about the magnitude and composition of the new immigrants, especially those who are 'undocumented'. In his article Clark raises local, national and global concerns. Writing from Southern California, he sees the heart of the problem on the local level in the very high direct costs that have to be borne by counties and cities which attract large streams of immigrants, while the state, and especially the Federal government, enjoy most of the benefits. On the national level, Clark joins those who argue that divisiveness and separation are rapidly growing in the receiving countries. Clark also draws global conclusions, according to which neither barriers nor changes in the immigration laws and programs can succeed in preventing the continuing stream of illegal migrants from arriving at their intended destinations. That means that international borders become permeable barriers for global redistribution of wealth in the post-industrial world. Because this is a central issue in many countries, it may justify global responsibility. Clark draws an analogy between global obligation for the environment and a desired global responsibility for handling international migration, because of the overwhelming impact of both on human welfare.

Part III focuses on the unique experience of Israel. This small, developed country is experiencing the arrival of a huge wave of immigrants (compared to its population), a large proportion of which constitutes a highly-skilled labor force, moving from its country of origin in search of better economic opportunities and more political freedom. In the first half of the 1990s, the five million citizens of Israel received 600 000 new immigrants, most of them from the former USSR. About two-thirds of these former USSR citizens came from the European republics, and one-third from the Asian republics. Compared with the Israeli population, they have fewer children, somewhat more elderly people, and a larger working-age population, with a dominant tendency to the upper part (45–64) of this age group. The most salient characteristic of this population of immigrants is its large 'human capital', expressed in its occupational distribution: about 75 per cent of those of working age declared that in their countries of origin they were occupied in academic and technical professions; some 20 per cent of those of labor age were engineers and 3 per cent medical doctors, doubling the number of persons with this kind of training in Israel.

Karnit Flug and Nitza Kasir examine the extent to which the Israeli labor market has succeeded in using this large amount of human capital which arrived so unexpectedly. Their point of reference is Israel's notable success in absorbing the former wave of immigrants from the USSR, who arrived during the 1970s with a similar occupational structure. In the former wave, there was little unemployment among the immigrants after 2–3 years in Israel, and 60 per cent of them were employed in their former occupations; most of the others remained in their occupational category but moved downward: engineers became technicians, technicians became skilled workers and so on. Both unemployment and the rate of change were expected to be much higher in the 1990s, because the current influx was much larger and the labor market had been saturated with the kinds of occupations the immigrants brought with them. As it turned out, the rate of unemployment among the immigrants was very high at the beginning, but dropped quickly, so that in their third year in the country the rate was similar to the general rate in Israel; however, most highly-educated immigrants – close to 70 per cent of those employed – could not find a job in their former occupation. This is a great loss for the country and a source of extreme personal agony for the immigrants. Although the authors, like most economists, do not support high intervention of the government in the market in general, and in immigrant absorption in particular, they do recommend governmental support for immigrant retraining programs. In order to make better use of the new human capital, not only should the immigrants change and adapt, but the local economy must do so as well. For this purpose, they recommend that the government facilitate processes of specialization in high-tech industries (processes which have already been developing in the Israeli economy) and by this indirect method increase the employment of professional immigrants, especially engineers, by the private sector.

Judith Shuval and Judith Bernstein studied one group of professional immigrants – medical doctors. In 1990–4, about 13 000 doctors immigrated to Israel from the former USSR, doubling the number of physicians in the country, that had already been higher than the per capita average in Europe before they arrived. This is a case of a highly-skilled group of professionals, with a high level of occupational commitment (as indicated by the empirical research), facing an extremely limited job market in their target country. The social system they enter continues to observe its own values and interests, which hardly change with the immigrants arrival. The burden of change is on them. They have to confront the painful choice between occupational change and unemployment. Women and older doctors are likely to be particularly vulnerable in terms of their occupational integration and consequent well-being.

Immigrants tend to concentrate in large cities. The larger cities of the post-industrial countries are going through processes of economic restructuring which involve changes in the structure of the job market; these changes occur in parallel with changes in the characteristics of the populations of the inner cities. While in the past the cities attracted poor immigrants who joined their poor incumbent populations, in recent years they have also been attracting local gentrifiers and highly-skilled immigrants. Such processes of change are taking place in Tel-Aviv, the city in and around which 40 per cent of the Israeli population live, and Gila Menahem studied them. She interviewed new immigrants and found that in accordance with what was expected in a post-industrial economy, it was difficult for them to find industrial jobs in the city, the economy of which tends towards advanced services. Moreover, the polarization typical of post-industrial societies also affected the immigrant job market; about a third found academic and professional jobs, a far smaller percentage held mildly prestigious jobs (clerks, sales people), while many, in spite of their high level of education, experienced sharp downward mobility. As for housing, the immigrants could find dwelling units in several central neighborhoods of Tel-Aviv, but wherever the process of gentrification had been gaining control, their penetration was blocked and they were pushed toward less attractive areas of the city. Menahem concludes that a deliberate rehabilitation effort in their neighborhoods is required, if the central and/or local governments are interested in making the new immigrants permanent residents of the city of Tel-Aviv.

Shlomo Hasson ends the Israeli section with a discussion of empirical research into the critical question of spatial dispersion of immigrants. It is critical, because the place the immigrant chooses to settle in determines to a large extent the opportunities open to him or her, and, from a different viewpoint, the potential of his or her positive or negative contribution to the host society. Hasson finds that unlike immigrants to other countries who tend in the first years, or even the first generation in the new country, to choose their place of settlement according to socio-psychological attachments, the new immigrants to Israel from the former USSR behave differently. Within a very short period of time, two to three years in Israel, they tend to change from social optimizers to economic optimizers; disregarding their social relationships with relatives and friends, they select a place of residence on the basis of job and housing opportunities. This finding may have relevance to other developed countries, which have recently received larger numbers of highly-skilled immigrants, whose behavior may differ from what we know from studies of unskilled immigrants. If governments want to influence the geographical dispersion of their immigrants, they will have a better chance of doing so with skilled laborers, and, according to Hasson, they may do it indirectly, by influencing the local availability of appropriate new jobs and inexpensive housing.

Finally, Part IV analyzes the experience of four highly-developed countries with a long tradition of integrating immigrants. Stanley Lieberson derives lessons from the US experience. From a historical viewpoint, he sees it as a success story. Based on empirical evidence and some speculation, he mentions several possible sources of this exceptional success: improvement in the quality of life in comparison with that in the sending country; large potential for mobility, especially inter-generational mobility; minimal legal and political distinctions made between older settlers and immigrants, including their children; and minimal official pressure on the immigrants to assimilate. He argues that government policies played only a small role in these processes. With a few important exceptions, the government was quite passive, despite considerable agitation from the receiving population. His arguments raise questions about the appropriateness of government policies for enhancing immigrant integration, and about the assumption that ethnic conflicts cannot be reduced without deliberate public intervention.

Although Australia is as much an immigrant society as the US, its experience is very different. Laksiri Jayasuriya analyzes its history and focuses on its current problems. He relates that until the mass migration of the post World War II period, Australia had succeeded in preserving its 'white Australia' policy and the philosophy of 'total assimilation' and 'Anglo' conformity. In the 1950s and 1960s, non-Anglo (but mostly European) immigrants were admitted, but it was not until the early 1970s that a non-discriminatory policy of immigrant recruitment and the philosophy of multiculturalism were established. As adopted by the Australian governments, multiculturalism legitimized cultural differences in the private domain, but disapproved group organization in the public domain, trying to prevent the formation of political ethnic interest groups. It seemed to work for some time, but the introduction of new factors that accompanied 'economic restructuring' – the talisman of a new socioeconomic era – have disrupted the relatively calm situation. The demand for a highly-skilled labor force that increased the arrival of immigrants of Asian origin and the downturn in the economy in the 1980s created new problems and aggravated older ones. According to Jayasuriya, multiculturalism – where limited to cultural pluralism – has failed as an experiment in social engineering, at least in the context of 'economic restructuring'. New ethnic collectivities are being created, especially when the offspring of immigrants grow; they have interests, needs and aspirations, and forcefully search for new ways to express them and fight for them in the public arena.

In the final chapter, John Crowley addresses the experiences of Britain and France. These neighboring European countries, both of which have received significant immigration from less-developed countries since the 1950s, particularly from their former colonies, are similar with respect to the formal rights of immigrants. However, they are quite dissimilar in that it is widely accepted in Britain, but overwhelmingly denied in France, that formal rights are not sufficient to ensure the integration they grant immigrants. Their attitudes to immigration remained influenced by opposite (albeit often implicit) paradigms. France has only slowly come to accept the broad irreversibility of migration and the contradictions of the long-dominant 'migration-labor' model. In Britain, on the contrary, immigration has (by elite consensus, if not public opinion) long been recognized as permanent. This goes some way towards explaining the centrality of race relations issues in British policy and, conversely, their marginalization in France. More generally, it links up with the broader ideological climate, France remaining faithful to an essentially assimilationist ideal that Britain has largely abandoned. Both countries are struggling with the difficulties of adapting their policies to the new circumstances of the post-industrial era, in which immigrants are legitimate social actors, rather than a socio-economic phenomenon.

In Britain and France, as in most other nation-states of the wealthier parts of the world, the issues of immigration and integration are very high on the national agenda. The democratic traditions of these countries predicate freedom of movement, and their economic policies support free transfer of means of production, including labor force; hence, they could have been expected to open their borders to all potential settlers. However, what the essays in this book teach us is that forecasts of extensive immigration of populations, which are very different from existing national, ethnic or religious majority, frighten large segments of the local inhabitants. In fact, the number of immigrants currently entering the wealthier countries is very modest (except in the US), but their enormous potential is frequently perceived as a great threat to national identity and political stability. Technical assistance and development investments are channeled to less wealthy parts of the world, with the aim of creating substitutes for emigration. But these efforts have achieved so little in comparison to the growing needs of those countries, that most experts doubt that anything can stop the redistribution of the world's wealth through mass migrations of its population.

A plausible scenario for the future is that economic globalization, which has already been very influential in post-industrial societies, will be followed by immigration-driven social globalization in these societies. Mass immigration movements and consequent intra-national diversification will create a more flexible global structure, composed of communities with various degrees of control over their members. Instead of clinging to their present citizenship, which currently is a necessary condition for attaining social security rights as well as for participating in the democratic process, the inhabitants of this new world will freely wander among its various communities, carrying their extended personal rights with them.

References

Alonso, William (ed.) (1987) *Population in an Interactive World* (Cambridge, MA: Harvard University Press).

von Laue, T.H. (1988) *The World Revolution of Westernization: The 20th Century in Global Perspective* (New York: Oxford University Press).

Part I

Immigration and Integration in a Changing World

Part 1

1 Immigration and Integration in Post-Industrial Societies: Quantitative and Qualitative Analyses
Naomi Carmon

The tendency to migrate is a basic human characteristic. The origin of *homo sapiens* has not been ascertained beyond all doubt, but experts seem to agree that our species first made its appearance on the African continent and that it has been spreading over the planet ever since. The current dispersion of people around the world has been created through many small- and large-scale migration movements: raids, invasions, conquests, slave trade and colonization as well as pilgrimage and settlement beyond frontier areas.

Throughout human history, migration movements have created problems and conflicts that have been studied by social scientists. Now, when we are entering a new stage in human history, the new post-industrial era, this chapter is intended to initiate discussion of the issues of migration in the context of a young, yet largely unfamiliar age. The chapter opens with a characterization of the new era, continues with quantitative and qualitative analyses of the economic, social and cultural aspects of immigration and integration and ends with a question: will the present economic globalization be followed by immigration-driven social globalization in post-industrial societies?

CHARACTERIZING THE POST-INDUSTRIAL ERA

For the purposes of this discussion, the new era is described in terms of five socioeconomic phenomena: demographic (age structure) changes, global orientation, restructuring of the economy, diversification of life styles and increasing disparities between haves and have-nots.

The salient demographic changes are decreasing fertility rates and aging of the population (UN, 1994). The average age of the population in the post-industrial societies is climbing, the number of labor-age persons is declining, and the number of the elderly, especially in the oldest subgroup, is increasing. This aging process stands in sharp contrast to the demographic evolution in the less developed countries.

Global orientation is a major trend and hallmark of the new era. This global orientation is most marked in the economic sphere, where market forces are pushing towards the lowering if not the total abolition of traditional trade barriers (mostly national boundaries) that inhibit free transportation of raw materials and finished products. Advanced communication technologies are making these changes possible, economically as well as culturally and logistically. The innovative use of mass media raises people's level of expectations and reinforces their inclination to move in order to realize these expectations; the development of modern means of transportation and the declining costs of transporting persons and goods make movement from place to place easier than it has ever been. A worldwide (global) search for opportunity has become a realistic alternative not only for directors of large corporations, but for non-skilled workers as well.

Restructuring of the economy is another main characteristic. For more than 200 years, the economics of Western societies was based mainly on industrial production of goods. In the last few decades, we have been living through the process of 'tertiarization' of the economy, that is, the rapid transfer of a large share of the labor force from industrial production to services. The deindustrialization process is accompanied by tough competition between large and small corporations and also between regions and cities. High unemployment rates seem to have become a permanent structural phenomenon. At the same time, the share of the informal (shadow) economy is growing in most highly-developed countries; according to several studies, it reached 5–12 per cent of the GNP in many OECD countries towards 1980 (Schneider, 1992), and has grown considerably since then.

Diversification of lifestyles is highly typical of our times. While in traditional societies there was usually one 'correct' and possible lifestyle for each person in a specific social group, in post-industrial societies there are more and more *legitimized* modes of life from which a person can choose. Mode of life is determined by a combination of choices in the following areas: value orientation (religious versus secular, for example), level of ethnic affiliation, family life, work patterns, leisure practice and residential preferences (Carmon, 1995).

Last but not least are the increasing disparities between the haves and the have-nots, and the absolute increase in the number of have-nots.

Economists have conventionally expected the benefits of development to 'filter down' to everybody. This may ultimately come true, but for now, rapid changes related to the transition from an industrial to a post-industrial society in the last quarter of the present century have caused unprecedented rates of unemployment in the highly-developed countries, a growing number of low-wage and non-secured jobs in their large cities (Sassen, 1991), and forecasts of worsening conditions for their middle-class populations (Kennedy, 1993). In both the US and Britain, inequalities in income are now larger than at any time since the 1930s (*Economist*, 1994). Disparities have been increasing within the post-industrial countries (especially within the large and prosperous 'world cities') as well as between them and the Third-World countries. The ratio of income level between the poorest and the richest 20 per cent of world population was 30:1 in 1960 and 59:1 in 1990 (UN, 1992).

These five characteristics of post-industrial societies are strongly related to the number of international immigrants and to the processes of their integration (or non-integration) in the receiving societies, as explained below.

MASS MIGRATION TO POST-INDUSTRIAL SOCIETIES?

The number of immigrants is growing worldwide. In the period from 1945–70, 100 million immigrants moved from country to country – an average of four million a year; by 1990, the number reached 120 million – an average of six million a year (World Media, 1991). Teitelbaum and Russell (1994) collected data from around the world and came to the conclusion that in the early 1990s at least 100 million immigrants were living outside their countries of birth or citizenship (including both permanent and temporary immigrants as well as refugees). About half of these immigrated to the developed countries of the world (approximately 23 million to Europe, 20 million to North America, and 4 million to Oceania). The present study focuses on this half.

The increasing number of immigrants to the developed countries is related first and foremost to the widening gap in the rates of unemployment and underemployment, as well as in the standards of living between the countries of the North and those of the South and (to a lesser extent) between countries of the West and East. However, had it not been for the declining work force in the rich countries, due to the above-mentioned demographic trends, and were it not for the need of these countries to recruit large numbers of workers, the new laborers would not have come (Alonso, 1987).

The restructuring of the economy of the post-industrial countries is creating a large demand for highly skilled workers, especially those trained in the natural sciences, computers, engineering and medicine. Young people in Western countries, however, prefer to attend schools of business, management and law; as a result, there are many openings in certain high-skill occupations. At the same time, and especially in order to cope with the tough competition in the international markets, there is a demand for unskilled, low-paid workers, to take the jobs that local residents spurn. This increased demand encourages immigration to the developed countries, both of university graduates, who find it difficult to land an appropriate job in their less developed countries, and of unskilled young men and women, who have only a scarce chance of making a living in the overpopulated countries of their birth.

Most of these trends are common to all of the developed countries, but there are also remarkable differences between North America and Europe. While the US and Canada have always been large importers of immigrants, Europe was traditionally an exporter. It was not until the twentieth century, and especially following World War II, that Europe became a region of net in-migration. In the last four decades, the area of net in-migration in Europe has progressively grown (Oberg, 1993). Waves of immigrants came to Northern and Central Europe in the 1960s and the early 1970s, at first from southern Italy, Spain, Greece and Portugal, and then from Yugoslavia and Turkey (King, 1993). In the late 1970s, 1980s and the early 1990s, Italy, Greece, Spain and Portugal joined the European countries which have a positive migration balance, and a much larger share of the new immigrants started to come from the Third-World countries. Most non-European immigrants come from North Africa; the former imperial nations (England, France, Holland) also take in immigrants from their erstwhile colonies of Asia and Africa.

Reliable statistics are scarce, mainly because the definition of foreigners, immigrants and citizens is not exclusive. All in all, the total number of immigrants in Europe is not large. France (1990), for example, had 4.13 million immigrants (with or without French nationality) among its resident population of 53 million (Ogden,1993); in England and Wales (1981) 3.5 million persons out of 48.5 million residents were born elsewhere (Coleman, 1992); in Italy (1990) there were about 1 million non-European immigrants (permanent and temporary) among 61 million (Barsotti and Lecchini, 1992). Oberg (1993) concludes a West European survey by saying that the present stream of immigrants includes just around one non-European immigrant per 2000 Europeans per year. He warns his audience, that 'without immigration and with a continuously low fertility pattern, almost every third inhabitant of West Europe will be over the age of 65 in 2050', and according to a more 'pessimistic' scenario, 44 per cent will belong to this age group (Oberg, 1992)

The numbers in the US, Canada and Australia are different. The US admitted more than 500 000 legal immigrants on a yearly average in the 1980s and is expected to admit around 1 million annually in the 1990s. Canada expects annual levels of immigration to rise to 250 000 in 1993–5. Australia's immigration was about 100 000 in 1992 (Teitelbaum and Russell,1994). These are far larger ratios of new immigrants to permanent residents than those of the Old World. Moreover, while in the 1920s around 95 per cent of the immigrants to the US were European in origin, in the 1960s about 50 per cent came from Third-World countries, and in the 1980s the share of Third-World immigrants grew to about 85 per cent of all immigrants to the US (Clark, 1996). Similar changes in the composition of the populations of immigrants have been reported from Canada and Australia.

A common phenomenon in the highly-developed countries of both the New and the Old World is the growing number of illegal immigrants. They tend to take the worst jobs on the market, jobs that native residents refuse to accept. When they cannot find ordinary jobs, they make their living in the growing informal market of the post-industrial societies. As of 1993, there were approximately 3.5 million illegal residents in the US, most of whom came from Latin America (Teitelbaum and Russell, 1994). The numbers (including relative numbers) are smaller in Europe, but the social tensions they create seem to be stronger. In France, for example, there were 300 000 *clandestins* (illegal immigrants) in the early 1980s; Silverman (quoted by Ogden 1993:114) claimed that 'the persistent and misleading confusion between "illegals" and "immigrant workers" has never been adequately resolved: not only has "immigrant" been increasingly reduced to "Arab", but also immigrants have continued to be identified "as a problem, outside the law and outside the nation"'.

The receiving countries have all tried to curtail illegal immigration. The US Congress passed the 1986 Immigration Act, with such an aim in mind. Following this Act, about 1.8 million persons filed applications for legalization on the basis of illegal residence in the United States prior to 1982; an additional 1.3 million seasonal workers also applied for legalization. According to Muller (1993), the Act and the following processes of legalization did not succeed in substantially reducing illegal entry. In anticipation of its partial unification on 31 December 1992, the

European Community strongly urged its member countries to tighten up their immigration policies and take special measures to reduce the number of illegal immigrants in so far as possible. In spite of these efforts, it seems that as long as the strong pressure generated by unemployment in the sending countries continues to exist and as long as there is a demand for cheap labor in the formal and informal economies of the receiving societies, even harsh measures will not be able to stop the flow of illegal immigrants.

While most of the workers among the illegal immigrants are low-skilled, the percentage of highly-skilled and very highly-skilled workers among legal immigrants to post-industrial countries is on the rise. According to a UN report (1992:55), the percentage of skilled workers among immigrants from the developing countries to the US was 45 per cent in 1966 and grew to 75 per cent in 1986, while in Canada the comparable figures were 12 per cent and 46 per cent. Both countries have recently changed their immigration regulations in order to admit a larger proportion of entrepreneurs and skilled workers. The brain drain is increasing, not only from the poor countries to the rich ones, but also from European countries to North America. This is another characteristic feature of immigration in the post-industrial era.

Thus, the number of immigrants is growing and their characteristics are changing. However, the data (especially European data) does not support the designation 'mass migration' that has recently been adopted by European books (for example: King, 1993) and conferences (for example: 'Mass Migration in Europe' held in Laxenburg, Austria, in March 1992). As Sture Oberg (1992), a specialist on world population, wrote, what we are witnessing is 'small numbers but large potentials'.

For the time being, only a little more than two per thousand are leaving the former USSR each year, and the same small proportion per year is received in Germany, the main target area in Western Europe for former citizens of the Communist countries (Ibid.). This ratio is expected to grow in the future, but the main population pressures on Western Europe as well as on the developed countries of the New World will not come from Eastern Europe, but rather from the developing countries. Some 38 million extra people join the labor force each year in the countries of the South, in which more than 700 million are already unemployed or underemployed; this means that one billion new jobs must be created or improved by the end of the decade – almost equivalent to the total population of the North (UN, 1992: 54). The fear caused by these facts has turned immigration and integration into one of the most contentious issues of the late twentieth century.

ECONOMIC CONSIDERATIONS

Does immigration bring about economic gains or losses? This question should be discussed both from the individual point of view of the immigrant and his/her immediate family, and from the national points of view of the sending as well as the receiving societies.

The common cause of international migration is the desire of the immigrants to improve their economic status. In the past, most of them succeeded in attaining this goal ultimately, if not immediately (i.e. inter-generational mobility). Will this trend continue in the post-industrial society? The answer may differ according to the assets brought by the immigrant, especially education and professional training. As mentioned above, there has been a large percentage of skilled and highly-skilled persons in the immigrating labor force in recent years; physicians and para-medics, engineers and technicians, trained managers and other professionals may still find open channels of economic mobility. For unskilled and poor immigrants the prospects are gloomier by far. If the poor immigrants are ready to take low-wage, long-hours, dead-end jobs, there are enough such jobs available in the present economy, and it seems that there will be many jobs of this kind in years to come. The shortage of jobs in post-industrial societies is at the intermediate level, the level that should be available to the children of the immigrants. Gans (1996) has developed the theory of 'second generation decline': it is anticipated that children of immigrants, raised under the cultural aspirations and work expectations of the receiving society, will refuse to take typical 'immigrant jobs'; this unwillingness, coupled with the scarcity of secure jobs in the primary labor market, is expected to make many of them – particularly young males – join the hard core of the unemployed, and consequently live on welfare, at the least, if they don't become involved with drugs and crime as well. Thus, faith in the nearly automatic straight-line advancement of immigrants, so common in American and other immigrant pools, is being shattered.

Gender is a salient issue in the context of economic adaptation of immigrants. Women make up nearly half of the international migrant population. In the European OECD countries, women constitute the larger part of foreign-born populations. Although women are often thought of as 'passive movers', who migrate to join family members, research has found that economic rather than personal or social considerations predominate. Despite strong evidence of women's occupation in the labor market, immigration policies still tend to assume that all migrants are men and that women are 'dependents'. Women's right to work may be severely restricted, access to support systems and social services may be limited, and rights to naturalization may be indirect and dependent on the status of the spouse. The level of expectation of immigrant women, like that of immigrant men, tends to be high, their prospects of finding some kind of job and bringing home some money are fairly good, but the road to progress is frequently blocked for them. Social networks, strong bonds of kinship and the extension of traditional social structures to the new settings, coupled with the special restrictions applied to married women immigrants in many countries and the general discrimination against women in the labor markets of the developed countries – combine to reduce the chances of success for women. Thus, unlike the situation for men, the before-after migration balance is showing just a slight (if any) improvement for women (UNFPA, 1993).

Consideration of macroeconomics in place of the micro-view of the individual immigrant leads the discussion into different directions. From ancient days, emigration has helped to reduce the number of persons who have to be fed in regions with limited resources. From this narrow point of view, emigration still assists poor countries. Now, however, the sending countries often lose skilled personnel and the problem of 'brain drain' may be severe. On the positive side though, wherever skilled immigrants keep in touch with their country of origin, cultural links are created which encourage much-needed technology transfers. In addition, they sometimes play a major role as investors in what they often continue to consider their homeland, even if a long time has passed since their forebears left it. Technology transfers and investments by ethnic Chinese citizens of the US and Canada, and even more frequently citizens of Southeast Asian countries (Singapore, Thailand, Indonesia, and others) have played a leading role in the recent rapid economic growth of the People's Republic of China (Financial Times, 1992).

Remittances – the hard currency earnings that immigrants send to family members and others in the country they left – compensate at least in part for the loss of a trained labor force. In 1990 alone, the official total was US$71 billion; the net transfer to the developing countries equaled US$31 billion (Teitelbaum and Russell, 1994). In Jordan, Pakistan and Sudan remittances were equivalent to more than 20 per cent of imports for that year; in Egypt, they were the most significant source of foreign currency income in the 1980s (UN, 1992). Individual households clearly benefit from money received from abroad. Less clear is the impact on the country as a whole. There has been criticism that most of these funds do not go into productive investment, but are used for speculative activities or to finance conspicuous consumption and import of luxury goods. But most expenditures can add to demand and stimulate the local economy. A study conducted in Egypt suggested a coefficient of 2.2 for remittances – that is, remittances of 1 million Egyptian pounds increased the GNP by 2.2 million pounds; a similar study in Pakistan found a multiplier of 2.4 (Ibid.).

In spite of this stream of cash to the sending states, the receiving countries are the main economic beneficiaries. For example: the US Congressional Research Service estimated that in 1981–2 the developing countries as a whole lost an investment of $20 000 for each skilled migrant – $646 million in total. Some of this returns as remittances, but not on a scale sufficient to compensate for the losses (UN,1992). Other economic benefits to the receiving societies take the form of revenues generated at all levels of government. Opponents of immigration frequently claim that the immigrants do not raise enough taxes to pay for the many services they use – social security benefits, health services and so on. Detailed studies in several countries have provided evidence to the contrary. Akbari (1989) studied the Canadian case and found that immigrants paid (slightly) more taxes than they received in transfer payments. Steinmann (1992) compared the contributed and received revenues of citizens and foreigners in Germany; he reported that the foreigners paid slightly more (taxes, health insurance, etc.) and received far less in transfer payments (mainly because of pensions received by citizens). A recent American study (Moreno-Evans, 1992, reported by Clark, 1993) shows that the Federal government of the US benefits directly from immigration because of the revenues collected from immigrants, but that local districts bear a disproportionately high cost for serving immigrants who arrive as a result of federal policies, laws and decisions. At issue are the disparities in geographic distribution, which create a heavy burden on regions and municipalities with large and often poor immigrant populations.

The dilemma stems from the tendency of immigrants to congregate in particular locations, especially in or near the large metropolitan centers of Western countries. In the 1980s and 1990s, ten metropolitan areas in the US, which housed 17 per cent of the nation's population attracted 55 per cent of its legal immigrants and probably a larger percentage of the illegal ones; first among them were Los Angeles and New York (Enchautegui, 1993). Figures from the 1980s show concentrations of 'foreign population' in certain large European cities: Luxembourg – 43 per cent; Geneva – 29 per cent; Frankfurt, Antwerp, Brussels and Amsterdam – 21–24 per cent (White, 1993). Voices in favor of closing the gates for additional immigrants are frequently heard in these large cities of mixed population.

In the highly-mixed regions, immigrants are frequently blamed for displacing veteran citizens in work places and for a potential decline in wages due to the excess labor force. Research does not support such claims. Studies by Simon (1989) and Borjas (1990) found that the American labor market was sufficiently segmented to escape noticeable influence by immigrant workers; both rejected the hypothesis that immigration caused unemployment in the US. Their studies were criticized for using aggregated data, but a desegregated analysis of the local areas that are large recipients of immigrants pointed in the same direction. Enchautegui (1993) made an ethnic-specific analysis of such local areas and showed that the wages of Anglo and Hispanic men increased in areas of high immigration; Blacks did not lose, but they did not gain, either.

The general conclusion is clear: the receiving countries and their citizens enjoy great economic gains which result from international migration. There is clear evidence of the financial gains, and also various indications of the contribution of immigrants to the economic vitality and the competitiveness of the highly developed countries. According to Sassen (1994), an expert on cities in the world economy, immigrants have contributed an enormous amount of energy to small-scale, low-profit entrepreneurship, which is necessary to meet the demand for goods and services that larger standardized firms can no longer handle, given the low profit levels and the increased costs of operation. One can see this in Paris, Tokyo, Toronto and Frankfurt, as well as in New York. In this context, she says, immigrants are almost akin to a rapid development force.

Yet, immigrants were not and are not welcome. The main reasons for this are to be found in non-economic spheres.

SOCIAL AND CULTURAL ISSUES

Veteran residents usually see and treat newcomers as intruders. The German writer and essayist Hans Magnus Enzensberger (1992) illustrates this by a story of two passengers in a railway compartment, who have made themselves at home for a long journey, their clothes hung up, their luggage stowed and the remaining empty seats next to them covered with their newspapers and bags. Suddenly, the door opens and two new passengers enter. Their arrival is not welcome. There is a feeling of reluctance when it comes to clearing the vacant seats to make room for the new arrivals. There is an air of solidarity between the first two passengers, even though they are not acquainted. They confront the newcomers as a group; it is their territory which is at stake. They behave as if they were natives who are laying claim to the entire space for themselves. Any new arrival is treated as an intruder. Enzensberger's conclusion is that group egoism and xenophobia are anthropological constants, preceding reason. The fact that these traits are universally present indicates that they are older than most known forms of social order. *Prima facie,* it means that immigration always causes a conflict.

The way to reduce the conflict is to facilitate rapid integration of the immigrants into the receiving society. However, for many – probably a majority – of the immigrants counted above, the concept of integration may be irrelevant. If integration is the process by which a person adapts himself to permanent settlement in a new environment, then it is irrelevant for most of the temporary migrant workers, for the asylum seekers, and for the numerous illegal migrants, many of whom are in constant mobility.

Even if our discussion is confined to long-term immigrants, researchers and policy-makers differ with regard to the desirable form and level of their integration. Through years of study and public debate, three models of integration emerged: assimilation, melting pot and cultural pluralism. Different versions of these models can be identified in different times and countries, but the three can be described in general terms as follows.

Assimilation is a process by which immigrants adopt the cultural norms and lifestyles of the host society in a way that ultimately leads to the disappearance of the newcomers as a separate group. In this model, contact between the minority group of immigrants and the dominant culture results in a gradual process of change in the minority group (and not in the receiving society), and its members gradually abandon their culture of origin in order to adapt themselves to the host society. This process has frequently been described in terms of conformity and/or acculturation. The numerical weight of the members of the dominant society, the frequency and intensity of the contacts and the passage of time were all considered assimilation-accelerating factors (Taft, 1963, 1985). The model was formulated by Robert Park (1928, 1950), the founder of the School of Sociology at the University of Chicago. He and his leading students, including Louis Wirth and Franklin Fraizer, assumed that assimilation was not only natural and inevitable, but would be all for the best (Glazer, 1993). Later researchers (Lieberson, 1961; Gordon, 1964; Barth and Noel, 1972) made the model more complex and more sophisticated, but generally agreed with respect to assimilation as the final result.

Social reality did not support the idea of inevitable assimilation. Empirical evidence, together with the unpopularity of assimilative ideas paved the way to the concept of the melting pot. The term had been known for decades: America was the great melting pot in which all the races of Europe were melted down and reshaped. But it was not until the 1940s that American researchers started to use it frequently as the title of a new model of integration, a model which allows two-way cultural influences. The final result is still a society which is culturally and ethnically homogeneous (allows for religious heterogeneity) (Herberg, 1955), but the construction of this new society is based on the interaction of all the existing cultures. The different ethnic groups of immigrants are not considered – as they were in the assimilation model – passive objects, but rather active subjects, who participate in the formation of the new nation (Glazer and Moynihan, 1963).

The ideal of a melting pot that included, in addition to a cultural mix, the creation of a new nation through biological interbreeding, seemed to work for most of the European groups in the US, but has never materialized for the Blacks, the largest minority group, with the deepest roots in America (with the exception of native American Indians). The Afro-Americans continued to suffer from segregation, discrimination and blocked social mobility. Many consider their suffering as proof of the failure of both the assimilation and the melting pot ideals.

Meanwhile, new ideas about coexistence of different ethnic groups were taking shape, with UNESCO leading its international dissemination. 'Union in Diversity' was the leading slogan of the Havana international conference in 1956 (Borrie, 1959), calling for cultural differentiation within a framework of social unity. Gradually, the model of cultural pluralism has taken center stage. It allows heterogeneity not as a transitory state, but rather as a permanent phenomenon in society. It assumes that the different groups of society influence each other reciprocally, that together they create the national space in which all participants are citizens with equal rights and with which all of them identify. The goal of the integration process was redefined as promoting civic unity while protecting ethnic diversity (Fuchs, 1993).

All three models take a macro viewpoint of the receiving society. They ignore the possibility that the process of immigrant integration can take different forms in different parts of the society (geographically and socially) or where it relates to different types of immigrants. They also ignore the wishes of the immigrants themselves as determinants of their integration or non-integration. The present behavior of immigrants in various developed countries indicates that disregarding their motivation is a mistake. It is especially so when immigrants of the same origin constitute a group in a particular locality which is large enough for their motivations to play a decisive role in the processes discussed.

Even though Glazer (1993) believes that the forces pressing towards assimilation have not lost power in American society, he admits that they have never worked for the Blacks. As for the Hispanics and Asian-

Americans, who seem to have been better accepted by the white majority, he found that they chose to establish or preserve an institutional base for a separate identity. The same tendency of preserving a separate identity, not only by means of religious and cultural institutions but also – at least to some extent – by having ethnic-based sources of livelihood (ethnic businesses) and political institutions, is reported by studies of Mexicans in Los Angeles, of Chinese immigrants in Vancouver and of Turks in Hamburg. It might have been encouraged by prejudice and discrimination derived from the majority population; but it seems to stem mainly from the free will of the immigrants and their ability to openly express this will in societies that have legitimized diversity of all kinds.

Diversification is the name of the game. It used to be an either/or situation: either you stay in your country of origin or you immigrate and integrate, that is, settle permanently and take upon you the identity of another nation. In the post-industrial era we are witnessing a multiple-alternative situation; the two main alternatives are temporary vs permanent migration, and within each of these there is a diversity of immigrants. Within the category of permanent international immigration, even within the same country, there is more than one pattern of integration; different groups of immigrants can make their choices between assimilation or the preservation of specific parts of their original culture, and even their original institutions. Within the temporary category, there are several common ways: a migrant may be part of the legal economy by having one of the permits for highly qualified personnel in the corporate sector (see the presentation of The Euroman in *World Media*, 1992), or by having a work permit for unskilled work in agriculture, construction and so on; another way of joining the sector of temporary migrants is to find a living in the growing shadow economy (the informal economy) of the developed countries. The lifestyles of people in these different immigrant groups vary greatly one from the other. Last, but not least, the world now has a new type of immigrant: people who have homes, careers and cultural roots in more than one society (see the report of the Puerto Ricans as multiple movers by Scheff and Hernandez, 1993). Where does this variety take us? The following discussion will cover this question.

CONCLUSION

Global orientation and diversification have been discussed in this chapter as megatrends of the post-industrial era. For conclusion, two hypotheses are suggested: the first is that the influence of these two megatrends will grow immensely, not only on the economy, but also on the direction and content of social and political changes in the twenty-first century; the second is that international immigrants will serve as major carriers of these changes.

It seems that the greatest cultural transformation of our civilization is that we now look to the future rather than the past. Traditional societies were based on the past; each generation was expected to add just a drop to the accumulation of human knowledge, and thus, the complete transfer of knowledge from one generation to the next was considered to be of the utmost importance. In our world, in the context of very rapid development of science and technology, a considerable part of human knowledge is created within the lifetime of each generation (25 years). People are born into a rapidly changing world and they expect it to continue changing even more rapidly. Therefore, attention moves from studying the past and organizing life by the experience of the past to attempts at adaptation to the uncertain future.

Migration implies leaving the past and present and concentrating on the future. Researchers used to believe that potential immigrants compare job openings, wages and standards of living in their home countries with those in their target areas, and make their decisions accordingly. But if this is the case, how can we explain the continued immigration to the huge cities of the developing countries that cannot provide reasonable standards of living for many, if not most, of their residents? And how can we explain the movements to cities of the developed world in which most immigrants experience a sharp decline in their socioeconomic status? The answer is that migration decisions are based on hopes and expectations for the future, rather than on considerations of the present. In this sense, immigrants are indubitably representatives of the post-industrial period, the era of the future.

But has this not been true of immigrants in the past? Is there something unique about the immigrants of the new era? At least three trends are worth mentioning here. One is that the search for new opportunities is frequently made on a global scale, and this becomes true for non-skilled workers almost as much as for highly-skilled immigrants. The second is that the legitimation of cultural diversity may encourage immigrants to maintain their separate identities in their new homes, and in consequence, gradually alter the nature of the existing nations. The third is the changing concept of rights: in the past, immigrants were either potential citizens, who could expect to receive full citizenship rights, or foreigners who came to work for a limited period of time and had very few rights; today immigrants enjoy many rights by virtue of their mere presence in a country: welfare, education for their children, instruction in their own language, and appeal against deportation. Rights are increasingly defined in universal terms; 'voting rights are human rights', claimed the 1990 migrants' voting rights campaign in Austria (Soyal, 1995). If trends continue to develop in the same direction and if the large potential of mass migration movements is realized, the outcome will be a new social and political order.

This chapter is devoted to the understanding of processes and does not deal directly with ways to ease the social turbulence caused by immigration, but let me note here that governments can – and to the best of my judgment – should play a major role in treating the issues discussed above. In spite of the rhetoric in favor of privatization and a reduction of the public sector, governments in the developed countries are highly involved in all spheres: service production (education, health, housing and welfare), guiding economic development (extensively, whether directly or indirectly), determining the standard of living of their citizens (through taxation and many other ways), and even shaping public and personal attitudes (appropriate nutrition and environmental conservation are two examples). These involved governments have no choice but to relate to issues of immigration: the number of immigrants, immigrant rights, and the dilemmas of integration and the appropriate governmental role in shaping it.

Other chapters in this book deal with these policy questions. This chapter ends with a theoretical question bearing on policy challenges: will the present economic globalization be followed by immigration-driven social globalization in the post-industrial societies? Following World War II, a hundred or so new nations were established which strengthened the semi-stable structure of a world composed of nation-states. Almost all of the human population was sorted and organized, not always neatly, according to principles of territoriality and citizenship. Will this structure give way to a more fluid one, in which national identities are blurred by affiliations transcending nationality? Will mass immigration movements, and the processes of intra-national diversification they cause, create a more flexible global structure, composed of communities of different size and various degrees of control over their members? Will the inhabitants of this new world move freely among its communities and, instead of clinging to their citizenship rights, carry with them wherever they go their extended human rights? These questions are left open.

References

Akbari, Ather H. (1989) 'The Benefits of Immigrants to Canada: Evidence on Tax and Public Services', *Canadian Public Policy,* 15 (4): 424–35.

Alonso, William, (ed.) (1987) *Population in an Interacting World* (Cambridge MA: Harvard University).
Barsotti, Odo and Laura Lecchini (1992) 'Social and Economic Aspects of Foreign Immigrants into Italy', a paper presented at the conference on *Mass Migration in Europe* (Laxenberg, Austria: IIASA).
Barth, E.A. and Noel, D.L. (1972) 'Conceptual Framework for the Analysis of Race Relations: An Evaluation', *Social Forces*, 50: 333–48.
Borjas, G.J. (1990) *Friends or Strangers: The Impact of Immigrants on the US Economy* (New York: Basic Books).
Borrie, W.D. (1959) *The Cultural Integration of Immigrants* (UNESCO).
Carmon, N. (1995) *Planning for 'Quality of Life for All'*, Vol. 9 of a series: Israel 2020 – Long Range Planning for Israel of the 21st Century. Haifa: Technion – Israel Institute of Technology, Faculty of Architecture and Town Planning.
Clark, William A.V. (1996) 'Immigration and Integration: Lessons from Southern California'. Chapter 5 in this book.
Coleman, David. (1992) 'The United Kingdom and International Migration', a paper presented at the conference on *Mass Migration in Europe* (Laxenberg, Austria: IIASA).
Enchautegui, Maria E. (1993) 'Immigration Impact on Local Employment and Ethnic Minorities', in Naomi Carmon (ed.), *Immigrants: Liability or Asset?* Haifa: The Center for Urban and Regional Studies, Technion – Israel Institute of Technology.
Enzensberger, Hans Magnus (1992) 'Remarks on the Great Migration', *Framtider International*, 2: 14–18.
Financial Times (1992) *China: an Open Door for Investments* (London: December 15).
Fuchs, Lawrence H. (1993) 'An Agenda for Tomorrow: Immigration Policy and Ethnic Policies', *The Annals of the Academy of Political and Social Science*, 530: 171–86.
Gans, H.J. (1996) 'Second-Generation Decline: The Post-1965 American Immigration and Ethnicity', Chapter 4 in this book.
Glazer, Nathan and Moynihan, Daniel P. (1963) *Beyond the Melting Pot* (Massachusetts: the MIT Press).
Glazer, Nathan (1993) 'Is Assimilation Dead?', *The Annals of the Academy of Political and Social Science*, 530: 122–36.
Gordon, M.M. (1964) *Assimilation in American Life* (New York: Oxford University Press).
Herberg, W. (1955) *Protestant–Catholic–Jew* (New York: Doubleday).
Kennedy, Paul (1993) *Preparing for the Twenty-First Century* (New York: Random House).
King, Russell (1993) 'European International Migration, 1945–90' in Russell King (ed.), *Mass Immigration in Europe* (London: Belhaven Press).
Lieberson, S. (1961) 'The Impact of Residential Segregation on Ethnic Assimilation' *Social Forces*, 40: 52–7.
Muller, Thomas (1993) *Immigrants and the American City* (New York: New York University Press).
Oberg, Sture (1992) 'Small Numbers but Large Potentials', *Framtider International*, 2: 5–7.

Oberg, Sture (1993) 'Europe in the Context of World Population Trends', in Russell King (ed.), *Mass Immigration in Europe* (London: Belhaven Press).
Ogden, Philip (1993) 'The Legacy of Migration: some Evidence from France', in Russell King (ed.), *Mass Immigration in Europe* (London: Belhaven Press).
Park, R.E. (1928) 'Human Migration and the Marginal Man' *American Journal of Sociology*, 33: 881–93.
Park, R.E. (1950) *Race and Culture* (Glencoe: Free Press).
Sassen, Saskia (1991) *The Global Cities: New York, London, Tokyo* (Princeton NJ: Princeton University Press).
Sassen, Saskia (1994) 'International Migration and the Post-Industrial City', *The Urban Edge*, 2 (3): 3.
Scheff, Janet and Hernandez, David (1993) 'Rethinking Migration: Having Roots in Two Worlds', in Naomi Carmon (ed.), *Immigrants: Liability or Asset?*, Haifa: The Center for Urban and Regional Studies, Technion – Israel Institute of Technology.
Schneider, Friedrich (1992) 'The Development of the Shadow Economy under Changing Economic Conditions: Empirical Results for Austria', a paper presented at the conference on *Mass Migration in Europe* (Laxenberg, Austria: IIASA).
Simon, J. (1989) *The Economic Consequences of Immigration* (Cambridge, MA: Basil Blackwell).
Soyal, Yasemin Nuhoglu (1995) *Limits of Citizenship: Migrants and Postnational Membership in Europe* (Chicago: University of Chicago Press).
Steinmann, Gunter and Ralf Ulrich (1992) 'The Impact of Immigrants on Economic Welfare of Natives: Theory and Recent Experiences in Germany', a paper presented at the conference on *Mass Migration in Europe* (Laxenberg, Austria: IIASA).
Taft, R. (1963) 'The Assimilation Orientation of Immigrants and Australians', *Human Relations*, 6: 279–93.
Taft, R. (1985) 'The Psychological Study of the Adjustment and Adaptation of Immigrants in Australia', in N.T. Feather (ed.), *Survey of Australian Psychology* (Sydney: George Allen & Unwin).
Teitelbaum, Michael S. and Sharon Stanton Russell (1994) 'International Migration, Fertility, and Development', in Robert Cassen (ed.), *Population and Development: Old Debates, New Conclusions*. US–Third-World Policy Perspectives, No. 19. (New Brunswick: Transaction Publishers).
The Economist 1994 (November 5th) 'Inequality', pp. 19–21.
UN (United Nations) Development Program (1992) *Human Development Report,1992* (New York, Oxford: Oxford University Press).
UN (United Nations) (1994) *Statistical Yearbook, 1993* (New York).
UNFPA (1993) *The State of World Population 1993: The Individual and the World: Population, Migration, and Development in the 1990s* (New York).
White, Paul (1993) 'Immigrants and the Social Geography of European Cities', in Russell King (ed.), *Mass Immigration in Europe* (London: Belhaven Press).
World Media (a special issue of a consortium of 15 national newspapers) (1991) 'Immigrants: In Search of a Better Passport', *World Media*, 2: 18.

2 Of Walls and Immigrant Enclaves
Peter Marcuse

The central problem of our times lies in the divisions among people. Immigrants historically have been on one side of a line dividing them from earlier residents, but the problem of divisions within nations and within cities is not limited to immigrants. Painful divisions may be found within the United States as within Israel, as the people of Los Angeles, New York City, and Washington, DC realize; they may be found within Western Europe as well as within Eastern, as Turkish and Algerian residents know too well; and within Canada as within Cambodia, as long-time French-speaking citizens sense.

Walls, physical and social, often mark these divisions, and behind them enclaves of one sort and ghettos of another sort have grown up, raising critical questions of public policy. Are divisions inevitable, and perhaps even desirable? Are immigrants particularly harmed by them, or do they perhaps benefit by being divided from the rest of society? Are enclaves of solidarity not different from ghettos of exclusion? Are there not differences among people that are naturally reflected in how they live, where they live, how they relate to others, how they mark the boundaries between themselves and the society into which they have newly arrived? Do not people in many circumstances, and perhaps particularly immigrants, want walls around them to divide themselves, at least in certain ways, from others outside those walls?

Walls, both real and metaphoric, are in fact a useful way to look at these questions. As I write this, the possibility of a wall, a real, tangible, impermeable wall around the State of Israel is under direct discussion; in the US presidential election, construction of a wall all along the almost 3000-mile US-Mexican border was seriously proposed to control immigration. My focus here is, however, on internal walls, particularly on walls within cities. I want to begin by looking at the question historically, and I want to move quickly through history from the national to the local and urban level, from early history to today. I want in particular to see whether looking at the roles walls have played in earlier times, their classification and the analysis of their purposes, may not clarify for us some of the issues we currently face.

Of Walls and Immigrant Enclaves

There have always been walls; walls of many kinds. One may imagine that walls were not needed within the Garden of Eden, although many paintings portray the expulsion of Adam and Eve from the Garden as their being sent out of the gates and beyond the walls surrounding the Garden, but it cannot have been long thereafter that they were used to provide shelter from the elements and protection from enemies; securing privacy was probably a later need. No one can object, on moral or social grounds, to such walls. They served basic human needs, and their social role was purely protective. Only aggressors could complain.

But those days are long gone. Since those early days, walls have come to play a much more differentiated role. They often reflect and reinforce hierarchies of wealth and power, divisions among peoples, races, ethnic groups, and religions, their hostilities, tensions, and fears. The use of walls has been aggressive as well as defensive; they have imposed the will of the powerful on the powerless and they have protected the powerless from superior force; they have isolated and they have included. In the process, they have come to reflect one of the chief ironies of our historical experience: that those that oppress are themselves limited by their oppression, that those that imprison are themselves imprisoned. Ultimately power dehumanizes those that exercise it, as well as those against whom it is exercised.

This is perhaps a heavy load to ask the metaphor of walls to carry. For walls are, after all, largely only a metaphor for the divisions of society, not their cause. But walls seem to me a striking metaphor. Walls at once exclude and confine. They exclude those on the outside, but also confine those on the inside. They represent power, but they also represent insecurity; domination, but at the same time fear; protection, but at the same time isolation. They are and have always been a second-best solution to the problems of our societies. One might indeed speak of an ideal society, one of peace and freedom, as a society without any walls other than the minimum needed for shelter and privacy. But we have come to accept this second-best solution as the best we can do. We accept walls that divide people and rigidify the relations among them as inevitable; they pervade our cities, they are visible (or block our sight) wherever we look; they symbolize status, rank, and power (or its lack), in fact they are taken for granted and accepted as desirable, in one form or another, by everyone.

Walls are boundaries, but they are more than boundaries. Boundaries also suggest divisions in society, or among societies, lines between groups and peoples. But walls are a particular kind of boundary. Boundaries are, after all, rather neutral; everything has boundaries, for all life and space is bounded. 'Boundaries' say nothing about the relations of those on their opposite sides; they can be friends and neighbors, sharing values and resources, or bitter enemies. 'Boundaries' is thus a bland term. Walls that act as boundaries, however, suggest a particular set of relationships between those on the opposite sides of the boundary they mark. They suggest distance, tension, fear, hostility, inequality, separatedness, alienation.

City walls whose physical strength provided protection for a community appear frequently in history, but the advent of the bourgeois epoch effectively ended that history in most of the world. This was partly because of the industrial revolution; with powerful artillery, walls could not stand a concerted onslaught for long. Another strong influence, however, was the ascendancy of capitalism and the advent of liberal democracy. Power no longer had to be exercised with the symbolism of superior force; the combination of a new economic and a new political freedom meant that hierarchical relationships of power and wealth could be put in place, protected and enhanced through more subtle means than walls of stone. Behind the invisible structures of the market, differences of wealth and power seemed natural and inevitable, rather than artificial and socially constructed. Technological and socioeconomic change combined to make city walls obsolete. Napoleon probably represented the historical turning point; as he swept through Europe, city after city demolished its walls, often replacing them with representative boulevards, parks, or highways. Vienna and Paris are today among the best-known examples of the reuse of earlier defensive walled space.

But let us come to the modern city, for in the complexity of its use of walls it far surpasses anything known in previous centuries. I will choose most of my examples from New York City and California, in each of which both extreme and typical examples can be found. What do we find there?

- Wide curved walls of white stucco around suburban housing estates.
- Barbed wire on the roofs of working-class tenements.
- Basketball courts surrounded by wire mesh fences with gates closed by heavy padlocks.
- Model, planned middle-income communities with ten-foot-high fences, business-like spikes pointing outward, surrounding them.
- Battery Park City, next to the World Trade towers in New York City, its skyscrapers protected on three sides by water and on the fourth by a highway and a controlled covered passage way from the city.
- The Martin Luther King Plaza, built by blacks in Watts, then the ghetto of Los Angeles, after the riots of 1964, now with a heavy but open cast-iron fence around it.
- Union sponsored housing on New York's East River surrounded by razor wire.

- Village Green, a prize-winning, integrated, liberal community in Los Angeles, replacing its inconspicuous fences with more obvious and sturdy ones, Private Property written on them, guarded by a private security patrol.
- Suburbs separated by walls of space from the central city.

The examples show both the proliferation and the diversity of walls now omnipresent in and around our society. But the effort to analyze, to categorize, to order these walls leads to some useful general conclusions. The most useful analytic distinction among walls is that of purpose.

A wall's purpose may be protection or confinement, insulation or limitation. Walls can insulate: against the weather, most obviously, but against the intrusion of threatening strangers as well. They can, for the individual, provide privacy; for a group, identity and chance of cohesion and mutual reinforcement. But walls can also be made to limit others, to keep them behind prison bars, in segregated ghettos, on exposed hillsides and river valleys, in overcrowded tenements or squatter settlements. The key questions are:

- Does the wall perpetuate power, or defend against it?
- Does it reinforce domination, or shield vulnerability?
- Does it isolate, confine, and denigrate, or does it protect, nurture and bring together?

Morally these are the important distinctions. For the wooden stockades built by native Americans may resemble the sharp pointed walls erected by the United States army when it came in to 'pacify' the Indians; yet one wall is for defense, the other for aggression. In today's cities, the poorer residents of the Lower East Side of Manhattan, or of Kreuzberg in Berlin, or of the area around the University of Southern California in Los Angeles, wish to keep wealthier gentrifiers out as much as the residents of the suburbs and luxury housing of Manhattan, Berlin, Los Angeles, want to keep poorer neighbors out; yet the two desires are not equivalent morally. One represents the desire of those poorer to insulate themselves from losses to the more powerful; the other represents the force of the more powerful insulating themselves from the necessity of sharing, or having exposure to, those poorer. One wall defends survival, the other protects privilege.

Walls of the type I have described can be tangible or intangible, physical or social or economic, official or customary. Walls can, and are usually thought of as being, of stone or concrete or barbed wire. But topographic divisions, highways, freeways can be just as much of a wall; the old phrase, 'on the other side of the railroad tracks', references a clearly visible and functional physical wall. Walls can also be of price and status, of rule and prejudice. These are more effective, perhaps, for intangible walls can be internalized, by force and custom, and their causes and functions hidden, the maintenance costs reduced, in the process. Sometimes walls are simply inscribed on a map and enforced by law or official practice: the red lines drawn around minority areas in United States cities in the 1930's, where mortgage loans were refused to anyone living in these 'red-lined' areas, effectively created ghettos; the curfew line drawn in Los Angeles during the uprisings in April of 1992 reflected, and reinforced, a similar ghettoization, even though both were only drawn on paper.

Bearing in mind these differentiations, one might define five types of walls:

1. *Ramparts*: castle walls, in my use symbolically named after the fortifications surrounding the medieval citadels.[1] Citadels are defined by the Oxford English Dictionary as a 'little city... a fortress commanding a city, which it serves both to protect and to keep in subjection'. Walls of domination, expressing superiority, typically today physically represented by superior height in the skyscraper apartments and penthouses that have replaced the mansions of the upper classes in the city, protected by technologically developed walls, gates, and security devices in the suburbs. They generally accompany representative architecture, an architecture of wealth and power. Such walls may be under-played, for similar representative reasons, as in the offices of a government wishing to portray itself as democratic; or they may be deliberately over-powering, as in the official buildings of fascist governments; or they may be treated as business-like and internalized as routine and sensible precautions in an irrationally dangerous world, as at all major airports and in the business districts of London or New York City. Ramparts, small and large, physical and human, pervade the world of those with much to lose. They defend, but against those below in the hierarchy. They define what I shall call, below, the *Dominating City*.
2. *Stockades*: as I would like to use the term, are named after the walls of pointed stakes typically used by army troops in the conquering of the American West from native Americans, similar in function to the walls built around the settlements created by the Roman empire in the lands of the 'barbarians', walls of aggressive superiority. Unlike ramparts, which protect a position already well established, stockades are used to expand territory, to intrude on hostile ground; stockades,

indeed, are likely to be attacked. The market may be the instrument of aggression, or the aggression may be direct and physical; in either case, it is clearly unwelcome. In the relatively tame context of gentrification in New York City, stockades both protect pioneers and secure their invasion, the analogy suggested by Neil Smith (1992) as appropriate for the process creating the *Gentrified City*.

3. *Stucco walls*: often gated, sometimes of glass, is the term I want to use for the walls that shelter exclusive communities whose residents are socially, economically, and politically established, where fear is attenuated by distance and status, but a symbolic demarcation remains necessary to reinforce a security which government already tries to protect. Here walls exclude for reasons of status and social control, symbolically protecting privilege and wealth from the threat of physical intrusion. Unlike ramparts, where walls are likely to be understated but dramatically effective when needed, walls in the *Suburban City* are likely to be pretentious; they are intended to denote comfort, security, and the superiority of those behind them to the world outside.

4. *Fences*: a not inappropriate term for walls that may not be walls at all, but demarcations of protection, of cohesion and solidarity, sometimes defined, as for immigrant quarters, simply by the language of street signs and spoken words, sometimes by the color of the skins of the residents, sometimes by the age and limited pretensions of the housing, sometimes by the social symbolism of the sign that says 'public housing' or the architecture of unornamented blank walls that spells 'project'. These walls may define the *Tenement City*, but they may also surround the trailer parks of migrant workers or the limits of a stable squatter settlement. But here the walls are reluctant, abashed, perhaps even put up with a guilty conscience. For the residents of the tenement city are used to seeing other people's walls aimed at keeping them out; walls more often mean to them, 'keep out' or 'watch out', rather than, 'you are safe inside'. Thus the attempt is to make them visible enough to serve their function, but transparent enough not to reflect hostility or exclusivity.

5. *Prison walls*: the obvious term for walls of confinement, walls defining ghettos and prisons and camps for the temporary warehousing of the unwanted; walls built for the control and re-education of those forced to live behind them. These are the physical walls of the ancient ghettos, the social and economic walls surrounding the modern ghettos, the blank walls of Andrew Cuomo's transitional homeless housing in New York City, the barbed wire surrounding the

camps of Cuban and Haitian refugees in the southern United States. They are the walls that racism has erected around the black ghettos of United States cities, often reinforced by ostentatious public actions, walls of public housing, highways, public institutions. These walls are entirely unwanted by those that are behind them; they are imposed from the outside on those without sufficient power to resist. They define what in the United States context can be called the *Abandoned City*.

What do such walls separate? With regard to the typical large city of the United States today, five distinctive types of quarters can be defined. While each type is represented in multiple neighborhoods, those neighborhoods fall into an ordered pattern, which form essentially separate cities within the city:[2]

- *The dominating city*, with its luxury housing, not really part of the city, but enclaves or isolated buildings occupied by the top of the economic, social and political hierarchy. In the United States, the dominating city tends to be all white, and disproportionately Anglo-Saxon Protestant in origin.
- *The gentrified city*, occupied by the professional/managerial/technical groups, whether yuppie or muppie, often dinks. Ethnically it is relatively open, being to a large extent a meritocracy; but since access to education is unequally distributed, members of dominant groups are heavily over-represented.
- *The suburban city*, sometimes single-family housing in the outer city, sometimes apartments near the center, occupied by skilled workers, mid-range professionals, and upper civil servants. Ethnic characteristics will vary widely by location; blacks and Hispanics will be under-represented, immigrant groups separated.
- *The tenement city*, sometimes cheaper single-family housing areas, most often rentals, occupied by lower-paid workers, blue and white collar, and generally (although less in the United States) including substantial social housing. Most immigrant groups will cluster in the tenement city, although individual members will leave it as their circumstances improve; blacks and Hispanics will, in the United States, be over-represented in most major cities. Whether specific areas in the tenement city should be called 'enclaves' or 'ghettos' we discuss below.
- *The abandoned city*, the end result of trickle-down, left for the poor, the unemployed, the excluded, where in the United States home-less housing for the homeless[3] is most frequently located. Here the poorest

of the poor, and overwhelmingly blacks and Hispanics, will be concentrated. Whether specific areas in the abandoned city should be called 'enclaves' or 'ghettos' we also discuss below.

Such a schematic description should not, of course, be taken as a scientific taxonomy. Boundary lines between them, the walls of the modern city, are dynamic; at the extreme case, as perhaps in Los Angeles, they may move from block to block, street to street, as one group moves in and another moves on or out, and only social or ethnic characteristics may separate one ethnic quarter from the other. But, for the residents of the tenement and the abandoned cities, the Koreatowns and the Watts and the barrios of Los Angeles, for instance, they are oppressively distinct communities, separated by socially palpable walls. If they are taken as separated ethnically but all components of a single 'sub-city' ranging from abandoned to tenement, the boundaries are easier to see.

For all but the cases at the extreme ends of the spectrum, walls will be ambivalent. Who ramparts help and who they oppress is clear; prison and ghetto walls imprison, and everyone knows it. But those in between, the stockades, stucco walls, fences, and barricades, may all be deceptive in appearance, with different meanings for different people, and sometimes even for the same people. Barbed wire protects, but it imprisons; stockades protect the invader, but confine as well; stucco walls and wrought-iron fences provide a sense of identity, but also reflect insecurity, betray vulnerability.

These ambivalences and ambiguities are not accidental. Most people are neither at the top nor at the bottom of the hierarchy of power, but in between. They are in daily contact with some above and some below them in the ladder of wealth and influence; they need both and are needed by both. Thus people may, at different times, both defend and attack, need protection and want to aggress, wish to exclude but wish not to be excluded. Those are the inevitable results of living in a society which is hierarchically ordered; one's position in the hierarchy needs to be continually established and reinforced in all directions. Hence the necessity of walls that reflect such hierarchical status.

But hierarchy is not an inevitable part of social organization. We live in a society in which the prosperity of one is often based on the poverty of the other. That need not be so; today we have the resources, the skills and the room to be able to combine justice with prosperity and mutual respect with efficient organization. Physical rearrangements such as restructuring, can help achieve such a society. Attacking walls of domination and walls of confinement, will help, but they need to be part of a broader effort to build a better society, physically, economically, socially and politically.

Would such a society have no divisions, no walls other than for shelter, within it? Or would there still be cases where fences become walls that are barricades against a foreign and threatening exterior, that might protect a tenement city from invasion from above and from below, from gentrification as well as from abandonment?

Or, to return to the question of immigrants in a society strange to them, might there not be walls that protect the cultural integrity of new arrivals with different traditions, different cultural patterns, perhaps a different language, from heedless incorporation into the dominant society, from loss of their unique culture and indeed identity? Could not walls of separation under such circumstances have strong positive values, without the negatives of walls that oppress?

'Enclaves' is the term often given to areas of spatial concentration, which are walled in socially if not physically, but which have positive consequences for their residents, as opposed to 'ghettos', which are entirely negative. But whether a particular area of racial or ethnic concentration is an enclave or a ghetto is not always so easy to say, even though the difference is crucial both for historic understanding and for public policy. The issue of immigrant 'ghettos' has become a highly visible one recently in the United States, in part through more detailed looks at the complexities of Los Angeles and its riots, and in part through work on specific immigrant enclaves, such as of Cubans in Miami. The situation is particularly complex in the United States because there are central differences in the experience of blacks and of immigrants. An understanding of the difference between the walling of black and the walling of immigrant spaces is an important one both for analytic clarity and for policy. The assumption that blacks should behave like immigrants, that black ghettos ought to be steps towards self-organization and upward mobility as immigrant enclaves are thought to be, plays a major role in attitudes towards blacks. Its ultimate expression is blaming the victim: 'if Koreans can do it, why can't blacks, its their own fault if they don't'. In the debate, the question of whether separation of immigrant spaces is really desirable and whether there really is a difference between ghettos and enclaves is often forgotten.

Like the walls that create them, enclaves and ghettos play different roles at different times for different groups. 'Enclave' is usually the word used for those areas in which immigrants have congregated and which are seen as having positive value, as opposed to the word 'ghetto', which has a clearly pejorative connotation. But, historically 'ghetto' can indeed have a

Of Walls and Immigrant Enclaves 39

positive aspect. Richard Sennett speaks, for instance of the ghetto as 'a space at once a space of repression and a space of identification',[4] and its residents have pride in Harlem whilst at the same time they condemn segregation. By the same token, 'enclave' has a negative aspect; its original use, derived from 'enclosure', was to designate part of a city or country surrounded by foreign territory, and typically referred to an imperial enclave in a colonial country. It was thus both dominant and defensive; it suggested power, but also fear and limitation.[5]

While both 'enclave' and 'ghetto' thus are two-sided concepts, 'enclave' is here used to describe those spaces given a primarily positive meaning by their residents, 'ghetto' those with a predominantly negative meaning. It is important to remember: all spaces of concentrated activity share some characteristics of a ghetto and some of an enclave. Pure types do not exist. While I am not concerned here with the colonial meaning of enclave, that is, the walled spaces of those in positions of superiority protecting their privileges, the two-sided nature of enclave walls is apparent even in those cases; while the walls of colonial enclaves permitted their residents to dominate their surroundings, they also confined them and reflected their fear of revolt and retaliation.

The ambiguity is found even in the archetype of the ghetto, the Jewish ghetto of the middle ages. Historically many of these early Jewish ghettos were clearly enclaves as well as ghettos. The first known legal segregation of Jews was in Speyer, where the bishop, in order to attract Jews to the city and thus 'add to its honor,' gave them the right to have a separate residential quarter where 'they might not be readily disturbed by the insolence of the populace' (Lestschinsky, 1928).

Immigrants in the United States have historically first settled in separate communities defined by their national origin, forming enclaves providing mutual support and an orientation to the new land. Perhaps because such communities have always been seen as voluntary and transitional, their characteristics are not normally considered in the context of ghettoization or segregation. It was assumed workers employed in them earned less than they would have if they had been in the mainstream work force, that they submitted to superexploitation because they saw it as a likely way out of the enclave and into the mainstream. In many cases the immigrant networks in fact supported the first entry of immigrants into contact with the mainstream, for example Korean grocery stores in non-Korean neighborhoods, Chinese restaurants catering to non-Chinese clientele.[6]

Some discussions about 'ethnic enclaves' today make a different point. Those today differ from these immigrant landing places in that those in enclaves confine their economic activity to within the enclave itself, but earn more than their compatriots otherwise similarly situated but living outside the enclave and employed outside it. This was the finding of Wilson and Portes (Portes et al., 1993), studying the experience of the Cuban community in Miami. They speculated that there was a productive attenuation of class relationships within the enclave, in which ties of ethnic solidarity resulted in employers providing training, skills, and upward mobility in return for initially lower wages:

> Ethnic ties suffuse an otherwise 'bare' class relationship with a sense of collective purpose ... But the utilization of ethnic solidarity in lieu of enforced discipline also entails reciprocal obligations. If employers can profit from the willing self-exploitation of fellow immigrants, they are also obliged to reserve for them ... supervisory positions ... to train them ... and to support their ... move into self-employment. (Portes and Bach, 1985: 343; see Waldinger, 1987: 445)

One might quarrel with the theoretical formulation of 'collective purpose' as a modification of class relationships, and there have certainly been arguments about the validity of the empirical findings. But the issue I want to raise here is whether these findings can be generalized to support the conclusion that the spatial separation of any immigrant group, or any ethnic group, is likely to be a positive pattern for that group. Not all concentrations of those with a common ethnic background are enclaves, in the predominantly positive sense in which the word is used here. John Logan and his colleagues point out, for instance, in a detailed analysis of the Los Angeles metropolitan area, that Japanese, Chinese, and Korean enclaves are significantly different in their economic structure than areas of concentration of Mexicans or Filipinos (Logan, Alba and McNulty, 1994). But, for the United States, the differences among immigrant groups pale in comparison to the differences between immigrant groups as a whole and blacks. The question can thus be formulated in very pointed fashion:

> Does the spatial separation of blacks have the same positive values that was found for Cubans in Miami? Are all ghettos potentially enclaves?

The traditional answer has generally been an implicit 'yes', although recognizing (or stressing) that the difference in degree is vast, with residential segregation being the primary culprit.[7] And that answer is true, in part: there is an identity derived from the ghetto as a localized space, a special cultural development, a support for political leadership, economic gains from retailing and services that meet local needs, that is analogous to that claimed for immigrant enclaves. But the links between these pluses and the existence of separated spaces is more and more questionable for the black ghetto. Saskia Sassen says flatly that the 'recent development in immigrant communities... the expansion of an informal economy... contrasts sharply with the growth of an underclass in black neighborhoods...' (Sassen, 1990). Today's black ghetto is a ghetto, not an enclave, even if those confined to it are sometimes able to marshal strength from that very confinement.

I have used the word 'black' here, rather than 'African-American', to highlight the question and avoid prejudging it.[8] While 'African-American' emphasizes a positive ethnic identity linked to a country or continent of origin, and thus establishes a basis for identity and a claim for equality of treatment that has strong positive value, the issue here is rather the relationship with the dominant group(s). For that purpose, African-American suggests a similarity with Korean-American or Italian-American that is misleading. Blacks are not immigrants, and their position is markedly different from that of other 'minority' groups. The black ghetto might thus logically be expected to be quite different in its characteristics from the immigrant ghettos as pictured by Portes.

Spatial patterns reflect the difference. The pattern for the black population is simple: in the areas in which most blacks are found, there are few or no whites; in the areas in which most whites live, there are few or no blacks. The distribution of the Asian population is quite different; it shows similar areas of concentration, but also shows much dispersion. And even in areas of concentration, there is substantial overlap with other population groups. This is not simply because there are fewer immigrants than blacks (in fact, the absolute numbers are quite similar, although of course immigrants belong to many ethnic groups, as indeed 'blacks' do), or because immigrant patterns are 'newer' and have not yet stabilized. Indeed, the more immigrants there are, and the longer they are here, the more dispersed their pattern is likely to be. The immigrant pattern is more that of a set of enclaves; the black reflects ghettoization in its harshest form.

How then does one tell a ghetto from an enclave? The two distinctions made above between blacks and Asians in New York City – economic position and spatial pattern – are at the core of the effort, but a more precise definition requires considerably more empirical work. A preliminary specification might involve answers to the following questions:

1. Are the walls that surround the cluster permeable from the inside, that is, can those living within them move out if they wish, or are they

confined within it against their will? The question is generally congruent with the question: were the walls created by those living within them, or by those outside?
2. Are those within the walls moving up within the hierarchy of wealth and power in the society, or are they largely excluded from the mainstream of society, at the bottom and, given existing relationships, relegated to stay there? The question is generally congruent with the question: are those within the walls receiving equal, or at least increasingly equal, treatment at the hands of the established society, or are they increasingly underserved by it and excluded from the benefits of membership?

So spatial separation is not in itself either a good thing or a bad thing for those thus separated; walls are neither inherently good nor evil. For immigrants in the United States separation has been, in many situations, a good thing; for blacks, it has been a largely negative experience, albeit with certain positive features. The difference between the two may be described metaphorically, as differences in the nature of the walls that create the separation.

All walls are boundaries, but all boundaries are not walls. Perhaps one way of defining a better society would be to speak of it as a wall-less society, a society in which the divisions among people were not equated to walls between them. We have sometimes, in recent years, attempted to justify segregation and even ghettoization by saying that it can be a source of strength for those within the ghetto: it can produce solidarity, creativity, bonds of mutual support, which a less confined environment might not permit. It is certainly true that ghettos have produced wonderful and heroic actions. But that is certainly no justification for the creation of ghettos. Those who have lost one arm or one leg can sometimes do wonders with the other; that is no reason to cut off an arm or a leg.

A wall-less society: but not a society without any walls. Walls for shelter, certainly; but perhaps also walls signifying boundaries between culturally distinct groups, walls preserving particular histories, asserting particular identities, creating particular communities? The dominant vision in the United States has shifted radically on these questions over the last hundred years. Beginning with the melting-pot formulation – still implicit in many circles – it has moved to multi-culturalism, an espousal of differences in community but in which equal treatment often results in a bland egalitarianism where the essence of differences are down-played or ignored; to a mosaic formulation, in which differences are highlighted but presumptively seen as parts of a larger pattern that makes sense as a whole.

The cultural questions involved are extraordinarily complex, and outside the scope of this chapter. But the political and policy questions are not. And on these, the previous discussion has, I believed, led to some answers. Cultural differences, multi-cultural patterns, or mosaic designs for which a society may aim may produce walls of various kinds. In and of themselves, such walls may have positive outcomes. But hierarchical, political and social walls, and the spatial boundaries that they represent, are always undesirable as a long-run pattern. Differences among equals are one thing; differences that reflect hierarchical relationships are quite another. Cultural multiculturalism[9] does not by itself produce political or economic equality (in the sense of fairness, not uniformity); quite to the contrary, political and economic equality are necessary for meaningful respect among cultures. Walls can sometimes promote such equality, help in the move towards it, as enclave walls do. But walls more often imprison ghettos, whose cultural development is but a poor compensation for the political, social, and economic inequality they reflect and increase.

In unraveling these complex questions the public treatment of the desirability of walls dividing groups plays a critically important role.

Notes

1. The term was first used in the juxtaposition suggested here by John Friedmann in Friedmann and Goetz, 1982.
2. I have discussed the concept of the 'Quartered City' in several other pieces (Marcuse 1989, Marcuse 1991). 'Quartered' is used both in the sense of 'drawn and quartered' and of residential 'quarters'; there are essentially four such quarters, the very wealthy not being bound by any specific spatial configuration as to where they live. See also Mollenkopf and Castells, 1991 (especially the Introduction and Conclusion) and Wallock, 1987.
3. For the concept of 'home-less housing' and discussion of its location, see Marcuse and Vergara, 1992.
4. Sennett, 1992, p. 40.
5. There are indeed other uses of 'enclave' which stress the 'positive' or 'voluntary' character to the exclusion of the negative. See, for instance, Vernoy's (1993) definition: '[An] enclave is an enclosed sector of the city, usually fairly small, that uses its separation from the rest of the city as a means to increase its potential land rent differential'. It is a usage, in real estate terms, parallel to the broader and richer concept of the 'citadel' introduced by John Friedmann (1982) much earlier.
6. The literature is replete with descriptions of such enclaves: Dahya discusses Pakistanis in Bradford, England, Suttles Italians in Chicago, for example. See Van Kempen, et al., p. 3.

7. For a more complex view, largely quantitatively based, see Logan, et al., 1994, pp. 12 and 16–17. The Clinton administration's empowerment zone program implicitly adopts the enclave rationale; for a critique, see Marcuse, 1994.
8. Following Herb Gans' logic, in Gans, 1991: '...African-American...is a term that seems to me to emphasize an ethnic heritage, and thus to deemphasize, if not intentionally, the racial issues inherent in the term black': p. x.
9. For a provocative and, in my opinion, sound discussion of the limitations of the traditional concept of multiculturalism see Jayasuriya, 1990.

References

Friedmann, John and Wolff Goetz, (1982) 'World City Formation: An agenda for research and action', *International Journal of Urban and Regional Research*, 6: 309–44.

Gans, Herbert (1991) *People, Plans, and Policies: Essays on Poverty, Racism, and Other National Urban Problems* (New York: Columbia University Press).

Jayasuriya, Laksiri (1990) 'Rethinking Australian multiculturalism: towards a new paradigm', *The Australian Quarterly*, Autumn: 50–63.

Lestschinsky, Jakob (1928) 'Ghetto', *Encyclopedia of the Social Sciences*, 650.

Logan, John, Richard Alba and Thomas McNulty (1994) 'Ethnic Economies in Metropolitan Regions', *Social Forces*, March: 691–724.

Marcuse, Peter (1994) 'What's Wrong with Empowerment Zones', *City Limits*, (May).

Marcuse, Peter (1989) '"Dual City": a Muddy Metaphor for a Quartered City', *International Journal of Urban and Regional Research*, 13(4): 697–708.

Marcuse, Peter (1991) 'Housing Markets and Labour Markets in the Quartered City', in John Allen and Chris Hamnett, *Housing and Labour Markets: Building the Connections* (London: Unwin Hyman) pp. 118–35.

Marcuse, Peter and Vergara (1992) 'Gimme Shelter: Homelessness in New York City', *Artforum* (Spring): 88–92.

Mollenkopf, John H. and Manuel Castells (eds) (1991) *Dual City: Restructuring New York* (New York: Russell Sage Foundation).

Portes, Alejandro and G. Bach (1985) *Latin Journey* (Berkeley: University of California Press).

Portes, Alejandro, Alex Stepick and Patricia Fernandez-Kelly (1993) *City on the Edge: Transformation of Miami* (University of California Press).

Sassen, Saskia (1990) 'Economic Restructuring and the American City'. *Annual Review of Sociology,* 16: 484.

Sennett, Richard (1992) 'The Origins of the Modern Ghetto', Paper delivered at Arden House Urban Forum on Place and Right, mimeo.

Smith, Neil (1992) 'New City, New Frontier: The Lower East Side as Wild Wild West', in Michael Sorkin (ed.), *Variations on a Theme Park: The New American City and the End of Public Space* (New York: Farrar, Straus & Giroux), 61–93.

Van Kempen, R.R. Teule and J. van Weesep (1992) 'Urban Policy and the Demise of the Dutch Welfare State', *Tijdschrift voor Economische en Sociale Geografie*, 83.

Vernoy, Andrew (1993) *The Enclave as a Strategy of Urban Revitalization*. Working Paper 039, School of Architecture and Planning, The University of Texas at Austin.

Waldinger, Rogers (1993) 'The ethnic enclave debate revisited', *International Journal of Urban and Regional Research*, vol. 17, no. 3, pp. 445–52.

Wallock, Leonard (1987) 'Tales of Two Cities: Gentrification and Displacement in Contemporary New York', in Mary B. Campbell and Mark Rollins (eds), *Begetting Images* (New York: Peter Lang).

3 Determinants of Immigrant Integration: An International Comparative Analysis
Myron Weiner

This chapter identifies the factors that affect the absorption of migrants in advanced industrial societies, particularly on the relationship between migrants and the native population. What determines whether the relationship will be hostile or supportive, and what differences do public policies make in influencing that relationship? Three factors are considered: (1) the willingness of the society to absorb the immigrants; (2) the commitment of the immigrants to their new society; and (3) the structure of the labor market. Particular attention is given to defining the nature of the social contract between a regime and the migrants it admits. Social contracts specify the conditions under which migrants may enter the country, including both what is expected from the migrants and what in turn is promised by the regime. Social contracts are embedded in rules of entry and in subsequent policies adopted by the government. Different kinds of social contracts are described. Before discussing them, let me present some basic questions, figures as facts.

Can Mexican migrants be made into Americans, Russians into Israelis, Algerians into Frenchmen, Turks into Germans, Koreans into Japanese, Chinese into Australians, Bangladeshis into Englishmen?

To raise these questions is to demonstrate what an extraordinary transformation has taken place in the demographic composition of many of the advanced industrial countries and how complex is the phenomena of changing national identities. In the last half of this century vast numbers of people have moved from the Third World into advanced industrial countries, and, in the post-cold-war era, from one European country to another. Western Europe alone has 16 million immigrants and non-nationals, largely from North Africa, the Middle East and Asia, and from East and Southeast Europe. The United States has 21 million immigrants (8 per cent of its population) and each year three quarters to a million new migrants enter. Nearly a quarter of the Australian population and 15 per cent of the

Determinants of Immigrant Integration

Canadian population are foreign born. Even Japan, perhaps the most homogeneous of the developed countries, has 1.2 million foreigners, including 700 000 Koreans.

How to absorb, incorporate, integrate, assimilate – the words themselves suggest complexity, ambiguity, and contention – migrants and refugees has become a major issue in dozens of countries. In country after country, population movements have spawned a new vocabulary to describe their complex and diverse character. Each country has its own often distinctive vocabulary to characterize these flows: in Germany the *Ubersiedler* or Germans from East Germany who fled to the West after the Berlin Wall was erected in 1961 and who came before the collapse of the East German Honecker regime; the *Aussiedler* or 'resettlers' – ethnic Germans from Poland, Rumania and the Soviet Union; *Auslander*, or non-German foreigners including *Gastarbeiter*, or guestworkers (Peck, 1992). The British Nationality Act of 1981 distinguishes among British Citizens, British Dependent Territories Citizens, British Overseas Citizens, British Subjects and British Protected Persons, and makes a distinction between two main types of immigration status, patrial (with the 'right of abode') and non-patrial. (Dummet and Nicol, 1990) The United States admits refugees, some as immigrants, others with 'temporary protected status', (TPS), and 'extended voluntary departure' (EVD), green card holders with the right to remain and become naturalized citizens, and 'replenishment agricultural workers' who can stay and work in the United States for a limited period. And each of these countries has illegal migrants – known in the United States as 'undocumented'.

All these terms (and we have given a sample from only three countries) matter for they tell us a great deal about who can be admitted into a country, their characteristics, whether they can stay permanently or not, whether they or their children can become citizens and how they are regarded and treated by the native population and by the state. These terms are indicative, in effect, of social contracts between governments and those they admit into the country. As we shall argue, these social contracts shape the relationship between the migrants and their host society; they are among the most critical factors in explaining the variations in the capacity of societies to absorb migrants. Social contracts are embedded in rules of entry and in subsequent policies adopted by the government toward the migrant populations. We can thus distinguish between two distinct, but related sets of policies – immigration policies and immigrant policies. The former refers to those policies dealing with admission, and the latter with the treatment of migrants once they have entered the country.

This chapter focuses on three factors that affect the relationship between migrants and the native population in advanced industrial countries. They influence what migration and migrant policies are adopted and, to a considerable extent, whether these policies succeed in facilitating migrant integration. The first is whether a society is willing to absorb migrants and, therefore, puts in place policies that grant migrants and their children the same legal status as that of the native population. The second, is the willingness of the migrants themselves to accept membership, both in the legal sense and by adopting a new identity. The third, is the structure of the labor market which enables the migrants to find a niche in the economy, one that frees them from excessive dependence upon the country's social services. We shall describe each of these in turn, in each instance suggesting some of the relevant policies which appear to be important in the migration absorption process.

Before turning to these factors it is necessary, however, to make two caveats. The first is that the relationships suggested here between specific policies and specific outcomes should be regarded as hypotheses rather than as research findings. There is sufficient comparative evidence to suggest that they are plausible, but not that they are demonstrable relationships. The second caveat is that even when a relationship between a policy and an outcome is established, one should be cautious in the application of these findings. The process of integration, varies so greatly from one society to another that transferring policy 'lessons' can only be done at some risk. What is a politically acceptable citizenship policy for the United States, a country of immigration, may not be politically acceptable in Germany, France or Japan. Ethnically heterogeneous countries deal with the issues of integration differently than do homogeneous countries. Each country faced with a large population influx must wrestle with the question of its meaning for national identity and cultural pluralism.

CITIZENSHIP RULES, RIGHTS AND BENEFITS

Not all countries want to absorb their migrants. Some countries want temporary workers, not citizens. Some countries are content to have migrants remain in the labor force for their entire lifetime, but are unwilling to extend them the rights and benefits, including citizenship, provided to the rest of the society. There are at least three distinct sets of policies that reflect and shape government attitudes toward migrant integration:

1. Migrants may be admitted to fill temporary positions in the labor force only for a limited period during which time they are given

access to those minimal welfare benefits (such as health care) that are essential to their effective economic performance.
2. Migrants may be permitted to stay indefinitely and given many if not all of the entitlements provided citizens, but they and their children are excluded (or nearly excluded) from citizenship.
3. Migrants and their locally born children may be readily admitted into citizenship.

Migrants cannot be incorporated into the host society as long as they are viewed as temporary residents – that is, the host society in effect rejects their permanent incorporation. Guest workers may be treated well, given accommodation, provided employment, and offered access to many of the benefits of the welfare system, but they will be regarded as outsiders in the cultural, social and political sense as long as they are seen as temporary sojourners. However, temporary migration arrangements have often proven to be more enduring than either the migrants or the government intended. What happens, then, to the children of the migrants who are locally born? Are they granted citizenship as a matter of birthright? Are they given the right to acquire citizenship at the age of maturity? Or are they faced with the same barriers to citizenship as their migrant parents? Does the host society educate the children in the local language and treat them in the same fashion as the children of the natives? Or is there enforced separation aimed at inducing migrants and their children to return to their country of origin?

The contrast between Germany and France in their treatment of guest workers and their children is instructive. Germany does not regard itself as a country of immigration (*'Deutschland ist kein Einwanderungsland'*) and does not automatically grant citizenship to German-born children of migrants, nor does it readily accept naturalized immigrants who seek to integrate into German society by becoming citizens. Only those who are of German descent, with ties of *blut*, are readily accorded membership in the German nation. (Hailbronner, 1989) and only Germans can be of German nationality. Thus, the German media described the three victims of a fatal firebombing of longtime Turkish residents in Molln, near Hamburg as 'Turks', including ten year-old Yeliz Arslans who was born in Germany and never lived anywhere else.

Germany is hardly alone in its reluctance to readily admit migrants and their children into citizenship. The oil-producing Arab states exclude their millions of guest workers from citizenship, Arabs as well as Asians. Palestinian refugees from Israel, and their children, are excluded from citizenship throughout the Middle East, with the notable exception of Jordan

(Weiner, 1982). Among European countries there are variations in how difficult it is for migrant workers to acquire citizenship; it is easiest among the Scandinavian countries, and difficult, costly, and time-consuming in Switzerland and in Germany. (Hammar, 1985; Hoffmann-Nowotny, 1985). Under German law naturalization is possible after ten years of residence, but it is not a right, and authorities have discretion in whether or not to grant citizenship. In the Netherlands only the third generation obtains citizenship at birth but migrants can become citizens, with some difficulty, after five years of residence and a demonstrable knowledge of Dutch (Hammar, 1985).

In contrast, the French do not regard nationality as a matter of blood and birth, but as a matter of acquired culture. If peasants can be made into Frenchmen, so can immigrants. Speak French, adopt French gestures and manners, identify with and take pride in French culture, and one can become French. Indeed, as Gerard Noiriel has written, (Noiriel, 1992) France absorbed large numbers of migrants from Italy, Spain, and Belgium in the second half of the nineteenth century, and Slavs from Poland, Czechoslovakia and the Ukraine during the interwar period, even though France does not regard itself as an immigrant country. While Germany continues to adhere to the principle of *jus sanguinis* and a restrictive naturalization process, the French grant citizenship to the children of migrants born in France and have a less restrictive naturalization process.

State policies toward citizenship are readily reflected in naturalization rates. Few of the 5 million immigrants in Germany (7.9 per cent of the West German population, prior to unification) have become naturalized citizens; a majority have resided in Germany for more than a decade and an estimated 70 per cent of the 1 million foreign children under age were born in Germany and are without citizenship. In France locally born children of aliens can become French citizens at the age of 18 if they have resided in France for five years and have not been convicted criminals. It should be noted, however, that the belief that nationality depended on blood was also widely held in France throughout the nineteenth century, until the passage of a French nationality law in 1889 which established the principle of *jus soli* in order to ensure that the children of Belgian and Italian migrants could be conscripted into the military (Brubaker, 1989).

Several other countries similarly provide citizenship to those they admit. Australia ended its White Australia migration policy in 1972 and since then has had a nondiscriminatory migration policy (Carens, 1988b), accords full rights to migrants (except voting rights) and easy naturalization after three years or residency. Over 23 per cent of Australia's population is foreign born, among the highest of advanced industrial democracies except for Israel. A study reveals that Asian migrants value Australian citizenship more highly than do immigrant Britons; immigrants from the Third World are twice as likely as immigrants from the English-speaking countries to become Australian citizens (Evans, 1987). Great Britain never had a guest-worker program; its migrants are largely from British Commonwealth countries who came under an elaborate set of rules that determined 'rights of abode' and citizenship. Today, an overwhelming proportion of the foreign-born in Great Britain are now citizens (Dummet and Nicol, 1990; Peters and Davis, 1986; on British immigration policy see Layton-Henry, 1985; Ivor Crewe, 1983; and Brown, 1983).

Immigrants to the United States can become citizens – indeed, have a right to citizenship – after five years of continuous residence if they pass a test in speaking, reading and writing English and a simple test on the US constitution and history. Approximately two-thirds of migrants living in the United States for five years or longer are naturalized. (On US naturalization see DeSipio, 1987 Easterlin, *et al.*, 1982; Gordon, 1990; North, 1987; Pachon, 1987; Portes, 1987) US laws also automatically confer citizenship on individuals born in the United States (Schuck and Smith, 1985), and provide legal rights to aliens (including illegal aliens) under the Fourteenth Amendment, and selected public benefits (Bennett, 1986).

Easy access to citizenship by migrants does not prevent the rise of conflicts between migrants and the native population. Opposition to the foreign-born has been a European-wide phenomenon, intensified in recent years by the economic down-turn and by the upsurge in an influx of asylum seekers from Eastern Europe and from the Third World. Virtually every Western European country now has an anti-foreign right-wing political party calling for an end to migration, barring refugees, denying citizenship to migrants and their children, and in some countries even advocating the forced repatriation of migrants. In most countries the debate is not over whether new immigrants should be admitted – the answer is uniformly 'no' – but whether existing migrants and their locally born children should be admitted into citizenship, whether the doors should remain open to refugees, and whether migration means multiculturalism.

Countries do, however, vary significantly in the level of conflict between migrants and the local population and in part these variations are related to naturalization and citizenship laws. The traditional countries of immigration, those with the most generous naturalization and citizenship laws, have been engaged in public discussions over immigration policies – who and how many to admit, and how to prevent illegal entry – but the question of how to treat legal immigrants has not been as divisive an issue.

It is hardly a coincidence that the most severe anti-foreign attacks in Western Europe have taken place in Germany, the country that is restrictive on naturalizing foreigners and where popular attitudes equate German nationality to German descent. Countries that facilitate naturalization and that grant citizenship to the locally born children of migrants are not without tensions, but integration has generally been smoother, especially for the second generation. The hospitality of the political system toward acquiring citizenship and nationality is by no means the only determinant of whether immigrants and their children are integrated into the political system and whether conflicts erupt between migrants and natives, but it is clearly one of the most important factors.

The willingness of the host society to incorporate migrants into the political, social and economic life of the country – and hence the ability of migrants to be incorporated – are substantially greater if citizens feel there is effective control over entry than if the flows are unregulated. A high rate of illegal migration, and an uncontrollable large-scale refugee influx will tend to heighten xenophobic fears in most societies. California provides a recent example of growing public resentment of the high rate of illegal migration. In November 1994 59 per cent of California voters endorsed a referendum to deny education, health, and social services to illegal immigrants by requiring service providers to identify all persons suspected of being an illegal immigrant. Many citizens were not motivated by xenophobic considerations, but by a concern over the maldistribution of these costs between the central and state governments, and over the inability of the federal government to control entry and access to the labor market. These concerns are by no means limited to California or to other American states, but are also present in Japan and in Western Europe. The world-wide growth in illegal migration and in unwarranted claims for asylum could have an impact in the attitudes of governments and their citizens toward legal migration and toward the incorporation of migrants into their societies.

MIGRANT PREFERENCES

A second determinant of integration is whether migrants wish to be incorporated. If migrants anticipate returning home, if they regard the host society merely as a temporary place to acquire income or as a temporary refuge from the violence and persecution of their homeland, then they are not likely to want to go through the process of redefining their identity, a process that is central to assimilation and incorporation. The willingness to acquire the local language is important, but in itself insufficient. As important is whether the migrant is prepared to acquire a new sense of identity, to declare oneself French, American, British, Israeli, or Australian. The willingness to change one's identity, or at least to add a second identity – perhaps among the more painful psychological experiences humans can encounter but also one of the most liberating – is shaped first and foremost by the willingness of the host culture to accept the immigrant into the community. As long as the host culture regards immigrants as permanent aliens and denies citizenship, then migrants will cling to their existing identities. Germans often make the point that Turkish migrants do not want to become German citizens so that it is unnecessary for Germany to liberalize its naturalization laws. The policy of exclusion, however, has promoted a reluctance to seek admission.

Another critical determinant of the attitude of migrants toward adaptation to the host society is whether they are socially or politically rejected by their home country. Refugees are likely to grasp the opportunity to acquire a new identity if they know they cannot return home. Examples abound: Jews from eastern Europe readily adapted to their American homeland in the latter part of the nineteenth and early part of the twentieth centuries. Armenians from Russia and Turkey, Greeks from Turkey, Bhais from Iran, Indians from Uganda, Hindus from Pakistan, Muslims from India, Jews from north Africa and other 'rejected' peoples have similarly eagerly sought citizenship and an identity in new homelands in the United States, Britain, Canada, Australia, Greece, India, Pakistan and Israel.

The creation of an enclave within the new homeland is sometimes regarded as an impediment to the process of assimilation, particularly to learning the language and culture of the host society. At the same time enclaves are often seen as a haven which enables the migrant to adjust to the new environment. It makes a difference, however, if the enclave is a permanent ghetto or a half-way station, whether socially mobile members of the immigrant community are freely able to move into the larger society or are restricted to the ghetto through the housing and employment practices of the larger community. Self-segregation into neighborhoods has not been a barrier to assimilation when the migrants and their children are able to acquire the same education as others in the society, and find employment outside the community; but self-segregation accompanied by limited education and employment opportunities will sustain separateness and often generate conflict between the migrants and indigenes and sometimes among the various migrant communities.

The process of linguistic assimilation is likely to occur more rapidly if the stream of migration is not a large and continuous one. When, for whatever reason, the migration stream has ended or been reduced to a trickle, ties to the homeland are likely to be reduced, and the process of assimilation will be accelerated. A continuous infusion of substantial numbers of people from the homeland, bearing with them their language and news of the homeland, particularly if many of the newcomers regard themselves as temporary sojourners, may weaken the migrant's resolve to acquire a new identity with their new homeland. Proximity, easy access to the homeland, and a high migration return rate may also slow the pace of identity formation. The central question to be asked is what are the incentives for migrants to learn the language of the host society and, more broadly, to adopt behavioral patterns that make them more acceptable to the host population? What opportunities are available to them, for example, with regard to education, housing and employment?

The willingness of migrants to be incorporated also depends, as we have suggested, upon the easy acquisition of citizenship, particularly for the children of migrants. It makes a psychological difference if native born children of foreigners are regarded by indigenes and by themselves as Americans, Australians, Israelis, or British at birth, than if formal citizenship must wait until the age of 18. Citizenship at birth implies, indeed, grants unconditional equality; individuals who must wait until they reach maturity, and then must decide their citizenship may be under pressure from friends, relatives, and the government of their parent's homeland not to 'surrender' the identity of their parents.

There is considerable disagreement as to whether migrants are more willing to be absorbed if the host society grants some value to the culture of the migrant community. Many French have argued that assimilation must be total, that the French government need not give any recognition to the migrant's language and culture, but rather that it is the task of the migrant to acquire the French language, learn French history and literature, and identify with French values. In contrast, immigrant societies, such as Canada, Australia, the United States, and Israel have been more willing to grant some degree of cultural autonomy to the migrant, to accept the organization of groups along ethnic lines and the articulation of ethnic claims as legitimate, and to assume that the host culture itself should take on some of the elements of the migrant culture – by accepting the cuisine, borrowing from the language, and most of all granting respect to the migrant's culture. An important unresolved question for research is whether pride in one's own culture makes assimilation easier or slows the process. Alternatively, if the host culture looks down upon the migrant's culture, will migrants lack the self-esteem necessary for social mobility, which will generate resentment, and, therefore, slow assimilation? Or does cultural marginality hasten a change in identity?

Determinants of Immigrant Integration

Few issues associated with migrant absorption have generated as much political controversy as the issue of 'multiculturalism', an ill-defined, contentious term that arouses passions among its supporters and opponents. Supporters see multiculturalism as a set of state policies aimed at enabling, even encouraging, migrant communities to maintain their own language, culture, identity, and especially their history, and to act as a cohesive political force. Thus, some multiculturalists call for bilingual education not as a transition to learning the language of the host society, but as a means of sustaining linguistic and cultural identities. Multiculturalists may also advocate state-funding for cultural activities by immigrant communities, and encourage migrant communities to organize themselves politically and elect their own members to legislative bodies. Critics of multiculturalism are opposed to state policies that induce a sense of separateness through bilingual education, and are concerned that separate education may marginalize the children of migrants in the labor market. They are also opposed to separate electoral representation which enables ethnic communities to elect their own leaders to legislative bodies and makes it unnecessary for politicians to try to win electoral support among the ethnic minorities.

The French continue to debate the question of whether Muslim girls can come to class covering their heads and faces with a scarf – an act interpreted by many French secularists as an attack against the secular basis of the French school system, and by feminists as a symbol of Islamic repression of women. Others defend the rights of Muslims to assert their religious identity even in public institutions. In Great Britain many Muslims have called for government-funding of private Muslim schools noting that the state already provides support to private Christian and Jewish schools. Others are concerned that the state may then be nurturing intolerant, religious fundamentalism. In the United States the debate over multiculturalism has in part centered on the issues of multicultural curricula in the schools, and on bilingual education, seen by advocates as a means of inculcating pride, and by critics as a way in which ethnic community leaders induce and even force young people to resist cultural assimilation. Within each of the migrant communities in the United States, and certainly between them, there are major differences in their attitudes toward linguistic and cultural assimilation. Russian and Asian migrants to the United States resist government programs to require their children to attend classes in their native tongue, preferring instead to immerse their children in English medium classes as the fast track toward higher education and economic advancement. But many (by no means all) Spanish-speaking Americans are eager to place their children in Spanish classes so as to strengthen their Mexican-American or Puerto Rican identity. Among Muslims in both France and Britain there are cleavages between those who are pressing for separate schools with Islamic content, and those who are committed to secularization and cultural assimilation. Moreover, everywhere there are generational differences: the young are sometimes more assimilationist than their parents, and at other times and places, more militant in seeking to assert their own cultural identity. These issues remain unresolved, in part because proponents of the various positions differ in what they regard as the desirable end points. Some are concerned with social mobility; others with improved inter-group relations; still others with preserving culturally distinct communities or with cultural assimilation.

What government policies, public attitudes, and external conditions influence the willingness of migrants to become integrated is a complex matter, but it is clear that the desire to be integrated is an essential feature of the process.

THE LABOR MARKET

The structure of the labor market is another factor in whether migrants and their children are economically and socially incorporated into the host society. Are migrants and their children confined to jobs that the natives do not want and which offer few opportunities for advancement? Is there an assumption by indigenous members of the host society that the children of uneducated migrants are fit only for the same menial jobs as that of their immigrant parents? Do the teachers of migrant children regard them as less able than the children of natives, and therefore fated for menial work?

The selective recruitment of migrants to fill menial positions in an economy where there is a rapid acquisition of new technologies and where cognitive skills and education are essential for mobility is likely to lead to a bifurcated society, with migrants locked into positions at the lower end of the labor market: helots in the economy and in the social and political order. Unskilled migrants to the United States at the turn of the century functioned in a very different kind of economy than unskilled migrants to the United States today. Individuals with little education, but personal drive, had far greater opportunities for mobility than at present when high levels of education are required for social mobility. For this reason some have argued for a selective immigration policy which gives priority to individuals with high levels of education, skills, and financial resources which will facilitate their integration into the labor market. Asian migrants to the United States – who now exceed the annual legal intake of migrants from Latin America (Gordon, 1990) – have been more readily incorporated into the American economy and society than the less educated migrants from Mexico, Puerto Rico, and most other areas of the Caribbean, not withstanding the long history of racial prejudice against Asians in the United States. A large proportion of the migrants from India, Hong Kong, Taiwan, South Korea, and the Philippines have educational levels that enable them to fit into high-wage positions in the labor market. The Asian Indian population in the United States, for example, has an average educational level that is higher than that of white Americans. They have high rates of naturalization and their children generally do better in schools and in the labor market than less educated migrants from Latin America. Intergenerational mobility is a key element in the assimilation process; its absence often reinforces ethnic and racial subordination even in the absence of discrimination.

Educated migrants may be more successful than the less educated, but the demand in most industrial societies is for the less skilled who can take care of the elderly, mind the children, work in restaurants and small businesses, clean houses and take on the many menial jobs that have become unattractive in countries in which welfare benefits are only marginally lower (if at all) than the minimum wages. The demand by many employers for low skilled, low-wage workers remains a critical determinant of the continued influx of illegal migrants into the United States, Japan, and Western Europe. The intake of the unskilled, both legal and illegal, has also had a negative impact on the willingness of societies to assimilate immigrants. The well-known proposition that cultural assimilation is largely related to the socioeconomic and educational status of immigrants suggests that an unskilled immigrant labor force, employed in the low-wage, dead-end sector of the economy, in some instances further marginalized by its illegal status, is unlikely to experience much generational mobility. Left to its own devices the labor market in advanced industrial countries is more likely to recruit the unskilled across international boundaries than the highly educated, precisely the opposite of what most scholars and policy-makers would regard as an optimum migration intake, both for national economic growth as well as for the ease of migrant integration into the country's political and social system. For this reason some industrial societies now have two distinct migrant classes, those legally admitted under a set of policies (such as family reunification, educational levels, financial resources, employment needs in universities and hi tech industries) likely to facilitate successful absorption, and a class of illegal 'undocumented' migrants or low-skilled, asylum-seekers who, by virtue of their characteristics and/or their legal status, are less able to be socially and politically absorbed.

Differences in mobility rates among various migrant groups within a country and between the children of migrants and the children of the native born can be the result of any one of a number of factors: discrimination in education and employment; the characteristics of the various communities of migrant origin, including how highly they value education; the aspiration level of members of the various communities; their sense of self-esteem; their aversion toward antisocial acts; whether family and community members support one another; and a variety of other group differences that are not easily identifiable but which enable some groups to overcome discrimination while others do not, and for some to have higher economic success rates than others. One of the most persistent but unresolved research issues is whether the success of one group and the failure of another is a result of differences among the groups or differences in opportunities and constraints imposed from without.

It is not self-evident that the rate of immigration is a particularly critical factor in the readiness of the native population to accept the migrants and their children as one of them. The high immigration rate into the United States in the 1980s (often as high as a million in a single year) did not result in a wave of xenophobia, while anti-migrant right-wing parties have flourished throughout Western Europe even after the rates of immigration had sharply declined. A variety of other explanations are more plausible: immigrant societies, with a history and (more important) an ideology of immigration are less likely to produce xenophobia than countries that do not regard themselves as 'immigrant societies' even if historically they have had large numbers of immigrants; multiethnic regions of a country are usually more likely to have a tolerance for the additional cultural diversity produced by migrants than homogeneous regions; diversity among the immigrants in their place of origin and in their culture is less likely to be perceived as politically and culturally threatening than if the migrants are predominantly from a single country or cultural region; an uncontrollable influx of illegal migrants and of refugees is perceived as more threatening than if the same number enters through a regularized immigration process; and a persistent high unemployment rate with no decline in sight will increase the hostility of the lower end of the native labor force to migrants even if there is little evidence of large scale displacement. Each of these generalizations warrants empirical study and to each, one can find some exceptions. However, the recent experience of most countries of immigration suggests that these are more significant determinants in how migrants and natives relate to one another than the magnitude of the migration flow. One generalization needs to be highlighted: in a slow growing economy, migrant communities are often visibly in competition with the native popu-

Determinants of Immigrant Integration

lation and with one another. There is competition for places in the educational system, for rental housing, for control over retail trades, and for jobs. Tensions are likely to be most acute during an economic recession; xenophobic anti-migrant political groups typically thrive in working-class neighborhoods during such periods, when they attract support from young native toughs resentful of state support for migrant minorities or for the successes of the migrants when they themselves are not doing well. The attacks against South Asians by white teenage skinheads allied with the British National Party, and the attacks against Gypsies and Turks by young neo-Nazis in Germany took place under these conditions. The competition for scarce housing and jobs may also exacerbate relations between the migrant communities and indigenous ethnic minorities not only because some groups are more successful than others but because the media may hold up the successful migrants to berate the unsuccessful indigenous minority. The attacks by blacks against Korean shopkeepers in the Los Angeles Rodney King riots of 1992 is a case in point.

The recent experiences of advanced industrial societies suggests a set of hypotheses as to the factors which facilitate the integration of migrants into the economy, the culture, the social system, and the polity of the host society:

- When the host society regards the migrants as permanent members of the society by readily granting citizenship, and the migrants in turn readily accept citizenship and a new identity;
- When the children of the migrants are at birth considered natives and provided with the same educational opportunities given to the children of the native born;
- When the characteristics of the migrants are particularly suitable for mobility within the host country's labor market;
- When the host economy is expanding, thereby providing opportunities for the migrants as well as reducing competition between those of migrant and those of native origin;
- When the structure of the labor market provides opportunities for migrants who seek occupational mobility;
- When the host society does not denigrate (even if it does not elevate, or even recognize) the culture and values of the immigrant community;
- When the migrant stream is sufficiently diversified, or the numbers from one source are not so large and continuous as to enable the migrants to build permanent self-contained enclaves where migrants can employ one another, speak the same language, and insulate themselves from the larger society;

- When the influx of migrants and refugees is regarded by the host society as controllable;
- When the state does not require or promote (though it may permit) separateness in schools, employment, or housing.

Plausible as these hypotheses appear, each one is in need of empirical comparative research.

It is striking to see how many of these factors – though by no means all – can be affected by state policies. Migration policies determine the educational and skill characteristics of those admitted into the country; governments determine the magnitude and sources of migration; governments influence (though they cannot always control) the level of illegal migration; governments decide who will be granted citizenship and what rights and benefits should be given to various categories of migrants; and governments can encourage or discourage integration though their housing and education policies. Still, when one considers how complex and often divided are the political forces in most countries to chose policies that can promote integration, and how difficult it is for governments to fine tune these policies especially in a slow growth economy, we can appreciate why the integration of immigrants in most countries remains so problematic and, especially in the short term, so conflictual.

References

Alvarez, Robert R. (1987) 'A Profile of the Citizenship Process Among Hispanics in the United States', *International Migration Review*, vol. xxi, no. 2, pp. 327–47.

Bennett, Douglas C. (1986) 'Immigration, Work and Citizenship in the American Welfare State', paper presented at the 1986 Annual Meeting of the American Political Science Association, Washington, DC, August 1986.

Brown, Colin (1983) 'Ethnic Pluralism in Britain: the Demographic and Legal Background', in Nathan Glazer and Ken Young, *Ethnic Pluralism and Public Policy* (Lexington: MA: Lexington Books, DC Heath and Company) pp. 32–53.

Brubaker, William Rogers, (ed.) (1989) *Immigration and the Politics of Citizenship in Europe and North America* (Lanham: University Press of America).

—— (1989) 'Immigration and the Politics of Citizenship in Late Nineteenth Century France,' Society of Fellows, Harvard University.

Carens, Joseph H. (1987) 'Aliens and Citizens: The Case for Open Borders', *The Review of Politics*, vol. 49, no. 2, pp. 251–71.

—— (1988a) 'Immigration and the Welfare State', in Amy Gutmann, (ed.), *Democracy and the Welfare State* (Princeton: Princeton University Press) pp. 207–30.

—— (1988b) 'Nationalism and the Exclusion of Immigrants: Lessons from Australian Immigration Policy', in Mark Gibney, (ed.), *Open Borders? Closed Societies? The Ethical and Political Issues* (New York: Greenwood Press) pp. 41–60.

—— (1989) 'Membership and Morality: Admission to Citizenship in Liberal Democratic States', 31–49 in William Rogers Brubaker (ed.), *Immigration and the Politics of Citizenship in Europe and North America* (Lanham: University Press of America).

Crewe, Ivor (1983) 'Representation and the Ethnic Minorities in Britain', in Nathan Glazer and Ken Young (eds), *Ethnic Pluralism and Public Policy: Achieving Equality in the United States and Britain* (Lexington Mass.: Lexington Books, D.C. Heath and Company) pp. 258–300.

DeSipio, Louis (1987) 'Social Science Literature and the Naturalization Process', *International Migration Review*, vol xxi, no 2, pp. 390–405.

Dummet, Ann and Andrew Nicol (1990) *Subjects, Citizens, Aliens and Others: Nationality and Immigration Law* (London: Weidenfeld & Nicolson).

Easterlin, Richard A., David Ward, William S. Bernard, Reed Ueda (1982) *Immigration* (Cambridge: Harvard University Press) chapter 4, 'Naturalization and Citizenship', 106–59.

Evans, M.D.R. (1987) 'Choosing to Be a Citizen: The Time-Path of Citizenship in Australia', *International Migration Review*, vol. xxi, no. 2, pp. 243–364.

Fuchs, Lawrence H. (1990) *The American Kaleidoscope: Race, Ethnicity, and the Civic Culture* (Hanover, New Hampshire: University Press of New England).

Gordon, Linda W. (1990) 'Asian Immigration Since World War II', in Robert W. Tucker, Charles B. Keely and Linda Wrigley (eds), *Immigration and US Foreign Policy* (Boulder, Colo.: Westview Press) pp. 169–91.

Hailbronner, Kay. (1989) 'Citizenship and Nationhood in Germany', 81–96, in William Rogers Brubaker (ed.), *Immigration and the Politics of Citizenship in Europe and North America* (Lanham, Md.: University Press of America).

Hammar, Tomas (ed.) (1985) *European Immigration Policy: A Comparative Study* (Cambridge: Cambridge University Press).

—— (1985) 'Citizenship, Aliens' Political Rights, and Politicians' Concern for Migrants: The Case of Sweden', in Rosemarie Rogers (ed.), *Guests Come to Stay: The Effects of European Labor Migration in Sending and Receiving Countries* (Boulder, Colo.: Westview Press), 85–107.

Hoffmann-Nowotny, Hans Joachim (1985) 'Switzerland', in Tomas Hammar (ed.), *European Immigration Policy: A comparative study* (Cambridge: Cambridge University Press) pp. 206–35.

Horowitz, Donald L. (1989) 'Europe and America: A Comparative Analysis of Ethnicity', *Revue Europeene des Migrations Internationales*, 5 (l), pp. 47–59.

Layton-Henry, Zig (1985) 'Great Britain', in Tomas Hammar (ed.), *European Immigration Policy: A Comparative Study* (Cambridge: Cambridge University Press) pp. 89–126.

Miller, Mark J. (1989) 'Dual Citizenship: A European Norm?' *International Migration Review*, vol. xxiii, no. 4, pp. 945–50.

Noiriel, Gerard (1992) 'Difficulties in French Historical Research on Immigration' in Donald L. Horowitz and Gerard Noiriel (ed.), *Immigrants in Two Democracies: French and American Experience* (New York: New York University Press) pp. 66–79.

North, David S. (1987) 'The Long Grey Welcome: A Study of the American Naturalization Program', *International Migration Review*, vol. xxi, no. 2, pp. 311–26.

Pachon, Harry P. (1987) 'Naturalization: Determinants and Process in the Hispanic Community: An Overview of Citizenship in the Hispanic Community', *International Migration Review*, vol. xxi, no. 2, pp. 299–310.

Peck, Jeffrey M. (1992) 'Refugees as Foreigners: The Problem of Becoming German and Finding a Home', Dissertation, Bergen: United Nations University, Wider, 16 and 22.

Peters, B. Guy and Patricia K. Davis (1986) 'Migration to the United Kingdom and the Emergence of a New Politics', *Annals*, AAPSS, 485, pp. 129–38.

Portes, Alejandro and John W. Curtis (1987) 'Changing Flags: Naturalization and its Determinants Among Mexican Migrants', *International Migration Review*, vol. xxi, no. 2, pp. 352–71.

Price, Charles (1973) 'Australia', in Daniel Kubat (ed.), *The Politics of Migration Policies* (New York: Basic Books).

Schuck, Peter H. (1985) 'Immigration Law and the Problem of Community', in Nathan Glazer (ed.), *Clamor at the Gates: The New American Immigration* (San Francisco: ICS Press) pp. 285–307.

Schuck, Peter H. and Rogers M. Smith (1985) *Citizenship with Consent: Illegal Aliens in the American Polity* (New Haven, Conn.: Yale University Press).

Weiner, Myron (1982) 'International Migration and Development: Indians in the Persian Gulf', in *Population and Development Review* 8 (1), pp. 1–36.

Part II

New Immigrants in New Circumstances: USA Experience

4 Second-Generation Decline: Scenarios for the Economic and Ethnic Futures of the Post-1965 American Immigrants*

Herbert J. Gans

'Second-Generation Decline' questions the current American faith in the myth of nearly automatic immigrant success. In discussing economic scenarios, positive and negative, for the future of the children of the post-1965 immigrants, it proposes the possibility that a significant number of the children of poor immigrants, especially dark-skinned ones, might not obtain jobs in the mainstream economy. Neither will they be willing – or even able – to take low-wage-long-hour 'immigrant' jobs like their parents. As a result they, and young males among them particularly, may join blacks and Hispanics among those already excluded, apparently permanently, from the mainstream economy. The paper also deals with the relations between ethnicity and economic conditions in the US, and with the continued relevance of the assimilation and acculturation processes described by 'straight-line theory'.This issue, as well as most others discussed in the paper, may also be salient for European countries experiencing immigration, especially those countries with troubled economies.

INTRODUCTION

The children of the latest 'new immigration' that began after 1965 are now in school, some are already in the labor force, and by the mid-1990s, their numbers will begin to increase rapidly.[1] Their entry into that force raises a

---

* This article appeared originally in *Ethnic and Racial Studies*, vol. 15, no. 2, April 1992, pp. 173–92.

host of significant questions about their economic future which are relevant both to public policy and ethnic theory.

Specifically, this chapter is impelled by the fear of 'second-generation decline,' that is, that if the American economy is not growing, some members of the second generation, especially those whose parents did not themselves escape poverty, could, in adulthood end up in persistent poverty, because they will either not be asked, or will be reluctant, to work at immigrant wages and hours like their parents, but will lack the job opportunities, skills and connections to do better.

Thus, they – including the Viet Namese and other Asian-Americans, Salvadorans and other Central and Latin Americans, as well as Haitians and others from the Caribbean, Africa and elsewhere – may join blacks, and the Puerto Rican, Mexican and other 'Hispanics', who came to the cities at an earlier time, as well as 'Anglos' (in some places) as excluded from, or marginal in, the economy. Indeed, even much of the joblessness, pathology and crime of today's urban poor is associated with second-generation decline on the part of young blacks and Hispanics whose parents came to the cities a generation or longer ago, and who are unable or unwilling to work in 'immigrant' jobs but are excluded, for skill or other reasons, from better jobs.[2]

Moreover, when the next spurt of economic growth rolls around, the second generation of the current immigration, as well as poor blacks and Hispanics, may be further marginalized by a new wave of immigrants ready to work under 'un-American' conditions. Bringing new workers into urban areas ready to work at low wages and for long hours from peasant areas overseas – as in the past from rural America – is an old American technique for renewing economic growth quickly and cheaply.

The theoretical concerns of the chapter are not limited to second-generation decline, but extend also to the relations between ethnicity and economy. Specifically, I am interested in the theories of acculturation and assimilation that were first developed in connection with the Southern and Eastern European immigration of about 1880 to 1925. These theories were formulated during a time in which the American economy was growing more or less continuously, especially with the employment of immigrant muscle labor.[3] Today, however, that economy has changed and the need for large amounts of muscle labor has ended. This raises the question of whether and how immigrant acculturation and assimilation will be affected by the change in the economy, if at all, particularly among the non-Caucasian immigrant population.

For example, the 'straight-line' assimilation theory associated with Warner and Srole (1945), in which each native-born generation acculturates further and raises its status *vis à vis* the previous generation is an almost entirely sociocultural theory, which pays little attention to the economy in which the immigrants and their descendants work. Looking back now on the classic research conducted in Yankee City, this emphasis seems strange, because the empirical work for the study took place between 1930 and 1935, in Newburyport, Massachusetts, never an affluent city at best. Nonetheless, Warner and Srole say little about whether and how the economy and economic problems affected ethnic upward mobility, and the Great Depression is not even an item in the book's index. In fact, Warner and Srole seem to assume that the state of the economy is not relevant, for they introduce the book as telling 'part of the magnificent history of the adjustment of ethnic groups to American life', and go on to predict that 'oncoming generations of new ethnics will...climb to the same heights that generations of earlier groups have achieved' (Warner and Srole, 1945, p. 2).

Most likely, the book, which began as Leo Srole's PhD dissertation, reflects not the Depression era but the upward mobility of the second-generation of the affluent 1920s, as well as the personal optimism of its authors and their colleagues. However, straight-line theory is still being applied, and its subsequent users, this author included, never built economic factors into it. Even so, it has remained valid for most immigrant populations so far (Alba 1990, Waters 1990).

To be sure, the line of the theory has not always been straight, and bumpy-line theory might be a more apt term. Moreover, the line will not necessarily 'decline' into final and complete assimilation and acculturation, and it is possible, perhaps even likely, that ethnic groups reach plateaus after several generations in which they still name themselves as members of an ethnic group but indulge mainly in a familial and leisure time ethnicity I have called symbolic (Gans 1979). And finally, changing economic and political conditions can produce generational 'returns', or at least interruptions in acculturation and assimilation processes, although the history of the descendants of the 1880–1925 immigrants suggests that straight- or bumpy-line theory operates quite independently of the economy, with assimilation and acculturation continuing even during economic downturns.

Straight-line theory has been under considerable attack in recent decades, not for ignoring the economy or even for distorting what has actually happened over the generations, but because it has conjured up too many impersonal and permanent forces or 'structures', not left enough room for human choice or 'agency', and perhaps most important, for ignoring the possibility of ethnic identity without much ethnic behavior or group participation. The new theorists are correct in pointing out that people construct their own ethnicity (e.g. Yancey, Ericksen and Juliani, 1976) or invent it (Sollors, 1989), but these theorists have not paid enough attention to the fact that people also construct their own acculturation and assimilation. Thus, whatever the faults of straight-line theory, including its lack of interest in identity, the outcome predicted by it, rapid cultural Americanization and slower familial and social assimilation, is still taking place, and may be occurring also among the new post-1965 immigrants.

So far the evidence for what is happening to the second generation is mostly anecdotal, and besides, that generation is still mainly composed of children and adolescents. It is, however, maturing into adulthood at a time when the lower or 'secondary' sectors of the national economy and especially the urban economies in which immigrant parents are working, is no longer growing as it did during the last European immigration. Moreover, many of the immigrants are dark-skinned and non-Caucasian and suffer from various kinds of ethnic and racial discrimination which now seem more permanent than those suffered by the white Southern and Eastern Europeans when they were characterized as races.[4] While dark-skinned immigrants from overseas cultures will also acculturate, racial discrimination will not encourage their assimilation, at least into white society. As a result, a number of questions can be raised about acculturation and assimilation, identity construction and other processes of ethnic adaptation among the second generation.[5]

Since this chapter is largely about the unknown future, it is organized in terms of 'scenarios' for the economic future of the second-generation; three positive for that generation and three negative, followed by a discussion of the primary policy and theoretical questions these raise. The three positive scenarios focus around the role of education, ethnic succession and niche-improvement respectively; the three negative ones deal with their opposites: educational failure, the stalling of ethnic succession, and niche-shrinkage.[6]

THE POSITIVE SCENARIOS

1. Education-Driven Upward Mobility

The extent to which education is a significant mechanism for upward mobility is difficult to ascertain. At the turn of the century, when less than 5 per cent of all Americans – and even fewer members of the second generation ethnics – graduated from high school, even a high school diploma must have made a big difference, especially for people who had no other resources for finding jobs and had no niches into which to enter. Today, high school diplomas are virtually taken for granted, and the college degree is quickly becoming a prerequisite for stable white-collar employment. Only a limited number of postgraduate professional and technical specialties are so short of workers that a degree in them can still guarantee upward movement via education alone.

Popular conceptions of the acculturation process have often ignored this reality, and instead assumed that the children of the European immigrants used education to move out of immigrant poverty. In fact, however, education was a major factor for the upward mobility of only a minority of the second generation, including some but by no means all of the Jews (Steinberg 1989, Chap. 3). For most other descendants of European immigrants, education probably did not make a major difference until the third and fourth generations (Greeley, 1974, p. 72).

This scenario may be repeated once more. Today's Asian-American second generation is currently being slotted into the role of the European Jews in the contemporary version of the ethnic success myth, although, as among the Jews, only a minority of the Asian-Americans can live up to the myth. In today's economy – as in past eras – it is the children of middle-class immigrants, Asian-American and other, who are most likely to be able to use education in upward mobility.

This time, the scenario may also apply to especially talented young people from non-middle-class homes, who will do so well in high school that they will be able to go to better-quality colleges, on scholarship and otherwise, and then on to professional or graduate school.[7] Institutions of higher education, public or private, are now so concerned with student body diversity, not to mention affirmative action, that they are opening their doors even to children of the immigrant poor.

A related but numerically more important version of this scenario can be constructed for the many immigrant children who will use high school graduation, technical training and perhaps some years of college to help them find, or certify them for, jobs better than those now being held by their parents, including stable and well-paid blue- and white-collar jobs in the mainstream economy. If the economy is healthy, they will probably constitute at least the plurality of the second generation.

In the longer run, education may become a more important means for upward mobility than it is today, for as firms become larger, the global economy more competitive, and the division of labor more specialized, the most up-to-date technical or professional education will become an ever greater job prerequisite, while parental social status may become less important.[8] For example, banks will be able to survive only with the most talented executives, and past requirements like an Ivy League background will pale into insignificance.

2. Succession-Driven Upward Mobility

During the European immigration, a typical second-generation scenario was the move into the relatively secure but low-status blue- and white-collar jobs which WASPs and the descendants of earlier immigrations would no longer accept because they could find better-paying and more pleasant work.[9] For that generation and its children, this kind of ethnic succession never ended, so that by the 1980s, white ethnics who were still in blue-collar and nonprofessional white-collar occupations probably held the best jobs in these strata.

Many of the kinds of jobs the second generation took over, first in the 1920s and then massively in the 1940s, have been disappearing in the last two decades, either moving out of the US into lower-wage countries, or being eliminated altogether by the computer. Thus, the ethnic succession scenario may be coming to an end in the manufacturing sector, although it will continue in two other sectors. One is the service sector, where immigrants, or the children of immigrants, are eligible as soon as they speak English and can live up to the status-based work and behavioral codes in service firms.[10]

A second sector which may open up to the children of the new immigration consists of the small manufacturing and service firms which have sprung up to fill gaps created by the departure of large ones overseas. So far, many of these firms seem to be able to survive only as long as they can hire immigrants at low wages and with inferior working conditions. These include the sweatshops that have replaced the old 'garment district' firms of New York and other American cities. In other industries they may be illegal firms, or legal firms staffed with illegal immigrants. Whether such firms can find sufficiently stable roles in their industries to hire second-generation people at higher wages remains to be seen.

3. Niche Improvement

The final scenario for second-generation upward mobility is to remain in and improve the economic niches which their parents occupied when they came to America (Waldinger 1986). Many children of the European immigrants took this route, staying in parental retail stores, taverns, contracting businesses and the like, both in their own ethnic neighborhoods, black ghettos and elsewhere. Their 'choice' (and it would be interesting to discover whether they chose or had to stay in ethnic niches) became part of the American ethnic success myth when the family food store became a regional supermarket chain; the small town dry-goods store, a big city department store; and the local contractor, a national development and construction company.

In most instances, the immigrant establishments grew more modestly, with the second generation perhaps taking over as owners but letting others, often from a later wave of the European immigration as well as blacks, Hispanics and others, do the work that required long hours and muscle labor.

A parallel working-class version of this scenario, closer to niche-retention than improvement, had immigrants in good industrial and municipal jobs passing these on to their children. Sometimes the jobs were virtually heritable via parental seniority or union rules, and sometimes there were informal arrangements in which managements seeking long-term stability encouraged their best workers to bring other family members into the firm (Newman, 1988, p. 182). Similar arrangements were found in some public agencies, notably police and fire departments.

The retail scenario is likely to be played out again among the children of immigrant store owners, although this time around, petty retailing may be a less successful niche, in part because of the continually growing role of national chains. However, since the large retail chains tend to locate in the suburbs and some shun the cities altogether, they have created an urban retail vacuum which is in part being filled by immigrants, and which the immigrants can at least try to hand down to their children. The expansion of the black ghettos has enabled a few black businesses to establish themselves, but it has also opened up new business opportunities for Korean, Indian, Yemenite and other immigrant storekeepers, and presumably at least some of them will pass their stores on to their descendants.

New retail niches were also created in the 1980s as a result of the decision of young professionals to remain urban. For example, since many of these professionals, as well as others in New York City's upper middle class, adopted 'health diets', Korean immigrants were able to develop urban fruit and vegetable retailing into a flourishing business.[11] This may have been an unusual instance of being in a profitable place at the right time, however. Moreover, the Korean storekeepers, many of whom had themselves obtained college and professional degrees in Korea, are sending their children to college here and may not even want the next generation to take over the stores. Similar preferences can be found among other immigrant groups, for example Soviet Jews (Gold 1989, p. 429).

In addition, the long hours required by storekeeping may discourage members of the second generation from continuing with the family stores, if they have any choice. This depends, however, on alternative opportunities, such as white-collar and technical jobs in manufacturing and service firms, or positions in public bureaucracies. Perhaps some second-generation people will find or develop opportunities in wholesaling or chain retailing or more prestigious forms of petty retailing, so that the children of the immigrants will move out of corner groceries and newsstands into appliance or clothing stores.

The old working class scenario is probably nearly irrelevant now, since civil service, affirmative action, the declining power of unions and other factors have reduced the heritability of all jobs considerably, including the ethnic niches established by the European immigrants in factories and public agencies.

THE NEGATIVE SCENARIOS

1. Educational Failure

Most European immigrants who were not from urban or middle-class backgrounds put little emphasis on their children's education. Just the reverse; children were expected to leave school as quickly as legally possible so they could contribute to the family income. This pattern began to change, however, in the 1960s, when future-oriented working-class parents first began to realize that their children would need to go to college if they wanted to get better jobs. Lack of money, opportunity, and cultural factors seem to have held many of the young people back, however, for the ethnic working class has not yet caught up with the middle class in college entry and completion, except perhaps at community and four-year city colleges.

Meanwhile, educational success and the right educational credentials become more important in the job market, but it is already evident that for some of the children of the new immigrants, school success and even a high school diploma are not in the offing. Studies of school performance are only just beginning and most of the data is in the form of grades rather than measurements of actual performance, but they suggest that as before, the children of urban and even nonurban middle-class parents perform the best, with the children of poor peasants and others from preindustrial cultures – as well as those from families disrupted by the Viet Nam war –

having the hardest time (Rumbaut and Ima, 1988; Rumbaut, August 1990). Thus, the Asian-American success myth notwithstanding, Asian-American children from poor and poorly-educated homes do not always obtain good grades, although they do far better than the children of Latin and Central American immigrants.

2. The Stalling of Ethnic Succession

When access to better jobs is difficult or when jobs are scarce, ethnic succession slows down. People hold on to their jobs as best they can, and the groups next in line in the queue have to wait. This pattern is probably most graphically illustrated by the length of time Italian-Americans have held on to both low and high-level jobs in organized crime. Being unable or unwilling to find alternative careers, they have let blacks and Hispanics, as well as newer immigrants, replace them mainly in the lower level and more dangerous jobs in organized crime, notably drug selling.

I have seen no studies of the extent to which succession has ended in the legal economy, but the journalistic and impressionistic evidence suggests that the urban queue has slowed down, except when firms use retirement, union-busting, and other devices to force higher paid workers out in favor of lower paid ones. As long as jobs remain scarce, this pattern will also affect, and shrink, the fortunes of the second generation.

3. Niche-Shrinkage

When jobs become scarce and the queue stops moving up, immigrant niches are also affected. They may not improve so as to provide job opportunities at decent wages, and they may even shrink, for a variety of reasons. Even in the best of times, ethnic retailing shrinks because of the loss of its most loyal customers, its own immigrants. The second generation generally speaks English and is thus not limited to the ethnic enclave; nor will it be as loyal to ethnic institutions or goods. It will not often read the ethnic newspaper and it will shop at the supermarket rather than at the ethnic corner grocery. If the original supply of immigrants is not replenished by newcomers, retail and service activities will decline considerably, unless they can, like today's Asian-American restaurants, attract non-ethnic customers.

The other source of niche-shrinkage is competition; not only can employers look for new immigrants who will work at immigrant wages, but new immigrants can themselves become employers, at least in industries which require little skill and initial capital. Thus, they can compete with existing firms. For example, just about every post-1965 immigrant group in New York City has gone into construction, and not only within its own ethnic enclaves. As a result, it seems unlikely that any single immigrant group can achieve the kind of success needed to improve the niche significantly, and provide enough good jobs for the second generation, and perhaps in other industries than construction.

SECOND-GENERATION DECLINE

Business cycles go up and down, but the long-term periods of economic growth, the first that began after the Civil War, and the second that started after World War II are not likely to return soon. The first helped to spur the arrival of the new European immigrants and enabled them to find more or less steady jobs so that many of them or their children could escape poverty by the end of the 1920s. The second enabled the descendants of that immigration to move at least into the upper-working and lower middle classes, and in many cases, firmly into the middle class.

Even if periods of long-term economic growth return, they will probably not be equally labor-intensive. No one expects a revival in muscle labor, and even many low-level service jobs may be computerized, sent abroad, or left undone. Such trends have special meaning for the new immigration and its second-generation, for among other things, they could lead to what I have earlier called second generation decline. This could happen if the children of the immigrants, having shed the immigrant parental work-norms, will not find the income, job security and working conditions they expect, but will not be asked to take or will turn down jobs involving minimal security, low wages, long hours and unpleasant working conditions, because they have become sufficiently Americanized in their work and status expectations to reject 'immigrant jobs'.

This fate is most likely to affect the children of illegal and undocumented immigrants. Although anyone born in the US is automatically an American citizen, the children of illegal newcomers are apt to come from poor homes, because their parents' origins and legal status gave them access mainly to low-wage work.

Two separate processes are involved in second generation decline. Either the second generation can be offered immigrant jobs and can accept them or turn them down; or the children of the immigrants can be denied the opportunity to make this choice. Who will have which of these choices and who then makes what choice remains to be seen, although such studies could be done now among the children of black migrants and of pre-1965 immigrants from Mexico or Puerto Rico.

If the young people are offered immigrant jobs, there are some good reasons why they might turn them down. They come to the world of work with American standards, and may not even be familiar with the old-country conditions (or those in the Deep South) by which immigrants and Southern migrants judged the urban job market. Nor do they have the long-range goals which persuaded their parents to work long hours at low-wages; they know they cannot be deported and are here to stay in America, and most likely they are not obligated to send money to relatives left in the old country. From their perspective, immigrant jobs are demeaning; moreover, illegal jobs and hustles may pay more and look better socially – especially when peer pressure is also present.

Whatever the processes that will be at work, however, the first to experience second-generation decline would be poor young men with dark skin, if only because all other things being equal, they seem to be the first to be extruded from the labor market when there are more workers than jobs (Wilson, 1987, p. 43).[12] Labor markets change, however, and they could also begin to extrude poor young Asians and whites of the second generation.

As long as they are young and single, and either do not have or can avoid family obligations, these young men could choose instead to hustle or work in the underworld economy, accepting steady immigrant and immigrant-like jobs only if and when they marry and have children to support. They can also remain unmarried and live off various women, or combine this with occasional jobs and hustles. And of course they can enter the drug trade, whether or not they also hold other jobs on the side.

In effect, some of the immigrants' children might react in the same way as poor young urban whites, blacks and Hispanics who have not been offered or turned down jobs of the kind that their immigrant or migrant parents took readily when they first arrived in American cities (Sullivan, 1989). One likely result of second-generation decline is higher unemployment among that generation; another is the possibility of more crime, alcoholism, drug use, as well as increases in the other pathologies that go with poverty – and with the frustration of rising expectations.[13]

Indeed, second-generation decline is likely to produce an early convergence between the present American poor and some second generation poor, for if immigrant parents are unable or unwilling to enforce strict school – and homework – discipline, if language problems cannot be overcome, or if the youngsters, especially those who have difficulty in school early on, see that their occupational futures are not promising, they may begin to get low grades, reject schooling, and eventually drop out or get themselves pushed out of the school system.[14] Should they join poor black, Hispanic and other youngsters in standing jobless on street corners, they will quickly be reclassified from the children of praiseworthy immigrants to undeserving members of the so-called underclass.

SOME POLICY AND THEORY QUESTIONS

Since most immigrants' children are now in school and not yet in the labor force, it is essential that the school careers and the future job possibilities of these children be understood as comprehensively as possible. The most urgent priority is to study – and then find help for – the children who are not likely to find a decent job either in an ethnic niche or the mainstream economy. I am probably being over-optimistic, but since there is still some interest in helping the immigrants, and since poor ones have not yet been dismissed by assignment to the underclass, perhaps some way can be discovered to divert those who are heading toward unemployment and/or the underworld before they leave school. The most important aspect of that diversion has to be a jobs policy: to discover what kinds of jobs these young people will take, and then to create them if they are not already available. And if the diversion is successful, perhaps something can also be learned to help the black, Hispanic and Anglo youngsters who are now heading for school and economic failure in large numbers.

Many questions, of both policy and theoretical relevance, need to be asked about the new immigrants and their children, but in what follows I will limit myself almost entirely to the poor among them. First, has selective migration been operating in the post-1965 immigration, and if so, is the poverty-stricken second generation apt to be less energetic and ambitious in adulthood than its parents? Or have immigrants been successful mainly because they came when jobs were available, while the second generation is less so because opportunities are scarcer. And is ambition spurred less when there is less to be ambitious about?

One of the differences between the last European immigration and the post-1965 one is that it is easier for many of the immigrants or their children to go back to the old country. Travel time is lower now, even if travel costs may not be, especially for the poor. Whether any members of the second generation are able or willing to go back to the old country if there is no economic future here remains to be seen. Perhaps sojourning, a temporary stay in the US, and the back-and-forth migrations of Puerto Ricans will become more widespread among other ethnic groups.[15]

What about the differences between immigrants who came for political reasons and those who came for economic ones? And assuming the former would go home if they could, would their children look at the old country through similar eyes? Do poor political refugees who have any chance of going home try to insulate their children from American culture – and to maintain old country work habits and standards? Or will poor political refugees – or their children – find economic reasons to stay here anyway?

In all of these cases, what immigrants want is not necessarily what their children do; thus, it is necessary also to ask who is, and is not, able to keep their children from becoming Americanized, including also with respect to work and income expectations. This is probably also a matter of the peer groups the young people encounter, and of the economic future they see for themselves. One study of poor Haitian immigrants, who are identified with a country that seems to mean little to their children, has suggested that the children are moving into the American black community, although the study did not report whether this had economic causes (Woldemikael 1989). Now, Waters (1991) has found the same pattern among other poor black West Indians. Conversely, the New York Chassidic community has insulated itself from America more successfully than perhaps even the Amish, but because their insulation also means that they will not work for non-Chassidim, they do not have enough jobs for all who need work, and many are on welfare.[16]

Second, the post-1965 immigration differs in class and race from the 1880–1925 one. This time, the proportion of immigrants of middle-class origin is higher, and this should affect the economic expectations – and perhaps success – of their children. Whether they will also be subject to second-generation decline, or whether this danger is limited to the children of the poor will have to be looked at – especially if and when the American economy is weak.

Today's immigrants are also far more diverse racially and ethnically. Many of the European immigrants of the 1880–1925 period looked 'swarthy' to the WASPs and the earlier Northern European immigrants, but their skin color seemed to brighten as they moved up in the economy. How today's second generation will be defined, and will define itself, is still unpredictable; even the variables which will influence definition and self-definition are not yet known. Once upon a time, Asian-Americans constituted a 'yellow horde' in the eyes of whites; today their skin color seems to be irrelevant, at least as long as they are middle class.[17]

Indeed, as long as class remains crucial to economic success, it may also shape who is defined and self-defined as a desirable or undesirable race and ethnic group. However, white definitional patterns also depend in part on the white ability to distinguish the middle class from the poor. As far as self-definition is concerned, Waters (1991) has found that middle-class West Indian young people tend to remain West Indian, at least in identity and social ties, both to retain their status and to discourage whites from treating them as American (read poor) blacks. Presumably the West Indian accent also helps. Conversely, 'Anglos' have a much harder time telling Asian-Americans apart; also Central and Latin American as well as Caribbean 'Hispanics'. However, in judging Hispanics, skin color may be more significant than class.

Third, what role if any does gender play? The European immigrants were thought to be patriarchally organized, and since many of the women did not work outside the home, they were relatively invisible.[18] Today, both genders have to work, and poor immigrant women appear to have an easier time in getting jobs than men; it is they who work in the sweatshops and as domestics. What tolerance the second generation has for such jobs remains to be seen. Women who do not want to hold 'immigrant jobs' may not wind up on street corners or in the drug industry, but what will they do? Whether they can avoid the single-parent family status found among poor American women may relate to how well women are sheltered by their ethnic culture, including even its patriarchal dominance patterns, nominal or real, if these persist into the second generation.

Fourth, what roles do various aspects of ethnicity play? Does the cohesion of an ethnic enclave, or the attractiveness of the ethnic culture, help poor children hold on to old work habits, or slow down their Americanization when that is occupationally useful? Will kin reciprocity patterns, mutual benefit associations and other ethnic sources of capital, as well as the availability of low-cost familial labor disappear by the second generation? Or can that generation obtain bank loans to go into business?

Among the poorer members of the second generation, will ethnic support systems or other features of ethnicity exist to help them through the crises of poverty? Will they, therefore, have easier times than appears to be the case among blacks and Hispanics, skin color being held equal? The experiences of poor immigrants in the nineteenth century as well as today would indicate a negative answer, since the destructiveness of poverty seems to overcome the strengths of ethnicity, even if poor ethnics suffered less than poor blacks because of lesser racial discrimination.

Fifth and last, what can be learned about acculturation: the effects of America, both formal Americanization, for example through schooling, and informally through peers, the media and the many other cultural influences which will impinge on the second generation? Here, the validity of straight-line theory is at issue, for this theory would argue that acculturation begins the moment the immigrants arrive in America and accelerates in the second generation, albeit inside ethnic families and networks.

Those who emphasize that ethnicity is a matter of self-selection or invention might disagree, but in the end only empirical research can tell. On the one hand, ethnic diversity is a higher national value these days than it was during the 1880–1925 immigration, when the pressures toward Americanization were strong, and not only if upward mobility was to be achieved.

However, in those days, the cultural differences between the immigrants and the native-born were more sharply defined. Since the end of World War II, and to some extent before, American popular culture and the consumer goods of the American Dream have been diffused internationally. Roger Waldinger suggests that because many of today's immigrants – especially those coming from Latin and Central America – are already familiar with much of US culture, the amount and stress of cultural change may be reduced.

Conversely, given the value now placed on ethnic diversity, and the possibility that upward mobility is no longer automatically available to the Americanized ethnic, perhaps some immigrants may try to persuade their children – or the children may persuade themselves – to hold on deliberately to all or some of the ethnic culture, language included, although today it is also possible to be mainly American in culture but to be so in Spanish.[19]

In effect, immigrants or their children may resort to 'delayed acculturation', an insulation from American work and consumption expectations so that they will not reject immigrant economic niches (Gold, 1989, pp. 421–2). Or, in the case of the West Indians being studied by Waters, to prevent identification with a racial group of lower status. Part of the new immigrant success myth is that Asian-American parents make their children study harder than is required by American school standards, and while some do it to assure their children's upward mobility, others may be trying to delay their acculturation as well (Rumbaut, 1990, p. 23).

These patterns are not new.[20] Poor black and Hispanic parents have insulated their children so that they devote themselves to school rather than to the adolescent street culture of the ghetto or barrio, and at the turn of the century, some Eastern European Jews and other immigrants delayed their children's acculturation in the same way with the same purpose. We do not know, however, how many tried and succeeded and how many failed.

Findings about this practice were not incorporated in straight-line theory, but, probably because of its macrosociological bias, this theory has never concerned itself enough with the microsociology of how the immigrants and their children actually acculturated.[21]

Whether delayed acculturation works on any but a small scale or among a very insulated population is unlikely, and success probably depends on at least four factors. First, parents have to be able to offer some reasonable assurance of future occupational and other payoff; second, the young people have to appreciate the parental effort and have enough reasons – or lack of choice – to obey.[22] Third, they must be able and willing to cope with countervailing pressure from peers, and fourth, they have to resist the sheer attractiveness of American culture, especially for young people.

Ethnic researchers nostalgic for old country cultures have often underestimated that attractiveness. It exists in part because American culture is in many ways a youth culture, and such a culture is still lacking in most of the countries from which the immigrants came.[23] America also offers freedoms to young people unavailable in the old country; among others, the ability to choose one's own friends, including 'dates' *sans* chaperons and even sexual partners; the right of young people to develop their own interests, cultural and occupational; and the freedom of young women from the dictates of either a patriarchal or matriarchal family.[24] In fact, the perceived attractiveness of American culture substitutes in part for the dim economic future that faces some poor young immigrants, and thus may help to generate second-generation decline.

The attractions of America become even stronger if the immigrants do not plan to go back to the old country. In that case, the old country and the immigrant culture quickly become irrelevant for the second generation – and the more so if the immigrants were exploited there and have little positive to pass on about it to their children, other than their family structure and norms.

This is why acculturation seems to have proceeded quickly in the past, and why I would be inclined to think that it will do so again in the future, more or less as predicted by straight-line theory. However, today's second-generation is growing up in a different economy and a different culture, and perhaps this time, the acculturation will be more partial or segmental, or what Rumbaut has called bicultural.

In fact, people do not acculturate into an entire culture, which only exists in textbooks. This is especially true in America, which is too diverse to be a single culture even for textbook purposes. Perhaps the researchers who will study today's second generation can break the host country down into the institutional and cultural sectors that will be most relevant in the lives of that generation, and the processes which will shape their relationships in and to these sectors.

Finally, the term acculturation is probably too narrow, for ultimately, it describes a process which combines adaptation with learning. As such, it is no different from the 'urbanization' of a rural migrant, or from the learning of newly minted American PhDs when they start teaching, or working in a corporation. Straight-line theory's teleological program hid the similarities between acculturation and other kinds of forced and voluntary learning.

CONCLUSION

Both the Warner-Srole straight-line theory and the more recent construction of ethnicity theories appeared during a period of affluence and economic optimism, a time that encouraged ethnics not only to acculturate into the affluent melting pot, but also to construct their ethnicity and their identity largely by non-economic criteria. However, many of the post-1965 immigrants are coming into a different economy, in which selective migration may count for nought after the first generation, and traditional opportunities for the upward mobility of later generations could be absent for some or many. Indeed, straight-line theory could be turned on its head, with the people who have secured an economically viable ethnic or other niche acculturating less than did the European second and third generations.

Conversely, those without such a niche or other opportunities, who acculturate out of their parents' immigrant jobs and end up experiencing the poverty and joblessness of second-generation decline might become more American faster than other second-generation ethnics, but they would be turning straight-line theory on its head in another direction, that of downward mobility. If I am right, then past and present ethnic theorizing would need to be re-evaluated, and the interrelationships between ethnicity and economy would have to be given more emphasis than they have been in the theorizing of the last half-century.

In any case, the popular optimism about new immigrant economic successes ought to be replaced by reliable information about which members of which groups actually succeed and why – and what can be done for the rest. The cities cannot stand a cohort of immigrants' children who will join very poor blacks, Hispanics, and Anglos on the corner or in the lines of the welfare agencies.

Acknowledgements

I am grateful to Ruben Rumbaut, Roger Waldinger and Mary Waters for helpful comments on an earlier version of this chapter.

Notes

1. Traditionally, new immigration has referred to the Europeans who came from about 1880 to 1925 but they stopped being new with the arrival of the Nazi refugees in the 1930s and the Displaced Persons who came after World War II. The terms new and old have long ago lost meaning and I will be discussing the second generation of the post-1965 immigration.
2. On the comparison of migrant blacks and their 'native-born' children, see Lieberson (1980) and the research summarized in Wilson (1987, pp 177–8).
3. Perhaps it would be more correct to say that these theories, which were initiated by the Chicago School of Sociology, paid particular attention to upward mobility, and therefore did not notice the downward phases of the business cycle during this period.
4. The relative success of the Chinese, Japanese and Koreans, who are non-Caucasian but also light-skinned, may thus not be accidental.
5. In an era in which downward mobility is being experienced by virtually all classes (Newman 1988), the connection between ethnicity and downward mobility can no longer be ignored.
6. My analysis focuses on the scenarios, but the various members of a second generation group can follow different scenarios.
7. Many will probably go to work in the more practical, less prestigious professions, in which skill is not affected significantly by language ability or parental social status, such as computer science, engineering, accounting, dentistry, and a variety of public service professions (Waldinger, personal communication). All but the first also attracted the first college-attending generations of the European immigration able to obtain a professional or technical degree. Then as now, the law, the academy, and often also medicine operate with an informal prerequisite that students should have college-educated parents of upper-middle-class status.
8. Parental social status may still influence the quality of pre-professional schooling, however, and as a result, occupational and parental status may remain correlated.
9. This succession scenario sometimes already began with the immigrants themselves, who could compete for the dirtiest jobs in mining, the steel industry etc., while the women worked in textile mills, food processing and other lowest-level 'pink-collar' work. (Howe 1977). Ironically, these jobs were at times taken from blacks, who then got them back when the ethnic succession process reached them once more during and after World War II, only to lose them again after 1965, either to deindustrialization or to the new immigrants who could be paid less.
10. In this case, they may once again be taking jobs away from blacks and Hispanics who, as Bourgois (1991) explains in a powerful but yet unpublished paper, are sometimes unable or unwilling to follow these work, and especially deference, codes.
11. Their ascent was also aided by the fact that the children of Italian and Jewish fruit and vegetable retailers did not move into the parental businesses, presumably because of long hours, low profits and poor working conditions. The same fate may overtake today's Korean immigrant storekeepers.

12. For some early data that second generation Filipinos, Mexicans and other Hispanics do more poorly in the second generation than other immigrants, see Gilbertson and Waldinger (1991). However, their data shows that judging by per capita income, intergenerational decline is taking place in the third generation, in this case among Mexican-Americans (Ibid., Tables 5 and 6).
13. Another possible effect is disillusionment with America, which might be expressed not in the desire to leave but a romantic or nostalgic view of the old country they have never known, or the politicized, almost nationalistic, ethnicity, rarely found among the descendants of the European immigrants, but visible among Mexican Americans, Puerto Ricans and others. The Chicano and Latino movements, for example, attract mainly the middle-class second and third generation, but much of their anger expresses the poverty and deprivation among their fellow ethnics. These movements are, needless to say, very different from the political parties which Asian, African and other immigrants bring with them and which are concerned with changing governments and economies in the countries of origin.
14. Rumbaut (1991) refers to studies which have found that Mexican-born immigrants do better in school and are less likely to drop out than American-born students of Mexican origin.
15. Roger Waldinger argues (in personal communication) that the ending of the last European immigration in 1925 helped the second generation because of the lack of competition from newcomers. The continuation of the present immigration, illegal and legal, may alter the situation for today's second generation – and of course for poor blacks and Hispanics.
16. This raises the question of what the Chassidim will do if there are further welfare cutbacks, or when they have to register for workfare jobs.
17. But what if Japan were to become an economic enemy of the US in the future; would the Japanese then turn into an economic yellow horde in white eyes?
18. There are scattered data to suggest that women held more power in the immigrant family than they or their husbands will admit publicly. Moreover, among the later generations, women do more of the 'kin work', thus doing more also to help maintain the ethnic group (di Leonardo,1984).
19. Rumbaut has suggested (personal communication) that among the California youngsters he is studying, acculturation may be bicultural as well as bilingual, replacing the straight line theory pattern he calls 'subtractive Americanization'.
20. Gibson (1989) has described this practice as accommodation without assimilation, but it seems to be similar to the acculturation without (social) assimilation which took place among the 1880–1925 immigration and has long been reported by writers following straight line theory.
21. Needless to say, the new immigrations provide a rare opportunity for microsociological ethnographic and interview studies among the immigrants and their children about all aspects of adapting to America, including the amount and degree of acculturation in the first and second generation. None of these could be conducted during the 1880–1925 immigration itself, and few were conducted afterwards because of the macrosociological emphases of the early ethnic studies.

22. This is of course directly contradicted by the ability of the Chassidic community to insulate its young people even without a promising economic future, but the Chassidim are a fundamentalist religious group and only secondarily an ethnic group.
23. This raises an interesting question about the extent of cross-cultural differences in national pressures and incentives for acculturation, and not only between the US and Europe.
24. Rogg (1974) reports that familial tensions between Cuban adults and teenagers about chaperons on dates developed shortly after they arrived. Evidently it did not take the young women, themselves immigrants, long to accept the desirability of romantic activities without chaperons.

References

Alba, Richard D. (1990) *Ethnic Identity: The Transformation of White America* (New Haven: Yale University Press).
Bourgois, Philippe (1991) 'In Search of Respect: The New Service Economy and the Crack Alternative in Spanish Harlem,' New York: Russell Sage Foundation, Working Paper No. 21, May.
di Leonardo, Micaela (1984) *The Varieties of Italian Ethnic Experience; Kinship, Class and Gender among Italian Americans* (Ithaca: Cornell University Press).
Gans, Herbert J. (1979) 'Symbolic Ethnicity: The Future of Ethnic Groups and Cultures in America,' *Ethnic and Racial Studies*, vol. 2, no. 1, pp. 1–20.
Gibson, M.A. (1989) *Accommodation Without Assimilation: Sikh Immigrants in an American High School* (Ithaca: Cornell University Press).
Gilbertson, Greta and Roger Waldinger (1991) 'Ethnic Differences in the United States', unpublished paper, April.
Gold, Steven J. (1989) 'Differential Adjustment Among New Immigrant Family Members', *Journal of Contemporary Ethnography*, vol. 17, no. 4, pp. 406–34.
Greeley, Andrew M. (1974) *Ethnicity in the United States: A Preliminary Reconnaissance* (New York: Wiley Interscience).
Howe, Louisa K. (1977) *Pink Collar Workers: Inside the World of Women's Work* (New York: Putnam).
Lieberson, Stanley (1980) *A Piece of the Pie: Black and White Immigrants Since 1880* (Berkeley: University of California Press).
Newman, Katherine S. (1988) *Falling from Grace: The Experience of Downward Mobility in the American Middle Class* (New York: Free Press).
Rogg, Eleanor M. (1974) *The Assimilation of Cuban Exiles: The Role of Community and Class* (New York: Abingdon).
Rumbaut, Ruben G. (1990) 'Immigrant Students in California Public Schools: A Summary of Current Knowledge', Baltimore: Johns Hopkins University Center for Research on Effective Schooling for Disadvantaged Students, Report No. 11, August.
—— (1991) 'Passages to America: Perspectives on the new immigration', in Alan Wolfe (ed.), *America at Century's End* (Berkeley: University of California Press) Chapter 10.

—— and Kenji Ima (1988) 'The adaptation of Southeast Asian refugee youth: a comparative study' (Washington: US Office of Refugee Settlement).
Sollors, Werner (1989) (ed.), *The Invention of Ethnicity* (New York: Oxford).
Steinberg, Stephen (1989) *The Ethnic Myth: Race, Ethnicity and Class in America*, 2nd edn (Boston: Beacon Press).
Sullivan, Mercer L. (1989) *'Getting Paid': Youth Crime and Work in the Inner City* (Ithaca: Cornell University Press).
Waldinger, Roger (1986) *Through the Eye of the Needle: Immigrants and Enterprise in New York's Garment District* (New York: New York University Press).
Warner, W. Lloyd and Leo Srole (1945) *The Social Systems of American Ethnic Groups* (New Haven: Yale University Press).
Waters, Mary C. (1990) *Ethnic Options: Choosing Identities in America* (Berkeley: University of California Press).
—— (1991) 'The Intersection between Race and Ethnicity: Generational Changes among Caribbean Immigrants to the United States', unpublished paper delivered at the annual meeting of the American Sociological Association, Cincinnati, Ohio.
Wilson, William J. (1987) *The Truly Disadvantaged: The Inner City, the Underclass, and Public Policy* (Chicago: University of Chicago Press).
Woldemikael, Tekle M. (1989) *Becoming Black American: Haitians and American Institutions in Evanston, Illinois* (New York: AMS Press).
Yancey, William, Eugene Ericksen and Richard Juliani (1976) 'Emergent Ethnicity: A Review and Reformulation,' *American Sociological Review*, vol. 41, no. 3, pp. 391–403.

# 5 Immigration and Integration: Lessons from Southern California
William A.V. Clark

INTRODUCTION

The topic of immigration has recently emerged as one of the most contentious social and political issues of the late twentieth century. The emergence of the immigration issue and particularly the current tension over the size of immigrant flows was unexpected two decades ago. There was no hint that international migration, would become a central topic on the political agenda. But in the last five years, in various forms, ranging from specific studies of illegal immigration, to studies of immigration control, the topic has exploded in both the research and policy arenas.

Although the immigration issue has always been of some concern in Southern California (there were studies of the impact of undocumented migration in the early 1980s) in general the world-wide focus on immigration stems from the fundamental political changes presently occurring in Europe, the continuing changes in Asia which followed the end of the Vietnam war, and the extensive and prolonged world recession of the 1980s. These events have created a situation in which the events in Southern California can be seen as part of a wide series of redistributive effects at a global scale, rather than the simple interaction of Mexico and Central America with Southern California.

In the past two decades, immigration flows have increased dramatically on all spatial scales, both within Europe and North America. The immigration flows from Asia and Central and South America to the United States are now nearly comparable to the flows from Europe to the United States in the first two decades of this century. The result of these very large flows is to raise questions about the process of immigrant absorption and assimilation. To what extent can a host society absorb and assimilate very large numbers of new immigrants and maintain the original social structure, levels of employment and citizen participation without creating a

Lessons from Southern California 87

balkanized and divided society? Will the sheer size of the late twentieth-century flows overwhelm the previous tendency, however limited, towards an integrated society? The general question creates specific sub-questions about labor force participation, about the provision of social services, and about political decision-making and the political process. These sub-questions focus on and crystallize the central arguments about an open-door policy for immigrants or of limits to immigration.

The first debate is focused around the issues of jobs, poverty and the discussions of the underclass. The argument takes the form that if there are not enough jobs for the unskilled and urban inner-city poor, continued immigration will worsen their situation. While Simon (1984, 1989), Borjas (1990), and Borjas and Tienda (1986) argue that general immigration causes little or no unemployment, Bouvier (1991) argues that it is the arrival of immigrants to fill low-wage jobs which removes the pressure on employers to upgrade the jobs or the wages. The few national studies of the effects of recent immigrant arrivals on the earnings of black workers suggest that there are no significant individual effects. However, there are probably regional and metropolitan effects to the extent that employers in one region have low-wage workers available, while other regions do not have such low-wage workers to fill jobs.

A second issue is perhaps the most debated topic of immigration: whether the immigrants' contributions in taxes outweigh the costs of education and health care. A third element of the debate about local versus global responsibility centres on the issue of political representation and political power. The issue is more intense with respect to undocumented than legal migration and it takes two forms. In the United States the decennial census is used to redistrict (to change the boundaries of voting areas) the congressional election system at least every ten years after the decennial census. At this point, the system of redistricting is based on the total population. Thus, if there are a large number of non-citizens who cannot vote, and they are not distributed uniformly then a smaller number of citizens in one district may have voting power which is greater than a larger number of voting citizens in a neighbouring district. A second component of the debate is related to the issue of entitlements and protected classes. As a result of a twenty-year period of civil rights litigation, the gains for the black population have been extended in a variety of affirmative action programs. Now, the protected classes have been enlarged to include Hispanics and Asians. Should the protected classes include recent immigrants? The political issue is not simply a US issue, the rise of the political right in Europe also speaks to the centrality of the issue of immigration, political power and the role of immigrants in the existing society.

IMMIGRATION IN A CHANGING AND SHRINKING WORLD

The United States is often described as a nation of immigrants.[1] Any reconstruction of historical immigration emphasizes the large scale immigration of the period 1881–1920 (Table 5.1) and the two decade period 1900 to 1924 (the year in which the United States ended an open-door immigration policy) is especially notable. It was a period in which 18.5 million immigrants were admitted to the United States. The migration in the most recent period approaches that scale. There were more than 10.3 million new legal arrivals in the period 1971–90. The size is an important aspect of the migration periodicities but the composition is equally important. While Europe dominated the flows in the 1900–24 period, Latin America and Asia dominated the flows in the 1970 and 1980 decades (see Figure 5.1). If undocumented migration is added to the numbers, the flows in the 1970s and 1980s may be as large as the flows in the earlier decades of the century.

It is important to put these flows into a legal context as well. There have been a succession of attempts, some more successful than others, to limit

Table 5.1 Legal immigration to the US: 1821–1989

Year	Number
1821–30	143 439
1831–40	599 125
1841–50	1 713 251
1851–60	2 598 214
1861–70	2 314 824
1871–80	2 812 191
1881–90	5 246 613
1891–00	3 687 564
1901–10	8 795 386
1911–20	5 735 811
1921–30	4 107 209
1931–40	528 431
1941–50	1 035 039
1951–60	2 515 479
1961–70	3 321 677
1971–80	4 493 314
1981–89	5 801 579

Sources: *Statistical Yearbook of the Immigration and Naturalization Service*, (1988) table 1; and *Advance Report: Immigration Statistics – Fiscal Year* (1989), table 1.

Lessons from Southern California

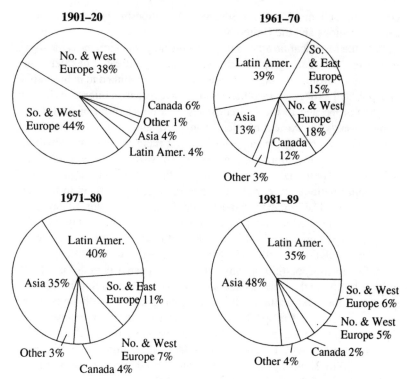

Source: *Statistical Yearbook of the Immigration and Naturalization Service*, 1988.

Figure 5.1 Origins of legal immigrants to the United States

immigration. In 1882 The Chinese Exclusion Act was passed to keep out Chinese laborers, but it was the quota acts of the 1920s which truly changed immigration policy. The Quota Act of 1921 limited immigrants from Europe to 3 per cent of their number in the 1910 census. The Immigration Act of 1924 further lowered the quota and included a provision which was designed to maintain the current ethnic structure of the United States. Until the introduction of the Bracero program during World War II (a program to allow agricultural workers to enter the United States temporarily) there were no significant immigration flows into the United States. In 1965 the Immigration Act changed the quota provisions of the 1924 Act and removed the link between entry quotas and the previous entry of groups into the United States. It was the 1965 act which changed the immigration policy together with the ethnic mix of the immigrants coming to the United States; it severed the relationship between European sending regions and the United States.

Both the historical flows and the more recent population movements are responses to demographic changes and political considerations. Immigration from one country to another is closely linked to demographic and political processes in other nations, and recent immigration both in and to Europe and to the United States, is a direct result of past demographic trends and current political change. Although it is often recounted, it is worth reiterating that high fertility and rapid population growth are *continuing* in developing countries. Even when fertility rates have dropped, the potential for continual growth is extremely high. Several developing nations are expected to double their populations in the next two decades. The country of most concern in a discussion of Southern California, Mexico, was only 27 million people in 1950. Today, in 1990, the country is close to 85 million people. But, even more critical, nearly half the population is under 15 years of age. Estimates of the effect of a youthful, fertile population range from an expected population of 110 million by the end of the decade and as high as 150 million by the first quarter of the next century. Other developing nations with links to the United States and Europe have similar trajectories. For example, the growth in middle eastern countries with the most potential impact on Europe include Egypt, which may grow from 55 million to 103 million in the next 30 to 35 plus years, and Iran which might grow from 54 to 130 million. Even if the projections are halved they are the context within which immigration issues need to be discussed.

Demographic change is paralleled by political changes. The reunification of Germany, the breakup of the Soviet Union, the restructuring of Europe and continuing instability in the Middle East and in South Asia have changed both political and social expectations. While some groups seek to reformulate or create new nation states, others have become political refugees. Some of the sociopolitical changes can be traced to our shrinking world. Both information technology and travel technology have joined to decrease the distance amongst populations and to increase the potential for contact. Just how these technological transformations are being played out is still uncharted but that they will have dramatic effects is without question.

What are the implications of the demographic and political changes? First, if the projections of continuing rapid population growth are correct then there is very little likelihood that the developing countries can create jobs at a sufficient rate to absorb the increase in the workforce. If, for example the workforce in Mexico doubles or triples in the next decade and Mexico cannot create the jobs, the probability of continuing large-scale migration to the United States is an almost certainty. Thus the health of the Mexican economy is inextricably linked with the levels of immigration from Mexico to the United States. Second, dramatic socioeconomic differences between developing and developed economies, especially in situations of proximity, will continue to stimulate migration. The proximity and the differences between Mexico and the United States is only one example, an example where migration is relatively unconstrained. But more generally, why would we not expect large-scale migration across international borders as poor, if not destitute populations, attempt to redress the differences between their lives and the lives of the well-off in the west.

GLOBAL CHANGE AND LOCAL OUTCOMES

California and the Los Angeles metropolitan region have changed fundamentally in the past two decades. The changes have been so dramatic that Los Angeles has been called the capital of the Third World to dramatize low-wage sweatshops, poor immigrant neighbourhoods and the rise of diseases largely eliminated from the United States as a whole. As recently as 1960 the population of Los Angeles was largely Anglo or more properly white/non-Hispanic. Now, in 1990 the County of Los Angeles no longer has a majority culture. It is close to 40 per cent Hispanic, 40 per cent white/non-Hispanic and approximately 10 per cent Asian and 10 per cent black (Table 5.2). Between 1980 and 1990 the

Table 5.2 Population of the United States, California and Los Angeles County in 1990

	United States	%	California	%	LA County	%
Anglo (white not-Hispanic)	188 128 296	75.6	17 093 961	57.4	3 504 553	39.5
Black	29 216 293	11.7	2 110 700	7.1	942 974	10.6
Hispanic	22 354 059	9.1	7 557 550	25.4	3 351 242	37.8
Asian/American Indian	8 762 132	3.5	2 944 669	9.9	54 485	10.8
Other race	249 093	.1	53 141		109 910	1.2
Total	248 709 873		29 760 021		8 863 164	

Source: US Census of Population, 1990.

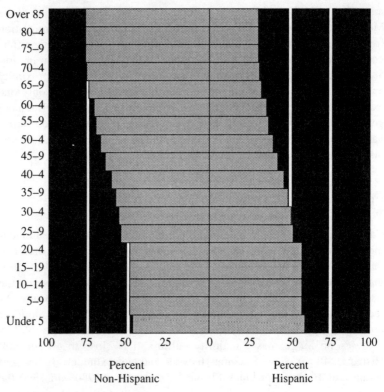

Source: US Census of Population, 1990.

Figure 5.2 Distribution of Los Angeles County Hispanic and Non-Hispanic population by age

County grew by more than one million Hispanics and over half a million Asians (particularly Koreans, Thais and Vietnamese). In addition the County is the recipient of a large proportion of all Hispanics and Asians in California and is quite different in composition from the United States as a whole. The difference between the County and the nation at large is a reiteration of the spatial variability in the impacts of immigration. Equally important are the differences in the age distribution on the immigrant and non-immigrant population (Figure 5.2). Using Hispanic as an overall proxy for the immigrant population we find dramatic differences in age distribution with concomitant implications for fertility and population growth. Indeed, the sheer numbers of new immigrant residents emphasizes the dramatic changes brought about by migration. The three immigrant groups, (1) legal immigrants (2) those granted amnesty by the federal government and (3) undocumented persons and their citizen children, make up about 25 per cent of the total population of the Los Angeles County in 1990.

The County is an extreme microcosm of the State. Some statistics drive home the role and impact of immigration. California is now estimated to have 31.3 million people and in the year July 91–July 92 the population of the State grew another 654 000, at a rate of over 2 per cent each year while at the same time the state was losing, not gaining jobs. An assessment of the growth provides further evidence of the impacts of immigration. A little over 300 000 were new immigrants, a one year *increase* of 22 per cent. A further complexity is that domestic out-migration was greater than in-migration, and much of the out-migration was non-Hispanic white and in the adult working-age population, while a large proportion of the growth was births to legal and undocumented immigrants (Hoag, 1993). In California's schools it is estimated that 17 per cent of the students, over 860 000, are the children of illegal and non-citizen immigrants. Three in ten of the students may not be citizens themselves.

A sizable proportion of the immigrant flows to the United States, and increasingly to European countries, is of undocumented migrants. While the numbers are always in dispute, the work of Warren and Passell (1987) placed some firm bounds on the size of the streams at the national level for the United States in 1980. They suggested that a minimum lower bound was about 2 million undocumented migrants counted in the 1980 census. A range for the United States as a whole is generally accepted as between 2 and 4 million undocumented immigrants. For Los Angeles county the numbers have been variously estimated as near 700 000 although this has been identified as a lower bound (Moreno-Evans, 1992). There are in addition about 1.1 million foreign-born residents including those who are legal immigrants and other persons who have legally entered the county since 1980. If the numbers counted in the census are any guide, then the total number of undocumented residents may be as high as 1.5 million in Los Angeles County alone, in 1990. There were at least 800 000 thousand applications for citizenship under the Immigration Reform Control Act of 1986 (IRCA) (Hoefer, 1991) which places the magnitude of the scale of immigration in perspective.

Much of the specific interest in the size of the legal and illegal flows revolves around *localized impacts* of the monetary costs and benefits of large scale immigration and around the extent to which the flows will create a 'separated' and 'disunited' society (Schlesinger, 1992).

Estimating Economic Costs and Contributions

Beginning in the mid-1980s there has been an increasing focus on the issues of the economic effects of increasing numbers of migrants in post-industrial societies of the west. Before the world-wide economic downturn of the 1980s there was little or no attention given to the economic costs which immigrants might pose for the receiving nations. But, by the mid-1980s with increasing unemployment in native populations, governments in Europe and in the United States were more concerned with the potential effects of continuing large scale immigration.

Much of the interest in legal and illegal immigrant-flows revolves around the issues of the monetary costs of large-scale immigration, especially when it is spatially concentrated. At various times there have been serious attempts to wrestle with the issue of costs. In the early 1990s, especially in the United States, the debate and rhetoric about the costs of immigration reached new heights with strongly held positions on the advantages (Simon, 1989) and disadvantages (Huddle, 1993) of continuing legal and undocumented migration to the United States. Of course, more nuanced studies note that while some immigrants do well, others have restricted opportunities and a gloomy future even when they enter legally (Sorenson and Enchautegui, 1994).

The initial studies of the economic effects of immigration focused in the main on issues of labor force participation. Indeed the major concern of much of the early work was on two related questions: (1) whether immigrant workers displace domestic workers from jobs, and (2) whether they cause a reduction in domestic wages? Almost all the studies suggest that the labor markets are sufficiently segmented, that there are no noticeable effects of immigrant workers, and that domestic workers are in large part insulated from the effects of immigrant workers. Studies by Bean, Lowell and Taylor (1988) Borjas (1987) and Simon (1989) all reject the hypothesis that immigration causes unemployment in the United States labor market. Some recent work by Borjas (1990) has suggested that a 10 per cent increase in immigration would have a $-.1$ per cent effect on the labor force participation rates of native white workers, and a $-.1$ to $.4$ per cent effect on African-American workers. Clearly the effects are small. At the same time, the impacts are regionally quite variable. Studies of Los Angeles and California show that there is evidence of wage depression due to immigrants (McCarthy and Valdez, 1986; Muller and Espenshade, 1985).

A second group of studies attempts to evaluate the use of services by immigrants as a way of assessing their "overall costs" to the economy.

Early studies by Blau (1984) and Tienda and Jensen (1986) compared the welfare and social insurance participation rates of recent immigrants and the native born and concluded that immigrants were *less* likely to be on welfare and *less* likely to be social insurance recipients than the native born population.

Studies which attempt an evaluation of both revenues and costs are more limited and often controversial. An often quoted study by McCarthy and Valdez (1986) examined costs and revenues for Mexican immigrants to Los Angeles county. The pool of immigrants included permanent and cyclical migrants to California and the assessment of the costs (or participation rates) were generated from assumptions about the use of services rather than from statistical estimation. The comparison of *per capita* costs and revenues generated a net deficit, that is, that immigrants generated more costs than revenues. Similar conclusions were provided from a Muller and Espenshade (1985) study of health care, welfare and public protection services. In contrast a study in Texas concluded that at the state level the revenues exceeded the costs, though in specific cities costs exceeded revenues (Weintraub and Cardenas, 1984). It is again an issue of scale and regional variability.

Addressing the issue of local costs and contributions, a case study (Moreno-Evans, 1992) provides a more detailed understanding of the issue of benefits and costs and addresses specifically the spatial impacts of these costs and benefits. Although there are a number of caveats which can be raised about small-scale local studies, for example the estimation of immigrant generated revenues may not take into account revenues paid by immigrant-owned businesses, even so the cost analysis is an important systematic attempt to assess the economic impacts of large-scale migration. The results are worth wider reporting as they provide a framework for understanding the costs and benefits of large-scale 'mass migration' (King, 1993).

Revenues generated at all levels of government (1990–91) by recent legal immigrants (immigrants since 1980), amnesty persons, and undocumented persons are estimated at 4.3 million dollars. The revenues are divided amongst the federal (60 per cent), state (28.6 per cent), the County (3.2 per cent) and other local cities and local governments (8.2 per cent). The federal government clearly receives the largest share. In contrast the County costs of services to the three immigrant groups (*documented*, illegal and refugees) are estimated at 946 million dollars. Additionally the education costs are estimated at 1484 million dollars but the education costs are largely state monies. The short fall in the County alone is about 807 million dollars. If we assume that the education costs are totally borne by the State then there is a short fall at the State level of about 250 million dollars. It is quickly apparent that the federal government is receiving the largest share of revenues and has a positive dollar flow. The local area, the County, 'bears a disproportionately high cost for serving immigrants who are in the country as a result of federal laws, and or policies and decisions, while most tax revenues collected from immigrants go to the federal government (Moreno-Evans, 1992). There is a clear spatial disparity which creates a burden on those counties with large and often poor immigration populations.

The implicit question which underlies much of the conversation about the costs of immigration is related to long term effects of immigration. Will the (temporary?) higher costs be balanced by increasing returns from an educated and entreprenurial immigrant population, or will the new immigrant population become a welfare and deficit cost on the host nation? It is these questions which are the most difficult to answer but some research suggests that more recent immigrants are less skilled, and less successful in the labor market than earlier groups (Borjas, 1990; Borjas and Trejo, 1991). At the same time we must recognize that revenue and costs do not measure the total contributions, nor 'costs' of large numbers of immigrants. The contributions of new immigrants who take 'low-end' jobs that no one else will accept, the contributions to international competitiveness by accepting low salaries and few if any social benefits and the costs of large numbers of unemployed new young immigrants who participate in alternate life styles, including gangs, cannot be measured in the terms we are using here.

At this point the evidence suggests that at the national level immigrants have been generating more tax revenues than the costs of services provided to them, but that at the same time the net gain is less than it was a decade ago. Local studies on the other hand show serious costs related to large scale immigration. Thus, areas with high levels of immigration may be bearing a disproportionate effect of the immigration patterns.

Immigrants and Integration

A central issue which emerges again and again and which is equally critical in Europe and the United States is the question of how will the new immigrants enter the existing society. The social and spatial mobility of new immigrants is an important part of the answer to the question of immigrant success. Is there evidence that the new immigrants are pursuing a similar process of occupational progress and spatial mobility as European migrants followed in earlier decades? A major 'local' issue of continuing high levels of immigration are the concentrated patterns of new immigrants in the metropolitan areas of initial entry. These patterns of immigrant concentration often create large homogenous areas of considerable separation from other ethnic groups and from the white/local populations.

In general, immigrant groups comprise low income and often very poor households which in turn influences their housing situation. For example, in the Los Angeles metropolitan area, 63 per cent of non-hispanic whites own their homes but only 22 per cent of Hispanics and only 5 per cent of recent legal immigrants. As a consequence large numbers of new immigrants are concentrated in the poorest sector of the housing market and are often quite segregated from other ethnic and racial communities.

Compounding the problem of inital poverty, many of the immigrants arrived during the 1970s not long before the world-wide economic downturn and a fundamental shift in the nature of the industrial enterprise. The old 'urban' industries in the center of major western metropolitan areas lost employment and thus no longer provided entry level positions and the possibility of upward mobility for new immigrant groups. The lack of employment opportunities further marginalizes new immigrant populations and increases the levels of separation. At the same time it slows, if not stops the possibility of upward social mobility and spatial geographic mobility.

Recent analyses of separation in Southern California confirms the overall pattern of separation for Hispanics, the largest and most recent immigrant wave into the region. Ong and Lawrence (1992) have noted the emergence of a mega bario now covering some 200 square miles and which has the majority of the three million Hispanics in Los Angeles County. Yet Hispanics are also moving to surrounding counties and there is evidence that some of this movement is integrative. Clark and Mueller (1988) have shown that those Hispanics who moved to suburban locations in Los Angeles County and to Orange county were more likely to have higher incomes. This is certainly support for the notion that Hispanics may follow the pattern of earlier European migrants. But at the same time the measures of concentration show that after an initial decline in the levels of separation there is evidence that the very large numbers of Hispanics may be creating re-segregation (Clark, 1995; Rolph 1992). It is the issue of separation which may in the long run be one of *the* critical factors in the local impacts of large scale immigration. Certainly, when the legal and political process emphasizes individual and group rights over the larger community of citizens there may be the potential for continuing, if not increased cultural seperatism (Clark and Morrison, 1992). The recent turmoil in the political arena highlights just this problem when special districts are created to ensure the representation of ethnic groups (Clark and Morrison, 1992). The combination of legal and political forces in the United States seems to emphasize cultural separatism rather than a united society (Schlesinger, 1992). The question which underlies so much of the debate on immigration and integration policies is perhaps best framed as the question about the future direction of a nation. The arguments for a bilingual, bi-cultural nation while seemingly responsive to different groups may not be the most attractive direction for a nation to follow if it strives for more unity, rather then separateness or even divisiveness.

An illustration of the tensions and divisions is contained in just such recent litigation over political power in Los Angeles County. A claim brought against Los Angeles County in 1988 centered on the demographic makeup of the five districts from which each of the County's five supervisors is elected. In 1980, Hispanics made up 27.6 per cent of all the County's inhabitants but only 14.6 per cent of all voting-age *citizens* (because many of the Hispanic residents are not citizens). In 1990 Hispanics made up almost 40 per cent of the total population (Table 5.2) but they are still only 19.8 per cent of all voting age citizens in the County. If 'persons' and 'citizens' similarly dispersed within the County, the disparity would be largely immaterial. In Los Angeles County, however, Hispanic non-citizens are noticeably more concentrated in certain parts of the County. (This is also visible in the concentration of Central American Hispanic applicants for legislation as shown in Figure 5.3.) Thus, it is possible to form majority-Hispanic election districts that encompass one-fifth of all *persons* in the County (to achieve representational equality) but nowhere near one-fifth of those who are entitled to vote (which undermines electoral equality). The essence of the problem is that one-fifth of the political voice went to an estimated one-fifth of all persons in Los Angeles County, but that district contained only 16.3 per cent of all *eligible voters* in 1990. Because the district did not have one-fifth of the County's eligible voters, it thereby disadvantaged other voters elsewhere in the County (Clark and Morrison, 1991). Had the district been widened to encompass one-fifth of the County's eligible voters, the district would then have contained well *over* one-fifth of the County's population. This distinction between the total population and the voter-eligible population lies at the heart of a tension within the law. In some jurisdictions, demographic realities force a choice between according either equal representation to all persons or equal voting power to all citizens. A third alternative would avoid the choice by equalizing the degradation of both (i.e., spreading the damage).

Lessons from Southern California

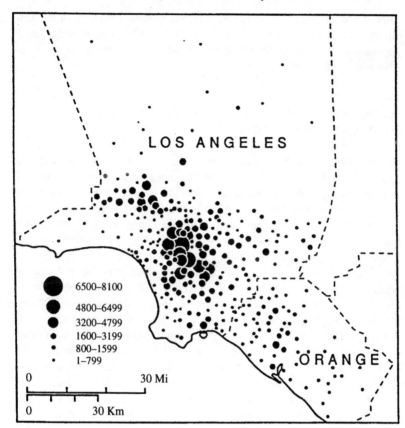

Source: Hoefer, M. (1991) 'The Legalization Program in California', Los Angeles Fourth Annual Demographic Workshop.

Figure 5.3 Central American legalization applicants by postal zip-code location in Los Angeles and Orange Counties

The tension is not simply one of citizens and non-citizens. The increase of one immigrant group, legal or undocumented, has impacts on other immigrant groups and on resident ethnic populations (Johnson and Oliver, 1989). When there is a rapid population increase of a relatively disadvantaged immigrant population, in the case being discussed here, Mexican and Central American groups, it is likely to occur in inner-city, socioeconomically poorer neighborhoods. If these same neighbourhoods are home to one or more other ethnic or racial groups the situation is set for inter-ethnic conflict. When political power is reorganized as in the Los Angeles County redistricting, there are potential impacts on resident ethnic populations from recent in-migration. The scene is set for further divisiveness and conflict.

IMMIGRATION POLICY: NATIONAL IDENTITY AND IMMIGRANT ABSORPTION

The flood of undocumented immigrants into the United States in the 1970s and early 1980s and the high levels of border apprehensions of illegal immigrants motivated the political process to attempt some reform of the immigration process (Baker, 1990). The Immigration Reform and Contral Act (IRCA) of 1986 was an attempt to take charge of the immigration process. The Act provided amnesty for all immigrants who were in the United States prior to 1982 and at the same time created sanctions for employers who knowingly hired undocumented workers. Several studies designed to evaluate IRCA have concluded that illegal migration has continued to rise in spite of IRCA's passage (Bean, Edmonston and Passel, 1990, p. 208). And, (Donato et al., 1992, p. 56) noted that 'the few small effects (of IRCA) we have uncovered are little to show for the millions of dollars and the thousands of hours that IRCA has invested in an effort to stem the tide of Mexican immigrants to the United States'. That immigration would have been even higher had there not been legislation is suggested by the portrayal of Espenshade (1992) who evaluated both the overall upward trend and the nature of the flow of undocumented aliens (Figure 5.4) and supports the earlier argument of the continuing potential for large-scale flows across the border.

Migration is inherently a dynamic social process. It is unlikely that laws like IRCA have the power to intervene against such a strong socioeconomic force. It is even possible that the decision to intervene may in itself have an expansionary effect on Mexican undocumented migration. By addressing only the current *stock* of undocumented migrants and by attempting to place ceilings on future migrants at the same time that the potential pool of migrants in Mexico and Central America is so large, may only have increased the pressure for further illegal immigration. It is this pressure and the attempt to control the flow which re-raises the issues outlined in the introduction to the chapter.

A guide for this discussion is a comparison of global environmental responsibility. We might argue that immigration policy is a central issue of global, social wellbeing just as environmental policy is a central issue

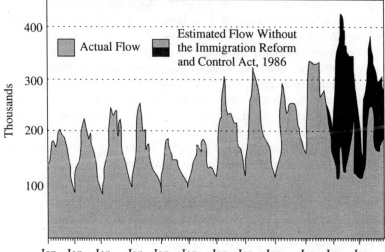

Source: Epenshade, T.J. (1992) 'Policy Influences on Undocumented Migration to the United States', *Proceedings of the American Philosophical Society*, p. 136.

Figure 5.4 Estimated monthly flows of undocumented immigrants to the United States

for global ecological wellbeing. In this context Layard *et al.* (1991) in the perspective of East and West Europe, argue that it is essential for the 'rich' European countries to provide, at least, conditional aid within the region. From their economic perspective, trade, as much as flows of capital and people will help living standards in the east and west converge. Without recognizing the disparities and without a regional perspective, the immigration pressures will rise and the flows will reach levels which will in effect change the rate and nature of absorbtion. The outcome may well be greater divisiveness and separation in the host societies. The evidence of history is that walls to keep people out have not been successful. There is no indication that barriers will be more successful in the late-twentieth century. Thus far, the evidence from Southern California is that neither barriers nor changes in the immigration program have been successful in preventing a continuing stream of undocumented migration to the metropolitan areas of the United states. By 1989 there were over 3 million applications under the IRCA program including 1.3 million from seasonal agricultural workers. Of the non-agricultural applications 1.2 million were from Mexico and .8 million applications were from Los Angeles County (Hoefer, 1989; 1991). We may be in the initial phase of what has been described as the process whereby international and continental boundaries become permeable barriers for the redistribution of wealth. Specific programs to deal with the flows of immigrants have included industrial and investment dispersal to developing countries, but in the end the problem of immigration will only be addressed when incomes are redressed at a world scale. In the end the immigration problem is a problem of resource distribution and it is likely that if the problem of resource distribution is ignored there will be major impacts on those nation states experiencing high levels of immigration.

Note

1. Immigration to and within the United States has been described as four waves (Muller and Espenshade, 1985). The first wave was the migration to the United States at the end of the last century an the beginning of this century. The second wave was the migration from rural to urban communities during the decades before the second world war. The third wave was the migration of the black population to the northern industrial cities of the United States and the fourth wave is the current migration from Central America and Asia.

References

Baker, S.G. (1990) *The Cautious Welcome* (Washington, DC: Urban Institute Press).
Bean, F., C. Lowell and L.J. Taylor (1988) 'Undocumented migration, Mexican Immigrants and the Earnings of Other Workers in the United States', *Demography* 25: pp. 35–52.
Bean, F., G. Vernez and C. Kelley (1989) *Opening and Closing the Doors: Evaluating Immigration Reform and Control.*
Bean, F., B. Edmonsto and J. Passel (1990) *Undocumented Migration to the United States: RCA and the Experience of the 1980s* (Washington, DC: The Urban Institute Press).
Blau, F. (1984) 'Use of transfer payments by immigrants', *Industrial and Labor Relations Review*, 37: pp. 222–239.

Borjas, G.J. (1990) *Friends or Strangers: The impact of immigrants on the US Economy* (New York: Basic Books).
Borjas, G.J. and M. Tienda (1986) 'The economic consequences of immigration', *Science* 235, pp. 645–51.
Borjas, G. and S. Trejo (1991) 'Immigrant Participation in the Welfare System', *Industrial and Labor Relations Review*, 44: pp. 195–211.
Bouvier, L. (1991) *Peaceful Invasions: Immigration and Changing America* (Lanham, Maryland: University Press of America).
Clark, W.A.V. and M. Mueller (1988). 'Hispanic relocation and spatial assimilation: a case study', *Social Science Quarterly*, 69: pp. 468–75.
Clark, W.A.V. and P.A. Morrison (1991) 'Demographic Paradoxes in the Los Angeles Voting Rights Case', *Evaluation Review*, 15, 712–726
Clark, W.A.V. and P.A. Morrison (1992) *Mirroring the Mosaic: Redistricting in a Context of Cultural Pluralism* (Santa Monica, CA.: The Rand Corporation) pp. 77–89.
Clark, W.A.V. (1992) 'Residential preferences and residential choices in a multi-ethnic context', *Demography*, 29: pp. 451–66.
Clark, W.A.V. (1995) 'Avoidance, assimilation and sucession: residential patterns in a multi-ethnic metropolis', forthcoming in R. Waldinger and M. Bozorgmehr (eds), *Ethnic Los Angeles* (Russel Sage).
Cornelius, W. (1990) 'The US demand for Mexican Labor' in W. Cornelius and J. Bustmante (eds), *Mexican Migration to the U.S.: Origins, Consequences and Policy Options* (La Jolla, CA.: University of California, San Diego Center for US–Mexican Studies).
Donato, K., J. Durand and D. Massey (1992) *Stemming the Tide: Assessing the Deterrent Effects of the Immigration Reform and Control Act* (La Jolla, CA.: University of California San Diego, Center for US–Mexican Studies).
Espenshade, T.J. (1992) 'Policy influences on undocumented migration to the United States', *Proceedings of the American Philosophical Society*, pp. 136.
Glazer, N. (1981) *The New Immigration: A Challenge to American Society* (San Diego: San Diego State University Press).
Heer, D. (1990) *Undocumented Mexicans in the United States* (New York: Cambridge University Press).
Hoag, E. (1993) 'Statistics from the State Department of Finance', Sacramento, California.
Hoefer, M. (1989) 'Characteristics of Aliens Legalizing Under IRCA', Baltimore: Paper presented at the Population Association meetings.
Hoefer, M. (1991) 'The Legalization Program in California', Los Angeles Fourth Annual Demographic Workshop.
Huddle, D. (1993) 'The Net Costs of Immigration to California', Executive Summary, Houston, Texas, Rice University Department of Economics.
Johnson, J.H. Jr and M.L. Oliver (1989) 'Interethnic minority conflict in urban America: the effects of economic and social dislocations', *Urban Geography* 10: pp. 449–63.
King, R. (1993) *Mass Migration in Europe* (London: Belhaven).
Layard, R., O. Blanchard, R. Dornbush and P. Krugman (1991) *East–West Migration: The Alternatives* (Cambridge: MIT Press).
McCarthy, K. and R. Valdez (1986) *Current and Future Effects of Mexican Immigration in California* (Santa Monica: The Rand Corporation).

Moreno-Evans, M. (1992) 'Impact of Undocumented Persons and Other Immigrants on Costs, Revenues and Services in Los Angeles County', a report prepared for the Los Angeles County Board of Supervisors.

Muller, T. and T.J. Espenshade (1985) *The Fourth Wave: California's Newest Immigrants* (Washington, DC: The Urban Institute).

Ong, P. and J. Lawrence (1992) *Pluralism and Residential Patterns in Los Angeles* (Los Angeles, UCLA School of Urban Planning).

Rolph, E.S. (1992) *Immigration Policies: Legacy from the 1980s and Issues for the 1990s* (Santa Monica: The Rand Corporation).

Rothman, E.S. and T.J. Espenshade (1992) 'Fiscal Impacts of Immigration to the United States', *Population Index*: 58, pp. 381–415.

Schlesinger, A. Jr (1992) *The Dis Uniting of America, Reflections on a Multicultural Society* (New York: W.W. Norton).

Simon, J. (1984) 'Immigrants, Taxes, and Welfare in the United States', *Population and Development Review*, 10: pp. 55–70.

Simon, J. (1989) *The Economic Consequences of Immigration* (Cambridge, Mass.: Basil Blackwell).

Sorensen, E. and M. Enchautegui (1994) 'Immigrant Male Earnings in the 1980s: Divergent patterns by race and ethnicity', in B. Edmonston and J. Passel (eds), *Immigration and Ethnicity* (Washington: The Urban Institute Press).

Tienda, M. and L. Jensen (1986) 'Immigration and Program Participation: Dispelling the Myth of dependency', *Social Science Research*, 15: pp. 372–400.

Warren, R. and J. Passel (1987) 'A Count of the Uncountable: Estimates of Undocumented Aliens in the 1980 United States Census', *Demography*, 24: pp. 375–93.

Weintraub, S. and G. Cardenas (1984) 'The Use of Public Services by Undocumented Aliens in Texas. A Study of State Costs and Revenues', Austin, Texas: University of L.B.J. School of Public Affairs Report, No. 60.

Part III

Coping with Mass Immigration of Educated People: The Israeli Experience

6 Short-Run Absorption of the Ex-USSR Immigrants in Israel's Labor Market
Karnit Flug and Nitsa Kasir (Kaliner)

INTRODUCTION

The economic literature on the absorption of immigrants in the labor market of the destination country has concentrated on the performance of their wages relative to that of the native population and over time (Borjas, 1985, Chiswick, 1978, LaLonde and Topel, 1992). Relatively few studies have dealt directly with the question of the preservation and transferability of immigrants' human capital. One such study is that of Friedberg (1991), which measures the transferability of schooling in the country of origin by measuring its effect on earnings in the destination country. Another is that of Ofer, Vinkoor and Ariav (1983), which studied the by-occupation absorption pattern and compared the earnings of those who retained and those who changed their occupation. Another direction of research is that of Beenstock (1993) and Chiswick (1992), which concentrated on language acquisition (as a complementary skill) and its effect on labor-market absorption (probability of finding a job and its quality). Other studies have shown that occupational convergence takes place over time: these include Chiswick (1977) for immigrants to the US, and Amir (1993) for highly educated immigrants from the Former Soviet Union (FSU) to Israel during the 1970s.

The present study also examines the transferability of immigrants' human capital to the destination country by looking at the by-occupation absorption pattern. To do this, we examine the actual pattern of absorption in employment of immigrants from the FSU who have reached Israel since early 1990, based on the analysis of data from surveys of immigrant employment and on the Labour Force Surveys of the Central Bureau of Statistics. In a previous article (Flug, Kasir and Ofer, 1991) we developed scenarios for absorption patterns based on the long-term absorption of immigrants who came in 1979–81. In this chapter we compare our predictions with observations of the actual absorption of immigrants in employment in 1991 and the beginning of 1992 that is, in the short run, as well as at the beginning of 1993. This enables us to address the question of whether the pattern of short-run absorption is consistent with its long-term aims or not.[1] Looking at the absorption pattern about two years after immigration (which can be considered the medium term from the point of view of absorption) enables us to assess convergence to a satisfactory long-run pattern.

The mass immigration from the FSU is particularly well-suited for studying occupational absorption and the transferability of skills because of its skill composition, which is relatively human-capital intensive, and because it can be compared with previous influxes of immigrants with similar occupational profiles and origins (e.g., Ofer, Vinokur and Bar-Haim, 1984, Stabatello, 1979). It is also enlightening because this influx was not selected in accordance with its labor-market properties as is usually the case with immigration elsewhere. Furthermore, the size of the influx – which amounted to about 10 per cent of the Israeli population at the end of 1993 – poses some specific problems, which have a bearing on our results and are referred to in the discussion.

The immigration and absorption policy in Israel, particularly with respect to the wave of the 1990's exemplifies a policy in which the government gave up control both with respect to the immigration wave itself and to the absorption process. First, by the 'Law of Return', which has been in effect since the establishment of the state, the government gave up its control over the number, timing and characteristics of the immigrants. This is in contrast to the typical approach to immigration in post-industrial societies. Second, by adopting a policy of 'direct absorption', whereby immigrants receive a monetary allowance but are free to choose any area to settle in and any activity to engage in, the government gave up control over the initial phase of absorption. Third, by adopting a private-sector based employment policy towards the immigrants, it also gave up control over absorption in employment. Both, giving up control of the initial phase of absorption and concentrating employment in the private sector represent deviation from the approach towards past immigration waves.

LONG-TERM ABSORPTION IN EMPLOYMENT – REVIEW OF PREVIOUS RESULTS[2]

In our previous article (Flug *et al.*, 1991)we examined the long-term absorption in employment of immigrants from the FSU and the implications for the economy of their entry into the labor force, using several scenarios for their distribution among occupations and industries. We assessed the economic desirability of each of these, their effect on the economy, and the investment required.

We reviewed various patterns of absorption in employment. At one end of the scale immigrants were absorbed in their original occupations. In this case, the economy adapts itself fully, creating jobs which match the immigrants' existing occupational distribution. At the other end of the scale immigrants change their occupations to match the existing structure of the economy, that is, all the adaptation is done by the immigrants. The interim patterns are those in which part of the adapting is done by the economy, enabling some absorption of the immigrants in their original occupations, and part is done by the immigrants. The actual absorption of the immigrants who came in 1979–81 serves as an example of an interim pattern.

Our paper analyzed the pattern of absorption in employment by occupation of the 1979–81 immigrants (using data from the census), which indicated possible and desirable patterns of absorption for the current influx of immigrants, based on certain assumptions about its size. The absorption in employment of the 1979–81 influx, which was quite small, but similar to the present one in occupational structure, served as an indicator of a minimum occupational-change pattern, reflecting mainly the redefinition of occupations to conform with their standard definition in Israel.

By analyzing immigration from the USSR in the 1970s and early 1980s we could make inferences about the immigrants' occupational absorption. This was associated with appreciable occupational change, even though there was not much pressure on the labor market, because of the small number of immigrants in relation to the size of the economy, and the relatively low unemployment rate. The main factors expected to exert pressure for occupational change in the current influx are its large size, Israel's high unemployment rate prior to the immigrants' arrival, and the high proportion of university graduates among the immigrants, of engineers in particular.

Some 40 per cent of immigrants from previous influxes employed in Israel changed their occupation. Among university graduates (excluding physicians) the rate was 42 per cent, while among physicians and paramedical occupations there was little or virtually no occupational change (3 per cent among physicians, 15 per cent among paramedics). For other professionals (lawyers, accountants, journalists, managers) the rate of occupational change was 54 per cent. When patterns of occupational change were analyzed, we found downward mobility. Thus, engineers became technicians, technicians became skilled workers, and most skilled workers went into service industries. The rate of change in the current influx is expected to be even higher, although in some cases this may be a temporary change, before a return to the original occupation after a training period. In others, downward mobility reflects the redefinition of occupations in accordance with Israeli norms.

The factors which determine the rate of change for different occupations are connected with the occupation's universal character and its appropriateness for Israel, the amount of additional training required in order to adapt to Israel's needs, and demand for the occupation in Israel. Among the 1979–81 immigrants, these factors were reflected in low rates of occupational change in medicine, teaching (especially non-university, post-high school), and unskilled labor. Immigrants who retained their original occupation usually had the highest level of education within their occupational group. (Because of the size of the current influx and the high proportion of physicians compared with demand, it is expected to display a far higher rate of occupational change.).

In the few years following the large influx, the supply of labor, by occupation, is the result of the continued trends for the established population in combination with the occupational structure of the immigrant population, while the demand side could develop to provide a rare opportunity to change the structure of Israel's economy, switching to a track which utilizes Israel's comparative advantage – its human capital.

Until 1990 the trend of occupational development in Israel was towards contraction in the tradables sector (agriculture and industry) and expansion in the nontradables sector (private and public services) – a typical move towards a post-industrial society. This trend was expressed by changes in occupational composition, with an increase in the proportion of graduates, members of the liberal professions, managers, clerical workers, and salespersons. At the same time, the proportion of laborers in industry and agriculture fell.

While the Israeli economy seemed to have been in a transition toward post-industrialism as reflected in the relative expansion of services and relative contraction of industry, the immigrants' occupation composition – biased towards industry – is more suitable for an industrial society. Therefore, to the extent that they will be absorbed into their original occupations, they may contribute to slowing down the transition process towards post-industrialism.

The immigrants' special occupational composition, with its high share of graduates in technical professions, is expected to bias the economy towards hi-tech industries, pushing up their proportion of employees. Among the hi-tech industries which are expected to grow and develop are chemicals, metals and electrical and electronic equipment. Such traditional industries as textiles may be modernized as tens of thousands of technically highly-trained individuals enter the labor force.

DEVELOPMENTS AND PROJECTIONS

In 1990–1, 375 000 new immigrants arrived in Israel mostly from the FSU, while only about 80 000 arrived annually in 1992 and in 1993. By the end of 1993 the immigrants amounted to some 535 000, approximately 10 per cent of the entire Israel population.[3]

The analysis of occupational composition[4] from the beginning of the influx of immigrants to the end of 1993 reveals a decline in the proportion of members of the scientific and academic professionals, particularly of engineers, physicians, doctors and members of the liberal professions, while the proportion of blue-collar workers increased.

During the current immigration, the proportion of academic–scientific professions fell from 39 per cent in 1990 to 27 per cent in 1993. The proportion of engineers fell from 25 to 16 per cent, and of physicians from 6 to 3.4 per cent. The proportion of blue-collar workers rose from 16 per cent to 26 per cent over the same period (Table 6.1).

These features – the slowdown in immigration and the change in occupational distribution – seem, to a large extent, to be a reaction to absorption problems and, in particular, to the difficulties encountered by immigrants in finding suitable employment. It may also reflect developments in the other potential destination countries, and expectations for the future. The slowdown in immigration may also derive from the reduction of pressure to leave these countries immediately. The change in occupational composition may also be affected by differences in occupational composition in the countries of the FSU, for example, and the uneven economic and political development of these countries. The change in the occupational distribution over time is also consistent with the phenomenon of 'Selectivity' typical of immigration flows in general. According to his phenomenon, those from a given pool of potential immigrants with the highest skills tend to move first.

DATA SOURCES

Our information on the absorption in employment of the current influx of immigrants is based on Labour Force Surveys and on three absorption surveys conducted by the Central Bureau of Statistics. The first, conducted

Table 6.1 Immigrants from the FSU who were employed abroad, by their occupations abroad

	Data from the Monthly Statistical Bulletin				
	1990	1991	1992	1993	1990–3
	(Thousands)				
Total	96.1	79.7	33.8	33.2	242.8
Academic scientific Professions	37.5	28.3	11.0	9.0	85.8
of which: Engineers and Architects	24.4	17.8	6.7	5.3	54.2
Doctors	5.9	3.4	1.3	1.1	11.7
Technical and Liberal Professions	33.0	25.9	11.1	11.0	81.0
Skilled and Unskilled Workers	15.0	15.2	7.8	8.8	46.8
Other Professions [1]	10.6	10.4	3.9	4.4	29.3
	(Per cent)				
Total	100.0	100.0	100.0	100.0	100.0
Academic Professions	38.8	35.1	31.7	26.8	29.4
of which: Engineers and Architects	24.8	22.4	18.9	15.3	18.5
Doctors	6.2	4.3	3.8	3.5	4.0
Technical and Liberal Professions	34.4	32.9	32.3	33.3	27.7
Skilled and Unskilled Workers	15.5	19.4	22.2	25.4	16.0
Other Professions[1]	11.3	12.6	13.8	14.4	10.0

1. Occupations included in this category: administrators and managers, clerical workers, sales workers and agricultural workers.
Source: Data from the Statistical Bulletin are based on the immigrant's statement regarding his occupation.

in the first quarter of 1991, reviewed immigrants who had arrived in the first half of 1990, that is 6–15 months (10 months on average) after immigration. The second was conducted at the beginning of 1992, and reviewed immigrants who had arrived in the last quarter of 1990, that is, after 12–17 months (14 months on average). The third survey reviewed the same immigrants as the second, one year later (that is, after an average of 26 months in Israel).

The level of aggregation of the data is far higher than it was for previous influxes of immigrants, as the survey is based on some 1100 family units, incorporating about 2700 immigrants of working age. Therefore, only broad groups of occupations can be examined. Our previous paper dealt with the pattern of occupational absorption among immigrants who had been in Israel for at least a year and a half (but an average of about 3 years) – a period which may be regarded as 'long-run' for that influx.

Investigating the situation of immigrants from the current influx about a year after their arrival means considering short-run absorption (see Note 1).

On the basis of the information currently available, two questions can be asked:

1. Have we reached a point on the path to a long-run absorption pattern?
2. What is the direction of occupational absorption over time?[5]

ABSORPTION IN EMPLOYMENT DURING 1990–3

The immigrants' average participation rates rose consistently with the average amount of time they had spent in Israel, and began to stabilize in the last quarter of 1991. In 1993 their participation rate was 64 per cent for men and 45 per cent for women (Table 6.2). Both men's and women's participation rate was higher than that of Israelis (62 and 42 per cent respectively). The high women's participation rate reflects their work habits in the FSU, and economic difficulties which make a second income necessary. The higher rates for both men and women also reflects their age composition – relatively few youngsters (15–18) whose participation rate is low.

There have been changes over time in the rate of labor-force entry. It was particularly high when the influx of immigrants began, and at the beginning of 1991 the labor-force participation rate was 59 per cent for immigrants who had been in Israel between 6 and 12 months. By the end of 1992 it dropped to 50 per cent for immigrants who had been in Israel for the same amount of time. During 1993 when unemployment was falling and the probability of finding employment improved, the pace of entry to the labor force accelerated.

The slowdown of the pace at which immigrants joined the labor force reflected growing difficulties in finding suitable employment. Lower participation rates may also reflect the fact that some immigrants despaired of finding work and therefore stopped searching and dropped out of the labor force. This, together with the immigrants' age-composition (a large proportion of elderly), also explains the fact that their participation rate steadied at a lower level than that of the previous immigrants from the USSR. During 1993 when the prospects of finding a job had improved, as reflected by the decline in the unemployment rate, the participation rates of immigrants had increased quite rapidly.

Table 6.2 Immigration 1990–3, labor market indicators

Period		Of working age	In the Labor force	Rate of labor-force participation				Unemployment rate		
				Total*	Males	Females	Total		Males	Females
				(Thousands)					(Per cent)	
1991		211.0	96.4	45.7	56.0	36.7	38.5		28.3	51.8
1992		295.9	153.8	52.0	62.1	43.6	28.7		20.3	38.5
1993		358.4	192.7	53.8	64.4	44.9	19.4		15.8	23.6
1990	IV	105	24	23	–	–	50		–	–
1991	I	159	59	37	50	25	42		30	60
	II	198	87	44	57	33	38		27	54
	III	238	112	47	54	40	39		30	51
	IV	266	133	50	61	42	36		27	47
1992	I	274	145	53	62	45	33		25	42
	II	290	151	52	60	44	28		18	40
	III	312	162	52	63	44	28		19	39
	IV	322	164	51	62	42	25		19	33
1993	I	346	180	52	63	42	22		19	25
	II	352	189	54	64	45	19		15	25
	III	381	209	55	66	47	20		16	26
	IV	372	201	54	64	45	16		14	19

Source: Central Bureau of Statistics, Labor Force Survey – Press releases.

The decline in the rate at which immigrants joined the labor market, together with their longer stay in Israel in general, and in the labor market in particular, are reflected in a sharp decline in their unemployment rate, which fell from 42 per cent at the beginning of 1991 to 25 per cent in the end of 1992 and 16 per cent at the end of 1993 (Table 6.2). If the time since the immigrants' arrival is held constant, the unemployment rate does not decline over time, however.

A comparison of the occupational absorption of men and women reveals that the situation of women is far worse (Table 6.2). The unemployment rate for women was about 24 per cent in 1993 compared with 16 per cent for men.

The problem of occupational absorption was exacerbated by the Mis-Match between available housing and jobs by geographic area. According to an internal migration survey, immigrants moved from the center to the periphery, where there is a large stock of unoccupied housing but a high rate of unemployment. Migration in this direction reduced the probability of finding employment. Moreover, about 35 per cent of all employed immigrants – and 45 per cent of those in the liberal professions – have to travel out of their district to work.

The by-industry distribution of immigrants' employment in 1991–3 shows that they are concentrated in industry and construction – 36 and 9 per cent respectively, compared with 21 and 6 per cent for Israelis. Relatively few are employed in the public sector – 19 per cent compared with 30 per cent for Israelis. This can be compared with the relatively high absorption of immigrants in the public sector in previous influxes. The large proportion of immigrants in construction is due to that industry's expansion in 1991–2, while their concentration in industry and construction in Israel is also related to the substitution of immigrants for workers from the administered territories. A comparison of the immigrants' by-industry employment in Israel with their employment in the FSU shows that their proportion in industry is relatively low, and in the services relatively high. This reflects both the difference in the structure of the economy and the relative flexibility of wages in the services, which are less unionized than industry.

THE OCCUPATIONAL ABSORPTION OF IMMIGRANTS IN THE 1990s

Two features characterize the occupational absorption of the current influx of immigrants (Tables 6.3, 6.4 and 6.5). First, rates of employment in the

Table 6.3 Matrix of absorption in employment of immigrants from the FSU – Survey No. 1

Occupation in the FSU	Total employed prior to immigration[1]	Total employed in Israel[2]	Academic professions	of which: Doctors	of which: Engineers	Liberal professions	Service workers	Skilled workers in industry	Unskilled workers in industry	Other occupations and not known
Total	100.0	100.0	8.8	2.4	4.5	13.3	21.6	36.3	11.0	9.0
Academic professions	33.7	23.6	32.6	9.8	16.2	14.2	14.7	23.1	7.9	7.6
of which: Doctors	7.5	2.8	82.7	82.7	0.0	3.4	13.9	0.0	0.0	0.0
Engineers	14.1	14.1	28.2	0.0	25.8	13.1	8.9	30.8	10.0	9.1
Liberal professions	21.6	19.1	1.5	0.6	0.0	30.5	22.6	30.8	6.7	7.8
Administrators and managers	7.7	7.7	2.6	0.0	2.6	18.7	10.7	39.8	14.9	13.3
Skilled workers in industry	19.3	24.7	0.2	0.0	0.2	4.5	11.9	63.7	14.1	5.6
Other occupations	16.8	25.0	2.4	0.0	1.8	6.5	40.9	24.3	12.7	13.2

1. Occupation in the FSU of immigrants employed in FSU.
2. Occupation in the FSU of immigrants employed in Israel.
Source: Central Bureau of Statistics – Survey of FSU immigrants' employment (immigration: Jan–June 1990).

Table 6.4 Matrix of absorption in employment of immigrants from the FSU – Survey No. 2

					Occupation in Israel				
Occupation in Russia	Total employment prior to Immigration[1]	Total employment in Israel[2]	Academic professions	of which: Doctors	of which: Engineers	Liberal professions	Service workers	Skilled workers in industry	Unskilled workers in industry	Other occupation
Total	100.0	100.0	7.1	1.0	3.4	8.8	26.6	33.7	13.4	10.4
Academic professions	36.1	27.8	20.0	3.7	10.6	7.6	22.7	27.6	10.7	11.4
of which:										
Doctors	7.5	2.4	44.5	40.2	0.0	5.4	18.5	11.3	8.2	12.1
Engineers	15.8	16.0	16.1	0.0	14.8	7.2	21.2	34.8	11.9	8.9
Liberal professions	18.8	16.9	(2.7)	0.0	0.5	27.3	33.0	20.9	9.2	6.9
Administrators and managers	9.1	9.7	–	–	5.5	–	14.5	41.8	16.6	15.1
Skilled workers in industry	21.0	23.8	–	0.0	0.0	–	18.9	58.0	16.0	5.8
Other occupations	14.9	11.3	–	0.0	2.4	–	36.1	24.8	18.3	17.0
Didn't work abroad		10.5	–			10.4	44.5	17.9	13.5	12.8

1. Occupation in the FSU of immigrants employed in the CIS.
2. Occupation in the FSU of immigrants employed in Israel.
Source: Central Bureau of Statistics – Survey of CIS Immigrants Employment (immigration: Oct–Dec 1990).

Table 6.5 Matrix of absorption in employment of immigrants from the FSU – Survey No. 3

Occupation in the FSU	Total employment prior to Immigration[1]	Total employment in Israel[2]	Academic professions	of which: Doctors	of which: Engineers	Liberal professions	Service workers	Skilled workers in industry	Unskilled workers in industry	Other occupations and not known
Total	100.0	100.0	12.8	3.5	5.5	11.9	22.6	30.6	9.3	12.9
Academic professions	36.2	30.7	30.0	10.7	11.3	13.3	15.8	20.7	7.2	13.0
of which: Doctors	3.0	4.4	69.5	69.5	0.0	7.4	8.2	1.8	5.1	7.9
Engineers	9.8	14.4	28.2	0.0	19.8	13.1	8.9	30.8	10.0	9.1
Liberal professions	18.9	18.0	5.2	0.5	2.0	29.7	28.9	20.8	7.3	8.0
Administrators and managers	17.4	9.2	39.1	16.9	5.0	9.1	0.0	12.4	8.6	9.1
Skilled workers in industry	8.1	11.3	61.3	14.6	2.5	1.8	0.0	2.2	20.4	21.0
Other occupations and not known	20.5	11.3	21.5	32.7	8.0	0.0	0.0	6.0	22.3	14.8

1. Occupation in the FSU of immigrants employed in FSU.
2. Occupation in the FSU of immigrants employed in Israel.
Source: Central Bureau of Statistics – Survey of FSU Immigrants' Employment (immigration: Jan–June 1990).

immigrants' original occupations for members of the academic, scientific, liberal and technical professions were low,[6] while the unemployment rate was high. The rate of occupational change consequently understates the difficulties of absorption in employment in these occupations. Second, employment opportunities for professionals deteriorated over time and improved only slightly with tenure in Israel. This means that the chances of finding suitable employment are lower for immigrants who arrived later in the current influx than for those who arrived earlier. Considering the fact that the immigrants reviewed in the second survey had been in Israel longer, the deterioration in the situation reflected by the two surveys, in fact underestimates its real extent. The improvement in the quality of employment for the same immigrants over time was modest.

The features described come as no surprise. It was to be expected that the rates of absorption of immigrants in their original occupations would be lower in this influx, particularly in the short-run. The reasons for high rates of occupational change in the short run are as follows:

1. There was no time to 'reconstitute' human capital – immigrants' skills are not yet adapted to the requirements of the Israeli economy. Human capital is 'reconstituted' by vocational training courses or on-the-job training (especially in the less skilled professions), and takes time.
2. As a result of the influx of immigrants, demand for the business-sector product in Israel was biased in favor of the nontradable sector, and of construction in particular. Employment in the latter increased by 42 per cent in 1990–2 while in industry it grew by only 8 per cent. The nontradable sector does not match the occupational composition of the immigrants. Furthermore, demand grew within industry, in the three-digit industries which serve the construction sector, rather than in the more technologically advanced industries whose skill composition is closer to that of the immigrants.

Reviewing the results of the third survey conducted on immigrants with an average length of stay of 26 months in Israel, shows that also in the medium term (after 2–3 years since immigration), for the current influx rates of employment in the original occupation are far lower than for the 1979–81 immigrants. It may reflect that a period that can be considered the long-run for a small number of immigrants is still the 'short-run' from the point of view of absorption of a very large influx. Only reviewing these immigrants after an additional period of time will allow us to assess whether the problem is mainly the 'speed of convergence' to the new permanent occupational pattern or also a far greater loss of human capital in the long run.[7]

While the number of employees in non-technological industries rose by 17 per cent in 1989–93, the number of employees in technological industries went up by only 6.5 per cent. During 1992 and to a greater extent in 1993, as the initial stage of immigrant-absorption came to an end, the structure of demand changed dramatically, contracting in construction and increasing in the tradable sector. These trends started to manifest themselves in the occupational composition of employment only in 1993.

Beyond the question of the time horizon, it was expected that the rates of occupational change would be higher for the current influx of immigrants, due both to its size and to the high unemployment rate prevailing before their arrival. The current influx contributed to an annual increase of 3 per cent in the labor force, compared with 0.5 per cent in the early 1980s. The current immigrants came to a country with an unemployment rate of 9 per cent, compared with 3 per cent in the early 1980s. These factors caused excess supply in most occupations; in some, it will not be possible to absorb all immigrants even in the long run.

The deterioration in the quality of absorption over time was due to the size of the current influx. The more 'congested' certain occupations became, the less likely it was that immigrants would find jobs in them. This was also reflected in the changeover time in the immigrants' occupational composition. Among immigrants, the proportion in occupations with large excess supply – particularly doctors and engineers – declined (Table 6.1).[8]

Data from the first survey show that only 40 per cent of physicians who arrived in Israel in the first half of 1990 had entered the labor market by the beginning of 1991, about half of them were employed and of those about 80 per cent as physicians (Table 6.3). In the second survey, still only about 46 per cent of the physicians had entered the labor force, and almost two-thirds of these were employed, but only 40 per cent of the latter as physicians (Table 6.4).[9] (Over 80 per cent of physicians who had to change occupation were employed in low-skilled occupations). In the third survey (looking at the same immigrants one year later), the rate of participation of physicians increased to 59 per cent of which 70 per cent worked as physicians (Table 6.5).

According to the first survey, about 15 per cent of all immigrants employed at the beginning of 1991 worked in the services, and approximately 13 per cent worked as cleaners (of streets, institutions, homes). At the beginning of 1992 (according to the second survey) these rates rose to 22 and 19 per cent respectively. In the third survey, their shares in these occupations were 23 and 10 per cent respectively. The actual rate may be even higher, as some of those who declare themselves to be unemployed are actually employed in these occupations. In the first and second surveys, 8 per cent of the immigrants were employed in occupations directly related to the construction industry; 3 per cent as engineers and architects, 5 per cent as skilled workers, and 0.5 per cent as unskilled workers. These figures match the immigrants' by-industry distribution – some 10 per cent were employed in construction in 1991–2.

Immigrants with occupations oriented towards expanding industries (mainly construction and the services) were absorbed in their original occupation or an allied one, while immigrants in other occupations, some with high levels of human capital, were absorbed in semi-skilled and unskilled occupations, mainly in the services.

Looking at employed immigrants gives only half the picture, since unemployment rates differ markedly between occupations. High unemployment rates among human-capital-intensive occupations, particularly among academics reveals severe absorption problems. There are low unemployment rates, however, in occupations related to the services and construction industries.

COMPARISON WITH THE IMMIGRANTS OF 1979–81

In our previous paper, we discussed the desired absorption patterns for the current influx of immigrants, on the basis of the experience of those who came in 1979–81. We regarded occupational changes of the previous influx as largely reflecting the 'standardization' of occupational requirements and the minimal necessary change, since this influx was relatively small, and unemployment was low. Consequently, immigrants whose skills matched the needs of the Israeli labor market had good chances of finding employment in their occupation. Considering the size of the current influx, its occupational distribution, and the unemployment rate which prevailed beforehand, rates of occupational change could have been expected to be higher in the long run. Since the period of time from the beginning of this influx can still be regarded as the short run, we would expect the rates of occupational change to be higher than those of the earlier immigration.

The higher rates of occupational change of the current influx can be seen by comparing Table 6.6 to Tables 6.3, 6.4 and 6.5. Of the immigrants of 1979–81, about 65 per cent of those in scientific and academic occupations found employment (after an average of about 2.5 years or so) within

Table 6.6: Absorption in employment[1] (Per cent)

Occupation in the CIS	Total	Scientific professions	Occupation in Israel							
			of which		Technical and Liberal	Service professions	Skilled workers in industry	Unskilled workers	Other occupations
			Doctors	Engineers					
Total	100.0	28.1	6.0	16.4	23.5	5.9	24.7	4.7	13.0
Scientific and Academic professions	40.6	65.6	95.5	76.8	8.7	1.0	12.0	0.7	12.0
of which: Doctors	6.3	0.0	95.5	0.0	0.0	0.0	0.0	0.0	4.5
Engineers	25.0	65.0	0.0	63.0	9.5	1.0	18.0	0.5	6.0
Technical and other Liberal professions	34.3	3.6	0.0	2.0	55.4	5.3	20.8	4.9	9.9
Administrators and managers	0.3	22.2	7.4	14.8	11.1	3.7	18.5	7.4	37.0
Skilled workers in industry	12.6	1.2	0.0	0.9	5.5	7.5	71.8	8.9	5.2
Other occupations	12.2	0.5	0.0	0.0	2.5	22.5	29.4	12.8	32.2

1. The matrix reflects a hypothetical absorption pattern according to which immigrants change their occupations as per the norms set by the immigrants of 1979–1981.
Source: K. Flug, N. Kasir and G. Ofer, 'The Absorption of Soviet Immigrants in to the labor Market from 1990 Onwards: Aspects of Occupational Substitution and Retention' (based on the population census of 1983).

their occupations, as compared with about 30 per cent in the current influx after about two years since immigration. In the technical and liberal professions, the figures are 55 and 30 per cent respectively. It is particularly noticeable that the rates of occupational convergence in most occupations increased only slightly between the second and third surveys.[10]

CONCLUSIONS AND POLICY IMPLICATIONS

When compared with the occupational absorption of previous influxes, the rate of downward occupational change of the current one is high, resulting in the loss of human capital, on the one hand, and dissatisfaction on the part of immigrants, on the other. Absorption difficulties are reflected in the decline of immigration and the change in occupational distribution towards occupations with lower human capital, and in particular a decline in the proportion of engineers and physicians.

In our previous study we concluded that in order to use the immigrants' human capital effectively the economy had to grow with a bias towards industry, and hi-tech industry in particular. These industries, in which the export component is dominant, are not limited to domestic demand and can expand if they are competitive. Their performance through mid-1991 did not reflect this objective, so that relatively few jobs have been created in these industries. The increase in economic activity in 1990–1 reflected a bias of domestic demand towards the construction sector typical of the first phase of absorption. Another factor which slowed down the expansion of industry is the time required to adjust the immigrants' human capital to the needs of Israel's industries. It could be concluded, therefore, that through 1991 the direction of growth was away from its long-run efficient equilibrium. However, 1992 seems to mark a turning-point, with the construction industry beginning to shrink and industry in general – and high-tech industry in particular – expanding. These trends have intensified in 1993.

There is a wide range of views regarding the desirability of governmental intervention in the process of absorption of immigrants. One view – advocating minimal governmental intervention (limited to providing education, including the acquisition of language skills) is expressed in this volume by Lieberson, based on the long-term experience of the US. In Israel, the authorities' view regarding the optimal degree of government intervention has changed in that direction over time. In the labor market this change manifested itself in the absence of expansion of public sector employment in reaction to the immigration influx in contrast to such expansion in reaction to previous influxes. The policies described below are based on the recognition that governmental intervention should be marginal and limited to facilitate the creation of employment by the private sector. It should concentrate on the provision of training which will expedite the process of adjusting the immigrants' human capital to the existing demand. The justification for governmental intervention in the provision of such training is related to its positive external effects and to the absence of perfect capital market which would allow the immigrants to finance such training on their own. The returns to training both measured in terms of workers' wages and in terms of firm productivity are quite high as reported in a survey by Lynch (1994) for a large number of studies, done in several countries. The return to the individual in the studies reported range 4–11 per cent, and those to the firm (productivity gain) range 10–17 per cent. The returns on training for immigrants were not studied specifically, but we suspect that they are even higher.

Since it has extensively subsidized investment in physical capital (via the 'law for the encouragement of capital investment'), the government should subsidize human capital as well, also in order to deter capital-intensive production technologies. In particular, the government should facilitate the 'rehabilitation' of immigrants' human capital by providing training courses in conjunction with potential employers. In this way, the content of the courses will fit industries' needs. It could also subsidize the acquisition of on-the-job training by subsidizing the initial period of employment.

To provide employment solutions which are successful for both the economy and immigrants, the government should focus on long-term solutions that match the immigrants' skills. Using 'make-work' solutions will not solve the problem of providing employment in occupations with high human capital, and may impede progress towards the efficiency equilibrium, since such solutions usually focus on low-skilled jobs. There is also a danger that it will be difficult to terminate short-term solutions.

Notes

1. In this paper the short run is defined as the period prior to the stabilization of immigrants' rates of participation and unemployment, and in which the individual immigrant has not yet found employment in his original occupation. The short run is thus not defined as a period of time, and can vary for different periods. The short run for the current, relatively large, influx is

likely to last several years, whereas the period of two years after the immigration referred to in the previous paper could be considered the long run.
2. See Flug, Kasir, Ofer (1991).
3. In our previous paper the distribution of immigration over time was not taken into account.
4. The occupational composition follows the breakdown of occupations used by the Central Bureau of Statistics.
5. It is difficult to make a comparison or study the 'cohort effect', because the two groups have been in Israel for different periods of time. Also, the difference between their immigration date is relatively short, 3–12 months. The samples are not large enough to consider partial samples by date of immigration.
6. Because of data limitations, the rates of occupational change refer to broad occupational categories. These rates of change would have been somewhat higher if the occupational break-down had been more detailed.
7. It should be noted that in other studies there was only a modest increase in the rate of immigrants employed in their original occupation between one and three years since immigration: (Beenstock, (1993)) for immigrants of the 1970s or even a slight decline (Sabatello (1979)) for the early 1970s.
8. Nonetheless, other factors may account for the change in occupational distribution over time. For example, immigrants with human-capital-intensive occupations may have left the CIS earlier. The shift in the distribution of the immigrants by country origin may also have contributed to the change in their occupational composition.
9. Participation rates of some occupations, especially physicians, might be low in the period reviewed because of participation in supplementary courses. Since 1987, physicians have had to take any examination in order to obtain a license, and many of them go on a one-year course (which includes Hebrew) prior to this. This may account for the very large increase in the proportion of those employed as physicians between the second and third survey.
10. This result is not unique to this influx. As mentioned earlier, Beenstock (1992) has shown (Table 6.5) that the rate of convergence for immigrants of the 1970s has increased only slightly for immigrants who were in Israel one and three years.

References

Amir, S. (1993) 'The Process of Absorption of Graduates from the Soviet Union in the Israeli Labor Market: 1978–84', Tel-Aviv: Israeli International Institute for Applied Economic Policy Review, Study Series (October).

Beenstock, M. (1993) 'Learning Hebrew and Finding a Job; An Econometric Analysis of Immigrant Absorption in Israel', Jerusalem: The Falk Institute, Discussion Paper No. 93.05.

Borjas, G. (1985) 'Assimilation, Changes in Cohort Quality and Earnings of Immigrants', *Journal of Labor Economics*, 4 (October).

Central Bureau of Statistics (1991) Survey of immigrants arriving in January–June 1990 (January–April) (Hebrew).
Central Bureau of Statistics (1991–2) Survey of immigrants who came in October–December 1990 (December–April) (Hebrew).
Central Bureau of Statistics (1992) Press release on internal migration of new immigrants, 1990–1 (Hebrew).
Central Bureau of Statistics, Press release on absorption in employment of new immigrants, from Labour Force Surveys (Hebrew).
Chiswick, B.R. (1977) 'A Longitudinal Analysis of the Occupational Mobility of Immigrants', Proceedings of the Thirteenth Annual Winter Meeting, Industrial Relations Research Association Series, New York (December).
—— (1978) 'The Effect of Americanization on Earnings of Foreign Born Men', Journal of Political Economy, 86 (October).
—— (ed.) (1992) Immigration, Language and Ethnicity (American Enterprise Institute, Washington, DC).
Flug, K., N. Kasir (Kaliner) and G. Ofer (1991) 'The Absorption of Soviet Immigrants into the Labor Market from 1990 Onwards: Aspects of Occupational Substitution and Retention', Discussion Paper No. 92.13, (November 1992).
Friedberg, R.M. (1991) 'You Can't Take It With You? Immigrants and the Return to Human Capital: Evidence from Israel', MIT, mimeo, July.
LaLonde, R.J. and R.H. Topel (1992) 'The Assimilation of Immigrants in the US Labor Market', in G.J. Borjas and Richard B. Freeman (eds), Immigration and the Labor Force, pp. 67–92.
Lynch, L.M. (1994) 'Training and the Private Sector', International Comparisons. The Introduction, edited by L.M. Lynch, The University of Chicago Press.
Ofer, G., A. Vinkoor, and A. Ariav (1983) 'Soviet Immigrants' Absorption into Employment: A Comparative Analysis', Falk Institute, Jerusalem (Hebrew).
——, and Y. Bar-Haim (1984) 'The Absorption and Economic Contribution of Immigrants from the USSR to Israel', in T. Horowitz (ed.), The Soviet Man and an Open Society (University Press of America).
Sabatello, E.F. (1979) 'Patterns of Occupational Mobility Among New Immigrants to Israel', International Migration (ICEU) volume xvii, no. 3/4.
Shaliv, A. (1989) 'The Occupational Composition of the Industrial Labor Force'. 1986–7, Research Report No. 5, The Industrial Growth Research Team (Hebrew).

7 Social Values and Health Policy: Immigrant Physicians in the Israeli Health-Care System

Judith T. Shuval and Judith Bernstein

VALUES AND IMMIGRATION IN ISRAEL

The chapter considers processes of interaction between social values and health policy as they are reflected in the entry of immigrant physicians into the health-care system in Israel. Data are presented regarding the most recent population of immigrant physicians who have immigrated to Israel from the former Soviet Union.

On the macro-level, two sets of values have played a role in molding these processes. The first concerns the high priority attached to Jewish immigration which is viewed as the central historic mission of the society and has been actively encouraged by means of an open, non-selective admissions policy. In practice, this value has overridden virtually all other values and goals of the society, with the exception of security needs. By way of contrast to other societies where migration has been controlled in terms of economic need, excesses and shortages in the labor force, levels of unemployment, pressures of interest groups and health criteria (Rose, 1969; Yochum and Agarwal, 1988; Zolberg, 1989), in Israel it has always been assumed that the society must seek ways of integrating immigrants into its social and economic structure regardless of the cost. Periodic protests voiced by groups which view themselves as deprived and who have objected to the substantial resources allocated to immigrants, have never changed the overriding priority accorded to free immigration.

The other value is associated with the high priority accorded to health in the society and is expressed in the importance attached to maintaining quality health care in an effort to approximate the most exacting Western standards. This value is reinforced by selective admission to Israeli medical schools, a rigorous curriculum in those schools, a pronounced elitism of the medical profession and by high expectations of the lay population with regard to health-care services (Shuval, 1992; 1995).

Starting with the macro-level, we will discuss policies regarding immigration of physicians and the implications of these policies, particularly with respect to the ambivalence induced by the two sets of high-priority values. Moving to the micro-level, we will discuss the impact of the policies on immigrant physicians' social construction of reality, with a specific focus on professional commitment. We will draw on our longitudinal study for relevant empirical findings.

POLICY REGARDING IMMIGRANT PHYSICIANS

Numbers of immigrants to Israel have varied at different periods depending on the countries of origin from which populations were emigrating. The open-door policy has meant that the number of immigrant physicians entering the country has been unplanned, uncontrolled and a function of circumstances extraneous to health needs of the society.

One of the results of this situation is the fact that Israel is characterized by one of the highest doctor to population ratios in the world: 363/100 000, a figure well above the European average (Anderson and Antebi, 1991; Rosen and Nirel, 1993).

Major efforts have been invested in past years to find employment for the large physician population. Indeed, until the 1990s almost all were employed in their profession in the health-care system (Ofer *et al.*, 1991). This was achieved by a flexible licensing procedure and by a number of allocative mechanisms concerned with the location of immigrant physicians in the health-care system. The two sets of values are jointly expressed in the fact that minimum formal barriers were set for the employment of immigrant physicians in general practice: basic knowledge of Hebrew, presentation of formal credentials indicating completion of training at a recognized medical school and a year of work under supervision were sufficient to obtain a license for general practice. However, such practice was most often located in settings which Israel-trained physicians viewed as less desirable. At the same time, quality control was stringently applied with regard to medical specialty status, which is almost universal among Israel-trained doctors and is accompanied by greater material rewards and prestige. This was granted sparingly to immigrant doctors and only after they succeeded in passing demanding specialty examinations (Shuval, 1985; 1990). These mechanisms provided an uneasy but relatively stable solution to the problem of employing large numbers of immigrant physicians while at the same time maintaining the elite status of the veteran professionals (Shuval, 1985; 1996).

During the 1980s there was a lull in immigration which made it possible for political and professional groups concerned with quality issues in medical practice, to exert pressure on the authorities to make the formal requirements for basic medical licensure more stringent. The set of values concerned with quality of practice was brought to attention at a time when matters relating to the admission of immigrants and their employment were not on the active public agenda. The result was that in 1988 the formal licensure procedure was made more rigorous. In addition to demonstrating language skills and credentials from a recognized medical school, immigrant physicians with less than twenty years of practice experience (reduced to fourteen years in 1992) were required to pass a basic licensing examination for general practice as well as the examination to attain the status of specialist. Those with more than twenty years of experience were required to work for six months under supervision before receiving a license for general practice.

The most recent influx of immigrant physicians began in 1989 when a large wave of immigration from the Soviet Union brought unprecedented numbers of additional physicians to Israel. Growing insecurity, fear of an uncertain future and the new freedoms of peristroika and glasnost resulted in the migration of over 600 000 persons from the former Soviet Union to Israel in the period 1989–95. Among these immigrants 2.5 per cent–3.0 per cent were physicians. By the end of 1994, over 13 000 physicians had arrived in Israel from the former Soviet Union, more than doubling the population of doctors in Israel.

Table 7.1 Immigration of health personnel to Israel: 1989–1994

	1989–91	1992	1993	1994*	Total
Total Immigrants	3 388	64 648	65 679	17 951	492 666
Physicians	9 818	1 430	1 337	292	12 877
Dentists	1 070	150	150	33	1 403
Nurses	7 888	1 580	1 784	511	11 763
Paramedicals	1 063	244	200	57	1 564
Pharmacists	957	163	170	30	1 320

* Through 4/94.
Source: Data are from the Ministry of Absorption and are based on the self-declared occupation of new immigrants and returning residents upon arrival. The Ministry of Health estimates that about 90 per cent of the physicians and dentists are from the former Soviet Union.

By the middle of 1993, 7863 immigrant doctors had registered with the Ministry of Health, thus initiating the procedures needed for licensure. 2607 (about 25 per cent of those who had arrived by that date) had taken no steps to initiate these procedures. Two ascriptive characteristics differentiate between these groups: gender and age. Table 7.2 indicates that female physicians registered less frequently with the Ministry of Health; the same is true of older immigrant physicians, specifically those over the age of 55. As in other situations where employment options are limited, it is women and older persons that tend to opt out in the competition for scarce jobs (Frenk, 1991; Ginzberg and Ostow, 1984; Ha Doan et al. 1990; van den Bussche, 1990).

In fact, some of those who declared themselves to be physicians upon arrival, were not medical doctors with full credentials from recognized medical schools. Others, in surveying the employment opportunities, apparently decided to opt out of the medical market or to bide their time rather than invest the effort needed to obtain a license.

As of the 1990s Israel joined the list of countries with a serious surplus of physicians. (Bankowski and Fulop, 1987; Ha Doan et al., 1990) Although quite a few countries have such surpluses, little research has been done regarding occupational change and unemployment among them (Branciard and Huard, 1988).

Table 7.2 Comparison of immigrant physicians who registered and did not register with the Ministry of Health, by gender and age 1990–1992

		Registered with Ministry of Health N = 7 863	Did not register with Ministry of Health N = 2 607
Gender			
Women	N = 6 098	72%	28%
Men	N = 4 372	79%	21%
Age			
Under 34	N = 3 719	78%	22%
35–44	N = 2 985	79%	21%
45–54	N = 1 936	77%	23%
55–64	N = 1 412	61%	39%
65+	N = 418	56%	44%

Source: Unpublished data from the Israel Ministry of Health, 8/1/95.

PATTERNS OF AMBIVALENCE AND THEIR IMPLICATIONS FOR SOCIAL POLICY

The ambivalent relationship between the two sets of values has led to some paradoxical policies that seek to resolve or reduce the inherent ambivalence. These may be seen in the structural and attitudinal barriers that immigrants confront in seeking employment.

The first structural barrier relates to the licensure examination. Considerable public investment has been made to assist immigrant physicians in their effort to pass this examination. They are offered a six-month preparatory course at public expense to up-date their basic knowledge of medical technology and practice. Participants receive financial subsidies during the course. Until the summer of 1992, an average of half of the physicians who participated in the course passed the licensure examination. This proportion decreased after that date possibly because the examinees included a higher proportion of persons who were retaking the exam after an earlier failure. This success rate contrasts with 8 per cent who pass the licensing examination in the United States and 15 per cent in Australia.

The value conflict is further reflected in a policy change in the number of years of practice required to obtain exemption from the licensure examination. In 1992 (only four years after the requirement for a licensing examination was established), the number of years of practice experience required of those exempted from the formal examination was reduced from 20 to 14. This had the effect of maintaining the formal barrier for a smaller segment of the population.

The second structural barrier concerns the limited job options and the fact that decisions regarding employment in the health-care system is controlled by veteran physicians in the employing organizations. It is estimated that, in the long run, regular positions in the medical profession will be available at most to only 20 per cent of the immigrants who were professionally qualified as physicians in the former Soviet Union. Preference for employment is given to younger immigrants who are viewed as more amenable to retraining in medical practice. A variety of publicly sponsored retraining programs are available to physicians for retraining in non-medical occupations, although little is known about how doctors respond to the need for occupational change. In 1992, despite the saturation of the market, the Ministry of Health made available 500 new posts in the hospital system for immigrant doctors to retrain to qualify for medical specialties.

The pool of candidates is kept large by the ongoing licensure examinations; neither is there a limit on the number of times an individual may sit for the exam. In 1993, three years after they had arrived in Israel, 57.1 per cent of the 1990 arrivals reported taking it once, 26.9 per cent twice and 11.3 per cent took it three or more times. Among those who hadn't passed or taken the exam at that time, 46 per cent stated that they 'definitely' planned to try again and an additional 35 per cent said they 'probably' would. Thus, by the time they had been in Israel three years, 78.6 per cent of those who attempted it, had passed the examination. Men and women were equally likely to pass (79.8 per cent and 77.5 per cent, respectively) (Shuval and Bernstein, 1994; 1995).

By the end of 1994, about 6250 immigrant doctors from the former Soviet Union held licenses to practice – a pool that includes over three times the number of doctors who are likely to be employed on a regular basis in their profession by the health care system. Such credentialling provides immigrant physicians with the satisfaction of legitimately using their professional title and reaffirms their self-identity by granting the symbolic trappings of professional status – even if they are not employed in their profession (Shuval and Bernstein, 1994).

The third barrier, which is an attitudinal one, can be viewed as an additional mechanism geared to make possible the existence of the open-door policy while controlling *de facto* competition in the market. This has been done by denigrating the standard of practice of immigrant physicians and is expressed in terms of a widespread negative stereotype regarding the level of medical practice in the former Soviet Union. The medical establishment has reiterated its view that the standard of medical practice of immigrant physicians from the former Soviet Union is, with some exceptions, lower than that acceptable in Israel. Like other stereotypes, this one is based on a core of objective fact which has been generalized beyond what these facts imply (Remennick, L. and N. Ottenstein, 1994; Rowland and Telyukov, 1991; Ryan, M. 1990).

One function of stereotypes is to block the perception of positive qualities that challenge its generality (Al Hadofek 1994; *Ha'aretz*, 1990; 1991). A negative image of immigrant physicians from the former Soviet Union serves the need of the Israel medical profession to assert its elitism in the face of a growing threat to Israeli doctors of competition for patients and erosion of professional status as a result of the increasing oversupply (Abel-Smith, 1987; Bankowski and Fulop, 1987; Meija, 1987; Rosenthal, Butter and Field, 1990).

THE SOCIAL CONSTRUCTION OF REALITY

Work commitment is enacted on the micro-level and helps relate behavior and attitudes to the exigencies of occupational change induced by the policies regarding migration. We refer to 'the degree to which a person is identified psychologically with his work or the importance of work in his total self-image' (Lodahl and Kejner, 1965, p. 24). Kanungo (1982) has referred to the degree to which a job is central to a person while Blau (1988) has applied these notions to the professions.

For many years, physicians have been described as an occupational group characterized by high professional commitment: medicine is a 'calling', 'a way of life', an occupation characterized by complete personal involvement that focuses on the intrinsic rewards of work and spills over to invade leisure-time leaving little space for extra-occupational concerns (Becker, 1960; Lopata, 1993).

Research on professionals employed in bureaucratic settings, which set limits on full autonomy, has been applied to physicians in the 1980s and 1990s, as medicine has been structurally transformed and widely bureaucratized (Anthony, 1977; Berthoud, 1979; Jones, 1991; Kennedy and Sadkowski, 1991; Krause, 1991).

In a situation of migration, in which loss of occupational status is frequent (Ofer *et al.*, 1991), commitment to work plays a role in determining psychological health and wellbeing (Borjas, 1989; Shin and Chong, 1988; Warr and Jackson, 1985). Thoits (1983) has noted that the more valued a position, the more committed an individual will be to it and the greater will be the psychological impact of its loss. With regard to physicians, it may be assumed that almost any occupational change will be viewed as downward occupational mobility.

Role theorists have noted that when a person has multiple identities, she/he is better able to cope with the loss of a specific role because viable alternative identities are available and can be given increased weight in defining one's self (Hoelter, 1983). There is evidence that downward occupational mobility is more frequent among women professionals than among men in similar occupations (Kats, 1982; Saunders, 1985; Shamir, 1985).

RESEARCH FINDINGS

The conflicts and ambivalences which characterize the macro-level are perceived on the micro-level and acted upon by immigrants in terms of their own needs and social construction of reality. Among immigrant physicians, perception of that reality is determined by two salient characteristics: gender and professional commitment which interact with each other in structuring attitudes, expectations and behavior. A little over half of the immigrant physicians are women. The commitment of physicians to their profession is threatened in a context that poses the possibility of occupational change but that threat may be differently constructed by male and female professionals. The data presented below explicate some of these issues.

In an effort to document the processes described, a multi-stage, longitudinal study was launched in 1990 with the goal of tracing the career dynamics of immigrant physicians who arrived in Israel in that year.

In Stage 1 of this research data were collected in 20 of the 28 courses given in 1991 to prepare immigrant physicians with less than 20 years of experience, for the licensure examination: about two thirds of the immigrant physicians were in this category. Russian language questionnaires were completed by 1142 participants. Data collected at this stage included personal, educational and professional background, practice experience before immigration, professional commitment and expectations regarding work opportunities in Israel. While not all immigrant physicians who were required to take the licensure examination participated in the prep course, a high proportion did attend regularly. Data are not available regarding the career patterns of immigrant physicians who did not participate in the preparatory course except for the fact that their failure rates in the licensure examination were considerably higher than among those who took the course (Nirel, et al. 1994; Shuval and Bernstein, 1994).

Stage 2 took place 2.5–3 years after arrival in Israel, 15 months after the physicians first took the licensure examination. Data were obtained by means of a Russian language, mail questionnaire sent to all of the respondents in Stage 1. Completed, useable questionnaires were received from 519 physicians. Examination of a variety of personal and professional characteristics shows that the respondents did not differ from the non-respondents (Shuval and Bernstein, 1994).

At stage 2 data included a detailed work history, outcome of the licensure examination, current work status, work satisfaction and a variety of other psycho-social behavioral outcome variables.

The data below present selected findings concerning gender differences and professional commitment drawn from both stages of the study.

The literature indicates that gender differences in practice characteristics of physicians in the former Soviet Union are similar to those found in other countries: they tend more often than their male colleagues to work in clinics rather than in hospitals and to attain high-status positions less frequently. They rarely specialize in surgery but are concentrated, more than male physicians, in internal medicine and pediatrics. Despite the egalitarian ideology, women in the Soviet Union occupied lower-status positions and were socialized to attitudes compatible with traditional gender roles (Ben Barak, 1989; Ryan, 1990; Shuval and Bernstein, 1994; Shye, 1991; Uhlenberg and Cooney, 1990; Walters, 1993).

At stage 1, before they had much direct exposure to the constraints of the job market, the immigrant doctors were asked about their expectations regarding employment opportunities in Israel. Table 7.3 shows that women were less confident than their male counterparts with respect to occupational

Table 7.3 Russian immigrant physicians' optimism regarding their professional future in Israel, by gender and age at stage 1 (percentages)

		Age 35 and older		Age 34 and younger	
		Men	Women	Men	Women
(N)		(200)	(278)	(251)	(307)
Chances of finding an appropriate job					
Very good/Good		30.0	17.3	47.4	26.7
Not too good/Poor		70.0	82.7	52.6	73.3
		Chi square = 10.07		Chi square = 24.79	
		D.F. = 1 P .01		D.F. = 1 P .001	
Chances for professional advancement					
Very good/Good		23.2	14.3	45.2	21.4
Not too good/Poor		76.8	85.7	54.8	78.6
		Chi square = 4.65		Chi square = 29.94	
		D.F. = 1 P .05		D.F. = 1 P .001	
Chances for getting along well with Israeli doctors					
Very good/Good		76.3	66.5	85.4	69.4
Not too good/Poor		23.7	33.5	14.6	30.6
		Chi square = 4.18		Chi square = 16.68	
		D.F. = 1 P .05		D.F. = 1 P .001	
Chances for getting along well with Israeli patients					
Very good/Good		87.0	81.7	88.7	85.1
Not too good/Poor		13.0	18.3	11.3	14.9
		Chi square = 1.73		Chi square = 1.15	
		D.F. = 1 P .10		D.F. = 1 P .10	

issues over which others exercise the primary control: finding a job, professional advancement, and getting along with Israeli colleagues. They did not differ markedly from their male counterparts when asked about interaction with patients – a process which is more within the boundaries of their own control. Controlling for age does not change the above pattern which confirms other research findings (Kats, 1982; Saunders, 1985; Shamir, 1985).

Table 7.3 also indicates that younger immigrant physicians, both male and female, tend to be more optimistic about their future than older ones.

In an attempt to explore the issue of professional commitment, a question was posed at Stage 1 regarding respondents' willingness to change their occupation – given the limited employment options for doctors. Hardly any physicians responded positively at this time (4 out of 180 physicians who responded to the question).

Furthermore, at Stage 1 only 12 per cent indicated that they would not chose to be a physician if they had to start their career over again. This is a lower percentage than that found among retired French physicians in the late 1980s: 25 per cent stated that they would not re-chose medicine (Herzlich *et al.*, 1993). Needless to say part of the difference stems from the difference in age in the two populations.

In a more systematic attempt to examine professional commitment, a scale was adapted from Kanungo (1982) utilizing six items which refer to the individual's feeling regarding the centrality and importance of professional work and goals, in this case focusing on medicine.

Table 7.4 shows scores on commitment at Stages 1 and 2. Mean scores range from 1 to 5; the higher the numerical score, the greater the level of commitment. While there is a slight decline in overall commitment from Stage 1 to Stage 2, it is negligible and the difference is not significant.

Table 7.5 shows the overall commitment scores by age and gender at Stages 1 and 2. At both stages, older physicians have higher commitment scores than younger. Both age groups reported lower professional commitment at Stage 2 than at Stage 1 but the decline was greater among the older respondents who had practiced for a longer period of time before leaving Russia and who were likely to have occupied higher-status positions in the medical care system there.

At both Stages men were slightly more committed to the profession than women but the difference was not significant at Stage 1. The scores of both groups were lower at Stage 2 but women's scores declined more and the difference in commitment between the genders, while small, is statistically significant at Stage 2.

We may, therefore, conclude that both older and male physicians are more committed to their profession than their younger and female col-

Table 7.4 Professional commitment* scores of physicians at two stages

	Stage 1 (N = 244)	Stage 2 (N = 495)
The most important things that have happened to me involve my being a physician	3.58 (1.22)	3.00 (1.35)
I have always lived and breathed my profession	4.07 (1.00)	3.96 (1.00)
Most of interests have been centered around my profession	4.04 (1.01)	3.93 (.99)
I have very strong ties with my profession which would be difficult to break	4.16 (.98)	4.22 (.93)
Most of my goals are profession-oriented	4.04 (1.02)	3.95 (1.01)
I consider my profession to be central to my existence	3.77 (1.25)	3.72 (1.16)
Overall Score	3.94 (.87)	3.81 (.85)
Cronbach's Alpha	.89	.88

* Items adapted from Kanungo (1982). Mean scores range from 1 to 5; the higher the score, the greater the professional commitment.

leagues. At the same time, the differences are small, even when they are statistically significant. Similar findings have resulted from other research (Rabinowitz and Hall, 1977).

DISCUSSION

The centrality of immigration in Israel preceded the emergence of its prominence as a factor in social change in post-industrial societies. While the historical and political context which determined Israel's open-door policy with respect to Jewish immigration is based on a number of idiosyncratic factors, its long experience with large-scale immigration and the integration problems it has faced for the past 50 years, can be viewed as a *proxy pre-view* of

Table 7.5 Professional commitment scores*** by gender and age at stages 1 and 2

	Stage 1	Stage 2
Age		
25–35 years	3.76 (.93)	3.67 (.84)
36+	4.14 (.76) $t = 3.42**$	3.95 (.82) $t = 3.64**$
Gender		
Men	4.03 (.84)	3.91 (.84)
Women	3.90 (.88) $t = 1.13$	3.73 (.85) $t = 2.14*$

* p .05
**p .001
*** Scores based on six items adapted from Kanungo (1982).

many of the issues that will be faced by post-industrial societies in which immigration is likely to become a major factor of social change.

It is striking that despite the stability of its open-door policy for Jewish immigrants, Israel has had to adapt to varying extremes of high and low numbers of arrivals; the changing numbers of immigrants over the past 50 years reflects a response to circumstances over which the host society has had little control. It seems probable that the dimensions of migration in the post-industrial world will follow this erratic pattern and that efforts at rational control of numbers can be only partially successful.

In the context of processes characterizing post-industrial societies, immigrants whose imported skills are irrelevant for the local job-market will become an increasingly frequent phenomenon. This is because criteria for admission cannot always be related directly to the rational economic needs of the host society. When the overriding criteria for admission are humanitarian or social, economic needs inevitably assume less priority and many persons enter a society with occupational skills that are poorly adapted to the needs of the host society. Among these, there are likely to be growing numbers of highly educated groups who will be faced with the need for occupational change. This chapter provides an Israeli case study of a situation in which a skilled group, characterized by a high level of occupational commitment, faces an extremely limited job market and the need to confront a set of complex and painful choices: occupational change or unemployment.

In all societies, the issues involved are likely to be exacerbated by value conflicts which reflect different, competing priorities. In the Israel case study we have pointed to two such values: one is expressed in the pro-migration policy; the other focuses on the priority accorded to health and high quality medical care. It seems probable that many post-industrial societies will find themselves enmeshed in a variety of value-conflicts regarding immigration. While these may differ in content, they are likely to produce ambiguities in policies, much as the Israeli value-conflicts have.

When the values are deeply entrenched as a result of historical circumstances or because they represent interests of powerful social or political groups, compromises may be difficult to attain. For example: the Israeli case shows that compromise with regard to the two sets of values on the policy level is unlikely.

Needless to say, individuals may – if they have a choice – opt not to migrate. In Israel this has in fact already occurred to some extent among physicians still in the former Soviet Union. In response to information regarding the limited job opportunities, fewer immigrated to Israel in 1993–4 than in 1990–1. However, in many post industrial societies, the pressures for migration may be so powerful that individuals' choices are constrained by circumstances over which they have little control. Thus it seems safe to suggest that sizeable immigration to Israel will in fact continue in the foreseeable future, as it will in other post-industrial societies.

Migration almost always involves some occupational change, most often a downward shift in occupational status at least in the short-run (Borjas, 1989; Shin and Chong, 1988). In the past, immigrant physicians to Israel have almost all been employed in their profession albeit not always in the precise type of practice in which they worked previously. In the 1990s it is clear that this will not be possible and large numbers of professional immigrants will have no choice but to shift to other occupations. Clearly this involves a price: on the macro-level there is a loss of valuable, skilled personnel; on the micro-level there is likely to be a cost in terms of psychological wellbeing and occupational adjustment problems in a population characterized by high professional commitment.

The findings of the research point to three variables which are critical in the social construction of reality by immigrants seeking to establish themselves in a new social setting: gender, age and professional commitment.

On the whole immigrant physicians are highly committed to their profession and at this early stage express little openness to the possibility of occupational change. Several studies reporting on immigrants from the Soviet Union to Israel in the 1970s, refer to high commitment to professional work (Bar-Yosef and King, 1989; Horowitz, 1989; Shuval, 1984; Toren, 1983; Voronel, 1982). In the early 1990s immigrants' reluctance to consider occupational alternatives contrasts with their pessimistic evaluation of the *de facto* job opportunities.

In a tight job-market, preference in employment is generally given to males and younger professionals. Women physicians, whose professional commitment is hardly any lower than that of their male colleagues, show an awareness of the realities of the job-market by their greater pessimism with regard to their own occupational options. Older physicians – who in the present study were only in their early 40s – for the most part held higher-status posts before coming to Israel and are most committed to the profession. They are likely to be under considerable stress in the context of a tight job-market in which preference is given to the employment of younger professionals. The Israeli findings indicate that in post-industrial societies experiencing large-scale migration of professionals, women and older persons are likely to be especially vulnerable groups in terms of their occupational integration and consequent wellbeing.

Further stages of the research will trace the dynamics of physicians' occupational patterns and will distinguish among those who have been able to maintain their professional roles and those who have shifted to other occupational options in the health field, or to other occupational areas. The consequences of occupational change become evident over a longer period of time; it is hoped that this research will serve to increase understanding of the processes involved and hopefully to contribute to some limitation of their dysfunctional effects.

References

Abel-Smith, B. (1987) 'The Price of Unbalanced Health Manpower', in Z. Bankowski and T. Fulop (eds), *Health Manpower Out of Balance* (Geneva: Council for International Organization of Medical Care) pp. 49–66.

Al Hadofek (1994) Magazine of the Alumni of the Hebrew University Medical School (Winter) (Hebrew).

Anderson, G.F. and S. Antebi (1991) 'A Surplus of Physicians in Israel: Any Lesson for the United States and Other Industrialized Countries?', *Health Policy*, 17, pp. 77–86.

Anthony, P.D. (1977) *The Ideology of Work* (London: Tavistock Publications).
Bankowski, Z. and Fulop, T. (eds) (1987) *Health Manpower Out of Balance* (Geneva: Council for International Organizations of Medical Care).
Bar-Yosef, R.W. and J.V. King (1989) 'Unemployed Professionals: The Case of Immigrant Engineers from Soviet Russia to Israel', in T. Horowitz (ed.), *The Soviet Man in Open Society* (New York: Lantham) pp. 185–219.
Becker, H.S. (1960) 'Notes on the Concept of Commitment', *American Journal of Sociology*, 66, pp. 32–40.
Ben Barak, S. (1989) 'Attitudes toward Work and Home of Soviet Immigrant Women', in T. Horowitz (ed.), *The Soviet Man in Open Society* (New York: Lantham) pp. 115–22.
Bernstein, J. and J.T. Shuval (1995) 'Occupational Stability and Change among Immigrant Physicians from the Former Soviet Union to Israel', *International Migration*, 33, 1, pp. 3–29.
Berthoud, R. (1979) *Unemployed Professional and Executives* (London: Policy Studies Institute) xlv, no. 582.
Blau, G.J. (1988) 'Further Exploring the Meaning and Measurement of Career Commitment', *Journal of Vocational Behavior*, 32, pp. 284–97.
Borjas, G.J. (1989) 'Economic Theory and International Migration', *International Migration Review*, 23, pp. 457–85.
Branciard, A. and P. Huard (1988), *Les Medicins Inscrits a l'Agence Nationale pour l'Emploi en 1987* (Laboratoire d'Economie et de Sociologie du Travail, Aix en Provence: Centre National de la Recherche Scientifique).
Frenk, J. (1991) 'Patterns of Medical Employment: A Survey of Imbalances in Urban Mexico', *American Journal of Public Health*, 81, 1, pp. 23–9.
Ginzberg, E. and M. Ostow (1984) *The Coming Physician Surplus* (Landmark Studies, New Jersey: Rowman & Allanheld).
Ha'aretz, 16/12/90, 8/2/91 (daily newspaper; Hebrew).
Ha Doan, B.D. et al. (1990) 'The Debates on the Numbers of Physicians', *Health Policy*, 15, pp. 81–9.
Herzlich, C., M. Bungener, G. Paicheler, P. Roussin and M.C. Zuber (1993) *Cinquante Ans d'Exercice de la Medicine en France* (Paris, Les Editions INSERM).
Hoelter, J.W. (1983) 'The Effects of Role Evaluation and Commitment on Identity Salience', *Social Psychology Quarterly*, 46, pp. 140–7.
Horowitz, T. (ed.) (1989) *The Soviet Man in Open Society* (New York: Lantham).
Jones, A. (ed.) (1991) *Professions and the State: Expertise and Autonomy in the Soviet Union and Eastern Europe* (Philadelphia: Temple University Press).
Kanungo, R.N. (1982) 'Measurement of Job and Work Involvement', *Journal of Applied Psychology*, 67, pp. 341–9.
Kats, R. (1982) 'The Immigrant Woman: Double Cost or Relative Improvement', *International Migration*, 21, pp. 345–57.
Kennedy, M.D. and K. Sadkowski (1991) 'Constraints on Professional Power in Soviet-Type Societies: Insights from the 1980–81 Solidarity Period in Poland', pp. 167–206 in Jones above.
Krause, E. (19910 'Professions and the State in the Soviet Union and Eastern Europe: Theoretical Issues', in A. Jones (ed.), *Professions and the State: Expertise and Autonomy in the Soviet Union and Eastern Europe* (Philadelphia: Temple University Press) pp. 3–42.

Lodahl, T.M. and M. Kejner (1965) 'The Definition and Measurement of Job Involvement', *Journal of Applied Psychology*, 49, pp. 24–33.
Lopata, H.Z. (1993) 'Career Commitments of American Women: The Issue of Side Bets', *The Sociological Quarterly*, 34, 2, pp. 257–77.
Meija, A. (1987) 'The Nature of the Challenge', in Z. Bankowski and T. Fulop, op cit. pp. 15–40.
Nirel, N., B. Rosen, G. Ben Nun, A. Shemesh and P. Vardi (1994) 'Stages in the Licensure of Immigrant Physicians: An Update', *Harefuah*, 125, A–B. pp. 19–22 (Hebrew).
Ofer, G., K. Flug and N. Kasir (1991) 'The Absorption in Employment of Immigrants from the Soviet Union: 1990 and Beyond', *Economic Quarterly*, 148: 135–171 (Hebrew).
Rabinowitz, S. and D.T. Hall (1977) 'Organizational Research on Job Involvement', *Psychological Bulletin*, 84, pp. 265–88.
Remennick, L. and N. Ottenstein (1994) 'Reaction of New Soviet Immigrants to Health-Care Services in Israel', JDC–Brookdale Institute, Jerusalem.
Rose, A. (1969) *Migrants to Europe* (Minneapolis: University of Minnesota Press).
Rosen, B. (1987) *The Health of the Israeli People: An International Comparison Based on the World Health Organization's 'Quantitative Indicators for the European Region'* (Jerusalem: Brookdale Institute of Gerontology and Adult Human Development).
Rosen, B. and N. Nirel (1995) 'Immigration and Medical Manpower in Israel: Partial Questions and Answers', Brookdale Institute of Gerontology, Hebrew, unpublished.
Rosenthal, M., I. Butter and M.L. Field (1990) 'Setting the Context', *Health Policy*, 15, pp. 75–9.
Rowland, D. and Telyukov (1991) 'Soviet Health Care from Two Perspectives', *Health Affairs*, 10, 3, pp. 71–86.
Ryan, M. (1990) *Doctors and the State in the Soviet Union* (New York: St Martin's Press), Chap. 3.
Saunders, E.A. (1985) 'Resettlement Experiences of Russian Jewish Immigrants in Vancouver, Canada between 1975 and 1982', *International Migration*, 23, pp. 369–80.
Shamir, B. (1985) 'Sex Differences in Psychological Adjustment to Unemployment and Re-Employment: A Question of Commitment, Alternatives or Finance?', *Social Problems*, 33, pp. 67–79.
Shin, E.H. and K.S. Chong (1988) 'Peripheralization of Immigrant Professionals: Korean Physicians in the United States', *International Migration Review*, 22, pp. 609–26.
Shuval, J.T. (1984) 'Soviet Immigrant Physicians in Israel', *Soviet Jewish Affairs*, 14, pp. 19–40.
Shuval, J.T. (1985) 'Social Functions of Medical Licensing: A Case Study of Soviet Immigrant Physicians in Israel', *Social Science and Medicine*, 20, 9, pp. 901–9.
Shuval, J.T. (1990) 'Medical Manpower in Israel: Political Processes and Constraints', *Health Policy*, 15, pp. 189–214.
Shuval, J.T. (1992) *Social Dimensions of Health: The Israeli Experience* (Westport, Connecticut: New York, Praeger).

Shuval, J. and Bernstein, J. (1994) *Doctors Who are not Doctors: Professional Commitment, Occupational Stability and Change amomg Soviet Immigrant Physicians in Israel* (Jerusalem: Jerusalem Institute for Israel Studies).
Shuval, J.T. (1995) 'Elitism and Professional Control in a Saturated Market: Immigrant Physicians in Israel', *Sociology of Health and Illness*, 17, 3, pp. 550–65.
Shuval, J.T. and J. Bernstein (1995) 'Patterns of Professional Commitment Among Immigrant Physicians from the Former Soviet Union in Israel', *Social Science and Medicine*, forthcoming.
Shye, D. (1991) 'Gender Differences in Israeli Physicians' Career Patterns, Productivity and Family Structure', *Social Science and Medicine*, 32, pp. 1169–81.
Thoits, P.A. (1983) 'Multiple Identities and Psychological Wellbeing', *American Sociological Review*, 48, pp. 174–87.
Toren, N. (1983) 'Attitudes toward Work: A Comparison of Soviet and American Immigrant Scientists in Israel', *Social Studies of Science*, 13, pp. 229–53.
Uhlenberg, P. and Cooney, T.M. (1990) 'Male and Female Physicians: Family and Career Comparisons', *Social Science and Medicine*, 30, pp. 373–78.
van den Bussche, H. (1990) 'The History and Future of Physician Manpower Development in the Federal Republic of Germany', *Health Policy*, 15, pp. 95–103.
Voronel, A. (1982) 'Aliya of the Jewish Intelligentsia from the USSR', in D. Prital (ed.), *In Search of Self* (The Scientists Committee of the Israel Public Committee for Soviet Jewry, Jerusalem: Mount Scopus Publications) pp. 21–131.
Walters, B.C. (1993) 'Why Don't More Women Choose Surgery as a Career?', *Academic Medicine*, 68, pp. 350–1.
Warr, P. and P. Jackson (1985) 'Men Without Jobs: Some Correlates of Age and Length of Unemployment', *Journal of Occupational Psychology*, 57, pp. 77–85.
Yochum, G. and V. Agarwal (1988) 'Permanent Labor Certification for Alien Professionals, 1975–82', *International Migration Review*, 22, pp. 265–81.
Zolberg, A. (1989) 'The Next Waves: Migration Theory for a Changing World', *International Migration Review*, 23, pp. 403–30.

8 Urban Restructuring and the Absorption of Immigrants: A Case Study in Tel-Aviv
Gila Menahem

IMMIGRANTS, URBAN ECONOMICS, AND URBAN CHANGE

Large cities have traditionally played a central role in shaping the opportunities of immigrants in industrial countries by offering employment and inexpensive housing. In past decades, manufacturing industries (i.e. textiles, metals) absorbed a large proportion of urban immigrants. These unionized industries offered immigrants an entry into the core sectors and provided them with the opportunity for political involvement (Merton, 1949; Shefter, 1976; Lupsha, 1976). Additionally, large urban economies offered employment opportunities through the development of ethnic economic enclaves based on entrepreneurial activities (Stark and Taylor, 1988; Bonacich, 1973; Light 1984). Research findings in the U.S. in fact indicate that immigrants settling in cities attained higher social standing than did those settling in non-urban areas (Lieberson, 1980; Chiswick, 1978). In those cities which serve as entry points for immigrants due to their abundant supply of inexpensive housing, urban ecological structure has been shaped to a significant degree by the very fact of immigration (Burgess 1925 (1967); Godfrey, 1988). Immigrants, for the most part, have found shelter in the inner areas of the cities, converting them into transition areas. However, in more recent decades, changes in urban economies and in the demand for space have occurred. Industrial and manufacturing activities have decreased and, simultaneously, communication, information processing and supervisory activities and legal, accounting, and insurance services have grown (Fainstein and Fainstein, 1982, 1989; Fainstein, 1990). These processes are termed *urban economic restructuring*.

The notion of economic restructuring contains a quantitative dimension, typified by the numerical reduction in manufacturing jobs and the growth of services; and a qualitative dimension, that is, the polarization of occupational characteristics suggested by the greater incidence of both low-skilled, low-wage and high-skilled professional jobs in service industries, a decline in wages and unionization rates in manufacturing jobs, and a feminization of the job supply (Sassen, 1990: 467). In addition, there is a growth in manufacturing activities performed in informal small operations (Sassen, 1986, 1991; Beauregard, 1991: 92).

Polarization of the urban employment market is a salient aspect of restructuring; expansion of the demand for both high-skilled, high-salaried jobs and low-skilled, low-salaried jobs, alongside a reduced demand for jobs demanding mid-range qualifications. Short (1989) indicated that along with the emergence of the new-middle class and young urban upwardly mobile professional (yuppies), restructuring is also characterized by growing numbers of young people who find mobility channels blocked and experience failure ('yuffies').

Urban restructuring also has a spatial dimension. It increases demand for office space (Feagin, 1988), gentrifiable dwellings (Zukin, 1987; Smith and Williams, 1986; Laska and Spain, 1980) and space to provide cultural services for gentrifiers (Whitt, 1987). Urban centers have been transformed into attractive locations for corporation headquarters, and have undergone gentrification (Smith and Williams, 1986). These functions compete for space with the traditional populations of these areas, namely poor native populations and immigrants, who have traditionally used these spaces for residential purposes.

Urban restructuring therefore has direct implications for patterns of immigrant absorption in urban centers. The purpose of this study, then, is to examine: (a) the occupational integration of new immigrants in a large city which is undergoing economic restructuring; and (b) the effects of urban spatial restructuring on immigrants' housing opportunities.

COMPETING APPROACHES TO THE RESTRUCTURING OF URBAN ECONOMIES AND THE INTEGRATION OF IMMIGRANTS IN URBAN AREAS

Several hypotheses have emerged regarding the impact of urban economic restructuring on immigrants' economic opportunities. The mismatch theory reasons that the transition to a post-industrial economy involves an increased demand for a highly-skilled labor force and a decreased demand for both low-skilled and manufacturing labor. However most immigrants have only low-level skills (Kasarda, 1983; Carliner, 1980). In other words, the occupational qualifications of most immigrants are incompatible with the labor-force demands of urban markets. This fact shrinks their employment opportunities within the urban economy and, consequently, their role in urban economic development.

An alternative hypothesis views immigration as complementing the process of urban economic restructuring. The theory of urban economic restructuring contends that although the change to a post-industrial economy creates demand for highly qualified workers, a corresponding higher demand for individuals with limited qualifications also arises in maintenance and service industries. These latter industries are tailored to answer the consumption patterns of highly-skilled employees in the globalizing economies while providing jobs for low-skilled immigrants (Sassen, 1986, 1988, 1991).

Accordingly, immigration complements urban economic restructuring in which the growth of services yields both high- and low-skilled jobs while increasingly excluding occupations with mid-level qualifications. The reduction of the proportion of mid-level jobs then increases polarization and inequality in large cities (Nelson and Lorence, 1985; Sassen, 1991; Harrison and Bluestone, 1988).

Another aspect of restructuring has to do with the globalization of operations and the expansion of control, command, and coordination activities. Apart from technical and professional expertise, these activities demand familiarity with the urban national and international contexts. This familiarity is not characteristic of most immigrants, even in cases when they possess high academic and occupational qualifications. It follows that immigrants with high academic and professional skills in industry will find it difficult to integrate into urban economies on the basis of these skills alone.

Taken together, these changes result – according to the restructuring hypothesis – in a reduced number of channels of entry for immigrants into the organized, unionized sectors of the economy, or mobility to mid-level occupations.

As the restructuring approach suggests a shrinking of the industrial sector, its implications should be tested in situations where immigrants display the full range of industrial skills. Therefore, an examination is needed of what opportunities exist for immigrants who were employed in highly-skilled positions in industry, such as engineers. When expanded to account for this group of immigrants, the restructuring hypothesis generates several propositions:

1. Immigrants with high-level professional skills of a traditional industrial nature (engineers, technicians, etc.) will experience a shortage of opportunities in the restructuring industrial urban context.

2. A larger proportion of opportunities will be concentrated in low-skilled personal services and unskilled industrial jobs.
3. As a result of the above trends in urban economies, immigrants' occupational opportunities in the restructuring economy will be polarized. Opportunities in mid-level occupations will be few. It follows that downward mobility will be rapid.

URBAN SPATIAL CHANGES AND THE INTEGRATION OF IMMIGRANTS

Two models describing the interrelationships between gentrification and housing opportunities for new immigrants and veteran populations in city centers may be discerned.

One model may be classified as a competition model. It suggests that the attraction of gentrifiers to city centers will negatively affect housing opportunities of both veteran low-status populations and new immigrants by increasing competition over available units. This rests on the assumption that the supply of gentrifiable housing in the centers of cities is limited.

Another model, which may be termed a complementary model, rests on the assumption that gentrifiers and gentrification enlarge the amount of residential units. According to this model, expansion of the supply of dwellings results from the following:

1. Gentrification effectively competes with other uses of dwelling units. Housing units which were transformed into various non-residential uses are returned to residential use.
2. New dwelling units are added to the area through construction.

The complementary model thus predicts that immigrants and low-status families may continue to find housing in the center of the city, thereby retaining the social diversity of the area.

The wave of immigration to Israel in the 1990s provides a suitable context for the testing of the hypotheses. The occupational composition of the immigrants on one hand, and the economic transformations experienced in Tel-Aviv-Yaffo on the other, provide an opportunity to test the hypotheses engendered by models of urban economic restructuring. A brief description of the immigrant population follows in order to set the stage for the study.

IMMIGRANTS IN ISRAEL IN THE 1990s

The occupational composition of the immigrants from the former Soviet Union in the 1990s is characterized by a large percentage of highly qualified professionals in fields typical of industrial societies. A sizeable proportion of the immigrants are university graduates, particularly scientists, engineers, physicians and technological specialists. Before immigrating, 38 per cent were employed in academic and scientific occupations, and another 34 per cent in professional and technical ones (Central Bureau of Statistics, Israel, Special Publication No. 900). The occupational composition of these immigrants enables us to examine the two dimensions of the restructuring process, which together have important policy implications (which will be discussed later in this chapter).

The social composition of the recent immigrants from the former Soviet Union may have potential impact on neighborhood processes in rundown areas in the city. The new immigrants have, on the one hand, favorable social and occupational characteristics yet, on the other hand, tend to look for residence in deteriorated areas in the city due to a lack of financial resources. Some of these areas are currently undergoing gentrification, while other low-status areas have experienced incumbent upgrading as a result of government renewal programs (Carmon and Baron, 1994). Thus, the recent immigration to Israel enables us to test some meaningful aspects of the relationship between gentrification, immigrants' housing opportunities in restructuring cities, and social processes in revitalizing urban centers, according to both competitive and complementary models.

THE PRESENT RESEARCH

The present study investigates the above urban restructuring processes and immigrants' absorption in Tel-Aviv in the 1990s. It is based on a survey sample of new immigrants households, administered in 1992, and statistical data relating to urban restructuring processes in the city, obtained from other sources.

The Sample

A random sample of 525 immigrants aged 21–60, who had arrived in Israel between December 1990 and January 1992, were interviewed in the summer of 1992. This means that at the time of the survey, the most veteran of the immigrants had resided in Israel for two years and nine months and the latest arrivals had been in the country for at least nine months. The sample was drawn from files listing all tenants eligible for property tax reductions due to their immigrant status. The files were arranged so as to reflect the distribution of the immigrants within the city's statistical areas. That is, the sample drawn reflected the proportions of immigrants residing in each statistical area in the city. The average age of the respondents was 39; the sample was composed of 48 per cent males and 52 per cent females. The interviews were administered in the Russian language, in the respondents' homes, by new immigrant university students.

The Research Site

Tel-Aviv is one of three largest cities in Israel, having a population of 327 000 residents. It is the center of the country's financial and business activity, and houses the stock exchange as well as the headquarters of the banks, insurance companies, and major entrepreneurial firms.

Since 1989, about 41 000 new immigrants from the former Soviet Union have entered Tel-Aviv; about 32 000 were still living there in 1992. They represent about 10 per cent of the city's population. A brief introduction describing the process of economic and spatial restructuring in Tel-Aviv is in place.

Economic and Spatial Restructuring in Tel-Aviv-Yaffo

The economic structure of Tel-Aviv-Yaffo has undergone far-reaching changes since the early 1980s. The manufacturing sector has been shrinking both in proportion and in the number of jobs. At the same time, financial and business services and commerce, restaurants and tourist accommodations have grown. Between 1978 and 1989, the number of jobs in industry declined from 53 600 to 44 700. The number of jobs in commerce, restaurants and tourism rose from 41 600 to 51 700, and in finance and business services from 46 400 to 62 700 (Nachmias and Menahem, 1993). During this period, the proportion of men and women in the manufacturing sector changed: the proportion of men declined while the proportion of women went up, probably due to the decrease in the volume of heavy industry. During the period of 1973–87, the inner city of Tel-Aviv became the managerial and financial core of the country, containing the headquarters of about half of Israel's major companies and 31 per cent of the country's trained managerial, academic and professional staff (Schnell and Graicer, 1993).

As of the 1980s, several areas in Tel-Aviv-Yaffo have undergone rejuvenation and gentrification processes. The central zones, which have experienced out migration until the 1970s, are now very attractive to young professionals.

In old Yaffo, which has unique architectural and historic values, a process of gentrification is also taking place. The newer sections of Yaffo were built mainly during the 1960s and the 1970s, as housing for low-status, eligible populations. Several neighborhoods in this section of Yaffo have been included in Project Renewal, but these areas do not attract gentrifiers. The southern areas of Tel-Aviv are also inhabited by a low-status population. The western part of the area is quite deteriorated, displaying a high proportion of industrial and commercial usages and a considerable proportion of empty residential and business units. However, some small subareas in the southwest have attracted gentrifiers. The southeast contains mainly residential neighborhoods, with little commercial or industrial usages, and some neighborhoods in this area have also been rehabilitated but without attracting gentrifiers.

FINDINGS

New Immigrants from the Former Soviet Union in Tel-Aviv

The occupational composition of the respondents in our survey, prior to immigration, is characterized by a high concentration in the academic, scientific and technical–professional occupations. As may be seen in Table 8.1, column 1, 37.8 per cent had been employed in academic and scientific occupations, and another 31.2 per cent in technical occupations. In this regard they are typical of the Russian Jewish immigrants to Israel of the 1990s.

What changes have taken place in the occupational structure of the immigrants after their arrival in Israel? We first turn to the descriptive data regarding the respondents' employment. 63 per cent of the respondents were employed, 27 per cent were unemployed and looking for jobs, and 10 per cent were unemployed but were not looking for jobs. Those unemployed and seeking jobs comprised 18 per cent of the males and 32 per cent of the females in the sample.

Table 8.1, column 2, shows the present occupations of the immigrants in Tel-Aviv. The proportion of those occupied in academic scientific occupations has decreased from 37.8 per cent to 10.7 per cent; in the technical occupations, the proportion has declined to 14.7 per cent. The largest

Table 8.1 Abroad and present occupation of employed immigrants and of veteran population in Tel-Aviv (percentages)

	Immigrants		Veterans (3)*
	Abroad (1)	Present (2)	
	100.0	100.0	100.0
Academic and Scientific Workers	37.8	10.7	11.7
Professional and Technical Workers	31.2	14.7	17.1
Managers	2.5	0.7	6.5
Clerical Workers	5.0	4.3	20.0
Sales Workers	2.0	3.3	12.2
Service Workers	6.0	24.4	12.7
Agricultural Workers	–	0.3	(0.4)
Skilled and Semi-Skilled Workers	14.0	20.0	18.0
Unskilled Workers	1.5	21.1	1.4

* Source: Tel-Aviv-Yaffo Statistical Yearbook, 1991, Table 3.14.

category is the non-professional service workers (24.4 per cent). Semi-skilled and skilled workers constitute 20 per cent and nonprofessional workers in industry constitute 21.1 per cent. Thus, the data show that about 65 per cent of the immigrants are employed in low-skilled non-professional industrial jobs or in low-status personal services. Most of the respondents have, therefore, experienced sharp downward mobility.

It is instructive to compare the sample with the occupational distribution of the veteran residents of Tel-Aviv. As may be seen in column 3 of Table 8.1, regarding academic and scientific occupations, the share of the new immigrants has in fact almost reached the level of the veteran residents of the city. The large difference between the occupational distribution of the newcomers and the veterans lies in the concentration of the latter in clerical, managerial and sales jobs versus the very small share of the immigrants in these sectors.

In order to further test the demand aspect of the restructuring approach, the method proposed by Morris et al. (1994) for measuring polarization in income was adapted to the measurement of polarization in the occupational distribution of the immigrants. A decile-based relative occupational distribution was constructed as follows. We first partitioned the occupational distribution of the veteran population into deciles. The fraction of veteran workers falling into each decile was then used as the baseline for comparison with the distribution of immigrant workers (see Figure 8.1).

As may be seen from the shape of the distribution (1 represents the lowest level of occupations and 10 the highest level in terms of an occupational scale based on occupation and income), when compared to veterans, immigrants are most represented in the lowest level, and least in the middle categories. It may be said that the data reveal a polarized distribution of immigrants' occupation in Tel-Aviv. This confirms the results predicted by the restructuring model.

The data showing the proportion of immigrants occupied in academic and scientific occupations is very similar to that of the veterans, even a short time after arrival. This supports the claim that restructuring economies experience an increased demand for high-skilled workers. At the same time, this approach claims that a reduction in demand for industrial skills in urban centers will negatively affect immigrants with high industrial skills.

This hypothesis is tested here by comparing the present occupational position of new immigrants having high industrial skills, such as engineers, with immigrants having high occupational skills of a nonindustrial nature, such as physicians and other scientific and academic occupations.[1] As may be seen from Table 8.2, which presents the distribution of immigrants' occupation in Israel by occupation abroad, a smaller proportion

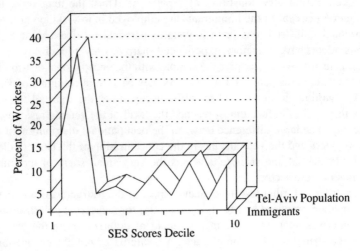

Figure 8.1 Decile-based relative occupational distribution of new immigrants – 1992

Table 8.2 Occupation of immigrants with academic skills abroad and in Israel

Occupation abroad	Percentage employed	Total	Occupation of employed in Israel							
			Academic and scientific workers	Professional technical workers	Managers	Clerical workers	Sales workers	Service workers	Skilled workers	Semi-skilled workers	Unskilled workers
Industrial Engineers N = 110	63.6 (N=72)	100% N=72	25.0	9.7	1.4	5.6	4.2	13.9	9.7	4.2	26.3
Other Academic and Scientific Professions N=78	59.0 (N=46)	100% N=46	37.0	10.9	–	10.9	–	32.6	4.3	–	4.3

(25 per cent) of those immigrants employed as engineers abroad are occupied in the same or a similar category when compared to 37 per cent of the immigrants with other academic or scientific skills.

Another claim made by the restructuring hypothesis is that the restructuring central city will offer fewer opportunities for academic and scientific workers in industry than will the surrounding localities (Sassen 1988). This claim is tested by the data in Table 8.3, which presents the occupational distribution of immigrants who work within the city compared to that of immigrants who work in the surrounding localities. As may be seen, 8.3 per cent of those who work within the city are employed in academic and scientific jobs as compared to 15.8 per cent of those who found jobs in other localities in the vicinity.

The interpretation of the data is not totally straightforward. It may be claimed that the higher share of immigrants who work in the academic scientific jobs in other localities results from a self-selective pattern which reflects costs of travel. This is at best a partial explanation, in view of the large proportion of immigrants (23.7 per cent) who commute to unskilled jobs outside the city, a proportion which is not significantly larger than those employed within the city, that is, 20.7 per cent (see Table 8.3, last column). The larger proportion of those employed in service jobs in the city reflects the fact that household cleaning provides many of the jobs in this category and that women tend to travel less for these jobs.

To summarize this section, it may be said that a polarized occupational distribution characterizes the immigrants during what might be called the short-term absorption stage. They have achieved the share held by veterans in academic and scientific occupations, yet are little represented in all the mid-level occupations and overrepresented in low-skilled jobs. Consistent with the restructuring approach, it appears that immigrants with academic skills of a traditional nature, such as engineers, faced more difficulties in integrating into the globalizing urban economy than did other high-skilled workers.

HOUSING PATTERNS AND PREFERENCES OF IMMIGRANTS IN TEL-AVIV

The new immigrants comprise about 10 per cent of the city's population. The policy of direct absorption, adopted by the Israeli government with regard to this group of immigrants, awarded each immigrant household a constant sum to cover the expenses of temporary rental housing for a period of three years. One of the side effects of this policy was an

Table 8.3 Place of occupation in Israel

Place of occupation		Occupation in Israel							
		Academic and scientific workers	Professional technical workers	Managers	Clerical workers	Sales workers	Service workers	Skilled workers	Semi-skilled workers	Unskilled workers
Tel-Aviv Yaffo	100.0 n = 218	8.3	11.5	0.5	4.6	5.0	29.7	9.6	10.1	20.7
Out of Tel Aviv	100.0 n = 101	15.8	19.8	1.0	4.0	1.0	11.9	14.9	7.9	23.7

increased demand for temporary housing; and prices of rental housing in the deteriorated areas of the city were raised to levels almost similar to those in the more affluent zones. As a result the immigrants dispersed throughout the city.

The spatial pattern of the socioeconomic distribution of the new immigrants in rental housing resembles that of the city's veterans. Immigrants with lower-status characteristics reside in the lower-status areas in the city. However, even in lower-status areas, a significant percentage of immigrants with high education and occupational skills can also be found. This reflects the socioeconomic composition of this group of immigrants, which is characterized by a higher level of education than is found in Israeli society.

From Rental Housing to Home Ownership

Inasmuch as eligibility for the subsidies provided by the Israeli government for temporary residence is available for only three years, newcomers are forced to make decisions regarding the purchase of a permanent dwelling relatively soon after arrival. Additional government subsidies and special mortgages are then made available to them.

About 20 per cent of the new immigrants had already bought flats at the time of the research, half of them within the city, and the other half in other localities. As previously mentioned, while new immigrants in Tel-Aviv found temporary residence in more and less expensive areas alike, the picture is very different with regard to permanent residence. 92 per cent of the flats bought in the city are located in the Yaffo (31 per cent) and the southern zones of the city (69 per cent).

As will be shown below, each zone of the city represents a distinct pattern of settlement with regard to both rental and purchased housing.

The pattern of the transition from rental housing to home ownership in the northern, affluent zone of the city and the gentrifying center reveals, first, practically no flats were bought there by the immigrants (Table 8.4, column 5), and second, a large proportion would like to buy in the area. As may be seen in Table 8.5, almost 89 per cent of the immigrants who rented flats in the center of the city searched for permanent flats there. However, only a handful managed to realize those preferences.

The picture is different in the deteriorated southwest. Among the immigrants residing in this area, 47 per cent of those who bought flats did so in the area. However, only 37 per cent of those who have yet to buy are looking for flats in the area. The main reason for purchasing in these areas is the presence of relatives who arrived in the previous wave of immigra-

Table 8.4 Proportion of those who bought flats in each area
(Percentage)

Present area of residence	Purchasing flat			Area where flat was purchased		
	Total (N = 510)	Yes (N = 117)	No (N = 393)	Total (N = 117)	Present area of residence (N = 64)	Other area (N = 53)
	(1)	(2)	(3)	(4)	(5)	(6)
North	100.0 (136)	8.0	92.0	100.0 (12)	–	100.0
Center	100.0 (53)	6.0	94.0	100.0 (3)	33.0	66.0
Old Yaffo	100.0 (25)	40.0	60.0	100.0 (10)	87.5	12.5
New Yaffo	100.0 (52)	48.0	52.0	100.0 (25)	89.5	10.2
Southwest	100.0 (111)	28.0	72.0	100.0 (34)	46.9	53.1
Southeast	100.0 (132)	25.0	75.0	100.0 (33)	38.5	61.5

Table 8.5 Proportion of those seeking permanent dwelling in present area of residence

	Present area of residence	Total	Search in present area	Search in other area
(1)	North	100.0	81.8	18.2
(2)	Center	100.0	88.9	11.2
(3, 4)	Old and New Yaffo*	100.0	71.4	28.6
(5)	Southwest	100.0	36.8	63.2
(6)	Southeast	100.0	73.4	26.6

* Old and New Yaffo were merged in this table because of the small N.

tion during the 1970s. In fact, an ethnic community of immigrants from the Asian parts of the former Soviet Union has emerged in the area. Those who do not belong to this ethnic community do not intend to stay in the area and look elsewhere.

The pattern in the southeast is different again. A large proportion of those who live there did not buy flats in the area, although their satisfaction with the area is much higher than in the southwest and in Yaffo, and the prices are considered to be reasonable. Only 38.5 per cent bought flats there, but a large proportion of those living in the southeast (73 per cent) are looking for flats in this area. It seems that the southeast is much more attractive to the immigrants than the southwest, but it offers few opportunities.

We may take the ratio between those who look for residence in the area and the number of flats actually bought by immigrants in the area as approximations for housing opportunities.

Figure 8.2 presents the patterns emerging in the different areas of the city.

The data reveal that three regional patterns can be discerned in this regard.

1. Areas in which the process of gentrification has progressed and are thus attractive to new gentrifiers. These include Old Yaffo and the central parts of Tel-Aviv. Hardly any new immigrants have bought flats there as prices have risen as a result of gentrification and renovation.
2. Deteriorated areas in the initial stages of gentrification and urban spatial restructuring, such as the southwest. These large areas contain much deteriorated housing; the availability of public services there is limited and of poor quality. The quality of life is also poor due to the mixture of industrial and commercial sites within the residential areas. Immigrants tend to live in rental housing and seek permanent residences elsewhere, as they claim that the social costs of living in these areas are very high. Table 8.6 shows the low satisfaction from various aspects of the area in the southwest.
3. Residential areas of low status incumbent residents, such as newer Yaffo and the southeast, evidence considerably better public services and quality of life. Although new immigrants are interested in permanent residence there, they must compete with the veteran residents, and hence have fewer opportunities open to them.

This interpretation of the attraction of the southeast and southwest and Yaffo is supported by data regarding the proportion of residents leaving

Area	Area Rating	Purchase Possibilities	Level of Demand	Pattern
Northern Area	High	Low	High	No Opportunities Extremely Attractive
Central City	High	Low	High	No Opportunities Extremely Attractive
Old Yaffo	Medium	Medium	High	Many Opportunities Very Attractive
Revitalized Yaffo	Medium	Many	High	Many Opportunities Very Attractive
Southwest	Low	Medium	Low	Many Opportunities Extremely Attractive
Southeast	High	Medium	High	Few Opportunities Extremely Attractive

Figure 8.2 Patterns of residential attractiveness selected Tel-Aviv/Yaffo neighborhoods – 1992

the different areas. As mentioned, the sample was drawn from a list of renters eligible for tax reductions due to their immigrant status. By comparing the list with current residents in the flats, we were able to determine how many immigrants had left the area. The data reveal that the proportion of immigrants who left the southwest and moved to other areas was highest (64 per cent), while in the southeast and Yaffo it was 48 per cent and 45 per cent, respectively (Table 8.7).

CONCLUSIONS

This study dealt with two aspects of immigrant absorption in a restructuring urban economy: the occupational aspect and the residential aspect. The data with regard to the occupational realm is consistent with hypotheses derived from the restructuring approach.

First, the data reveal that Tel-Aviv's restructuring economy offers immigrants job opportunities in high-level jobs. A short time after arrival, the proportion of immigrants in academic and professional occupations was similar to that of the veteran population of the city. At the same time, a very large proportion of immigrants were occupied in non-skilled occupations and experienced sharp downward mobility.

Table 8.6 Percentage of satisfied immigrants from various aspects of neighborhood by zone of residence

Zone	Percentage of satisfied immigrants from						
	Location	Population	Cost of housing	Schools	Environment	Transportation	Service
North	77.6	85.3	12.6	61.1	73.7	79.3	86.0
Center	88.9	66.0	16.3	56.0	51.1	71.4	74.0
Old Yaffo	89.4	40.0	29.4	33.3	28.0	80.0	72.0
New Yaffo	68.4	36.5	11.8	21.2	53.8	86.6	82.3
Southwest	66.0	36.9	7.5	25.3	16.4	70.3	51.9
Southeast	64.7	60.6	22.7	50.0	63.9	85.0	85.6

Table 8.7 Proportion of respondents who were located and who moved out in each area

	Located	Moved out
North	68%	32%
Center	65%	35%
Yaffo	55%	45%
Southwest	36%	64%
Southeast	52%	48%

The polarization which characterizes restructuring economies is reflected in the polarized job structure of the immigrants. A very small proportion is employed in the mid-range occupations such as clerical and sales jobs. The greater bulk of the immigrants are employed in non-professional and low-status personal services and low-skilled industrial jobs.

The data also showed that immigrants with high-level industrial skills, such as engineers, had relatively few opportunities to find jobs in the changing urban economy. Their chances were smaller than those of immigrants with high-level skills of a non-industrial nature. Restructuring is said to be characterized by increasing job opportunities in communication, information processing and supervisory activities and legal, accounting, and insurance services. Most of the highly qualified immigrants from the former USSR were not trained in these jobs, which are typical of post-industrial and globalizing economies. Also, consistent with the restructuring hypothesis, it was found that the employment opportunities of immigrants with high industrial skills were better in the surrounding localities, than in the central city.

We can therefore conclude that the pattern of the occupational opportunities available to immigrants from the former USSR corresponds to the predictions of the restructuring approach.

The second aspect of immigrant absorption deals with housing. The data indicate that new immigrants must confront two types of competition for housing in a restructuring urban context – with gentrifiers on one hand, and with low-status incumbents on the other.

From this perspective, the data reveal that immigrants have very few housing opportunities in areas with advanced gentrification. Thus, for immigrants, the relationship between gentrification and housing opportunities is one of competition. Restructuring, therefore, decreases immigrants' housing opportunities. However, deteriorated areas in which gentrification has only begun, such as the southwest, offer immigrants more opportunities although, at the same time, they hold little attraction for them.

These findings support the view that the relationship between gentrification and immigrants' housing opportunities evolves in two phases. In the first phase, when gentrification in an area is just commencing, immigrants may still have housing opportunities available to them. As gentrification proceeds, housing costs in the whole area rise and opportunities for immigrants drastically decline. These findings have important policy implications.

POLICY IMPLICATIONS

The policy implications of the research follow from the two main themes of the study. With regard to the occupational aspect, it appears that in a restructuring urban context, policies designed to absorb immigrants cannot be confined to dealing with immigrants solely on the individual level.

Proponents of the restructuring approach claim that the problem lies with the type of jobs being generated by industrial restructuring. That is, the demand is dichotomized into low- and high-level skills. This suggests that in order to increase the immigrants' occupational opportunities, efforts have to be directed to changing the economic structure, and not simply toward retraining. In order to enlarge the proportion of those occupied in high-skilled jobs and to avoid sharp downward mobility, what is needed is on the one hand a growth policy regarding high-skilled sectors and, on the other, a retraining policy that takes into account the changing nature of urban economies.

The second policy implication refers to the activities designed to reduce the social costs of residence in deteriorated areas. In the restructuring urban context, immigrants compete with gentrifiers over housing opportunities. In areas where gentrification has already progressed, immigrants can no longer afford permanent housing. This leaves the neighborhoods where gentrification is only beginning as the major sources of housing opportunities. The largest potential supply of flats for immigrants is concentrated in the deteriorated areas, only at the edge of gentrification. It seems, however, that for the immigrants from the former Soviet Union, the social costs of living in these areas is very high, and they prefer to leave the city. In such areas, immigrants are warded off by the poor condition of the infrastructure. It follows that in order to facilitate the policy of direct absorption adopted by the Israeli government, that is, the integration of a large portion of these immigrants in the urban setting, some modest form of public intervention is needed in order to retain the immigrant population within the urban setting.

In cases where municipal policy is to attract immigrants as permanent residents, such as that of Tel-Aviv, government intervention to upgrade the public services in deteriorated areas may prove to be an important means in advancing this goal.

As a parting word, following the restructuring approach, we can hypothesize that the experience of Russian immigrants who arrived in Israel in the 1970s may be only partially relevant in predicting the occupational opportunities and mode of integration of the current wave of immigrants (see Flug and Kasir in this volume).

References

Beauregard, R.A. (1991) 'Capital Restructuring and the New Built Environment of Global Cities: New York and Los Angeles', *International Journal of Urban and Regional Studies*, vol. 15: pp. 90–105.

Borjas, C.J. (1987) 'Self selection and the earnings of immigrants', *American Economic Review*, 38, pp. 538–94.

Bonacich, E. (1973) 'A Theory of Middleman Minorities', *American Sociological Review*, 38, pp. 538–94.

Burgess, E. (1925; 1967) 'The Growth of the City', in R. Park, E. Burgess and R. McKenzie (eds), *The City* (University of Chicago).

Carliner, G. (1980) 'Wages, Earnings and Working Hours of First, Second and Third Generation American males', *Economic Inquiry*, Jan. pp. 87–102.

Carmon, N. and M. Baron (1994) 'Reducing Inequality by Means of Neighborhood Rehabilitation: An Israeli Experiment and its Lessons', *Urban Studies*. vol. 13, no. 9, pp. 1465–80.

Chiswick, Barry (1978) 'The Effects of Americanization on the Earnings of Foreign-Born Men', *Journal of Political Economy*, October, 86, pp. 897–921.

Clay, P.L. (1979) *Neighborhood Renewal: Middle-Class Resettlement and Incumbent Upgrading in American Neighborhoods* (Mass: Lexington Books).

Fainstein, S.S. (1990) 'The Changing World Economy and Urban Restructuring', in Judd Dennis and Michael Parkinson (eds), *Leadership and Urban Regeneration. Urban Affairs Annual Reviews*, vol. 37, pp. 31–51 (Sage Publications: Newbury Calif).

Fainstein, N.I. and S.S. Fainstein (1982) 'Restructuring the American City', in N.I. Fainstein and S.S. Fainstein (eds), *Urban Policy under Capitalism*, vol. 22, (Sage *Urb. Aff. Ann, Rev.* Beverly Hills, Calif) pp. 161–89.

Fainstein, S.S. and N.I. Fainstein (1989) 'Technology, the New International Division of Labor and Location: Continuities and Disjunctions', in R.A. Beauregard (ed.), *Economic Restructuring and Political Response* (Sage Publications: Newbury Park. Calif).

Feagin, J.R. (1988) *Free Enterprise City* (New Brunswick: Rutgers University Press).
Flug, K. and N. Kasir (Kaliner) (1996) 'Short-run Absorption of the ex-USSR Immigrants in Israel's Labor Market', Ch. 6 in this book.
Ginsburg, Y. (1993) 'Revitalization of two urban neighborhoods in Tel Aviv', in D. Nachmias and G. Menahem (eds), *Social Processes and Public Policy in Tel Aviv-Jafo* (Ramot Publishing House, Tel-Aviv University) (Hebrew), pp. 147–67.
Godfrey, B.J. (1988) *Neighborhoods in Transition: the Making of San Francisco's Ethnic and Nonconformist Communities* (Berkeley, Calif: University Calif. Press).
Harrison, B. and B. Bluestone (1988), *The Great U-turn: Corporate Restructuring and the Polarization of America* (New York: Basic Books).
Kasarda, J.D. (1983) 'Entry–Level Jobs, Mobility, and Urban Minority Employment', *Urban Affairs Quarterly* 19: pp. 21–40.
Laska, S.B. and D. Spain (1980) *Back to the City: Issues in Neighborhoods Renovation* (New York: Pergamon).
Lieberson, S. (1980) *A Piece of the Pie: Black and White Immigrants Since 1880* (Berkley: University of California Press).
Light I. (1984) 'Immigrants and Ethnic Enterprise in North America', *Ethnic and Racial Studies*, vol. 7, no. 2, pp. 195–216.
London, B., B.A. Lee and S.G. Lipton (1986) 'The Determinants of Gentrification in the United States: A City-Level Analysis', *Urban Affairs Quarterly* 21(3): pp. 369–87.
Lupsha, P.A. (1976) 'The Politics of Reform', in A. Callow (ed.), *The City Boss in America* (Oxford University Press), pp. 233–238.
Menahem, G. and S. Spiro (1989) 'Urban Neighborhoods and the Quest for Community: Implications for Policy and Practice', *Community Development Journal*, vol. 24, no. 1, pp. 29–40.
Merton, K.R. (1949) *Social Theory and Social Structure* (Glencoe, Ill, The Free Press).
Morris, M., A.D. Bernhardt and M.S. Handcock (1994) 'Economic Inequality: New Methods for New Trends', *American Sociological Review*, vol. 59, no. 2, pp. 205–15.
Nachmias, D. and G. Menahem (1993) 'Tel-Aviv: Continuities and transformation', in D. Nachmias and G. Menahem (eds), *Social Processes and Public Policy in Tel-Aviv-Jafo* (Ramot Publishing House, Tel-Aviv University) (Hebrew), pp. 15–28.
Sassen, S. (1986) 'New York City: Economic Restructuring and Immigration', *Development and Change*, 17, pp. 85–119.
Sassen, S. (1988) *The Mobility of Labor and Capital* (New York: Cambridge University Press).
Sassen, S. (1990) 'Economic Restructuring and the American City', *Annual Review of Sociology*, vol. 16, pp. 465–90.
Sassen, S. (1991) 'Cities in a World Economy: New York, London Tokyo', paper presented at the AESOP International Congress Oxford, UK.
Savitch, H.V. (1988) *Post-Industrial Cities: Politics and Planning in New York, Paris and London* (Princeton, New Jersey: Princeton University Press).

Schnell, I. and I. Graicer (1993) 'Causes of in-migration to Tel Aviv inner city', *Urban Studies*, vol. 30, no. 7, pp. 1187–207.

Schnell, I. (1993) 'The formation of an urbanite life style in central Tel-Aviv', in D. Nachmias and G. Menahem (eds), *Social Processes and Public Policy in Tel Aviv-Jafo* (Ramot Publishing House, Tel-Aviv University) (Hebrew), pp. 41–60.

Shefter, L. (1976) 'The Emergence of Political Machines: An Alternative View', in W. Howley and N. Lipsky (eds), *Theoretical Perspectives on Urban Politics* (Englewood Cliffs: Prentice-Hall Inc.).

Short, John R. (1989) 'Yuppies, yuffies and the new urban order', *Transactions Inst. Br.Georg.* N.S., 14: pp. 173–188.

Smith, N. and P. Williams (1986) *Gentrification of the City* (Boston: Allen & Unwin).

Stark, O. and E. Taylor (1988) 'Relative Deprivation and International Migration', Discussion Paper Series, Migration and Development Program, Harvard University, Discussion Paper No. 36.

Tel Aviv-Yaffo Municipality, *Statistical Year Book 1990*.

Varady, David P. (1986) 'Neighborhood Confidence: A Critical Factor in Neighborhood Revitalization', *Environment and Behavior*, vol. 18, no. 4, pp. 480–501.

Wilson K.L. and A. Portes (1980) 'Immigrant Enclaves. An Analysis of Labor Market Experiences of Cubans in Miami', *American Journal of Sociology*, 86: pp. 295–319.

Waldinger, R. (1989) 'Immigration and Urban Change', *Annual Review of Sociology*, 15: pp. 211–32.

Whitt, J.A. (1987) 'Mozart in the Metropolis – The Art Coalition and the Urban Growth Machine', *Urban Affairs Quarterly,* Sep., pp. 15–36.

Zukin, Sharon (1987) 'Gentrification; Culture and Capital in the Urban Core', *Annual Review of Sociology*, 13: pp. 129–47.

9 From International Immigration to Internal Migration: The Settlement Process of Immigrants from the Former Soviet Union in Israel
Shlomo Hasson

INTRODUCTION

This chapter examines the settlement pattern of Jewish immigrants arriving in Israel from the former Soviet Union. The settlement process for recent immigrants is conceived as a lengthy one comprising several stages. It commences with a geographical decision made upon arrival as to where to settle, and continues with a series of subsequent decisions that may lead to internal migration within the receiving country. The ensuing patterns of settlement thus reflect a series of decisions made at different stages: international immigration and internal migration.

The study concerns four general problems. First, what are the patterns of settlement at the stages of international immigration and internal migration? Second, what are the motives underlying the choice of residence at the stages of international immigration and internal migration? Third, are there any sociodemographic differences between those recent immigrants who chose to stay in their first place of residence (stayers) and those who choose to move from the first place of residence (movers)? Finally, what is the government's role in shaping the geographical pattern of immigrant settlement?

The study is divided into six sections. First, it presents the theoretical background underlying the study. Second, it provides a short description of the demographic and socioeconomic characteristics of the immigrants, thus providing a general framework for the study of the group. Third, it analyzes the geographical distribution of the immigrants. Fourth, it charts the patterns of internal migration. Fifth, it analyzes the motives underlying the choice of residence at the stages of international immigration and internal migration and examines the sociodemographic characteristics of movers and stayers. Finally, it explores the government's policy with regard to immigrant settlement.

The chapter focuses on recent immigrants who arrived in Israel from the former Soviet Union between September 1989 and September 1992. It is based on three surveys taken in June 1990, May 1991 and September 1992. The three surveys were based on proportional stratified samples, where the stratifying factor was the region of settlement. The samples thus represent the geographical distribution of the immigrants when the surveys were taken. The June 1990 survey comprised 609 immigrants, the May 1991 – 809 immigrants and the September 1992 – 826 immigrants. The samples were based on official lists of immigrant residents supplied by the Absorption Ministry. The sample unit was the household. One person in the household was interviewed using a questionnaire written and administered in Russian. The questions included in the three questionnaires were the same. The only exception was questions on internal migration, which were included only in the September 1992 survey. In other words, the September 1992 survey is the only source for internal migration. Besides the surveys, additional data were gathered from the Central Bureau of Statistics. Finally, information on government policy was gathered from the Absorption, Interior and Housing Ministries.

THEORETICAL AND EMPIRICAL BACKGROUND

The decision where to settle during the stage of international immigration is, as Nogle (1994) has observed, made under conditions of extreme uncertainty and is occasionally constrained by language barriers and limited knowledge about alternative locations and opportunities. The most common geographical tendency noted among recent immigrants is to locate close to previous immigrant concentrations (Glazer and Moynihan, 1970; Trovato, 1988). Here the newly arrived immigrants can maintain a sense of community and identity, and reduce the social and psychological strains of immigration. This tendency is closely associated, as Gurak and Caces (1992) have noted, with the existence of social networks of friends and relatives in the receiving country. The networks may play an important role at this stage, by addressing housing, employment and other needs of the immigrants upon arrival, leading ultimately to spatial concentration in immigrant enclaves. In certain cases spatial concentration serves a cultural need of preserving identity. The Chinese and Jews maintained their ethnic identity through concentration in segregated areas.

The impact of government policy on the geographical distribution of recent immigrants is a debatable issue. As Zlotnik writes: 'The more economies became export-oriented, the greater the influence of global forces on the spatial distribution of population' (Zlotnik, 1994: 183). Nevertheless, there is some evidence which shows that government policy may affect geographical patterns. Thus, for example, a side-door policy for guest workers, a policy which favors a relatively small yet constant stream of alien laborers, may facilitate the concentration of immigrants in large or rapidly growing cities, where there is a large demand for cheap labor. On the other hand, a government policy which favors counter-urbanization or the settlement of marginal areas may lead to spatial dispersal of the population (Martin, 1994).

The tendency to concentrate in large cities may have a significant effect on the geographical distribution of the population. It has been recently suggested that international immigration played a significant role in stopping counter-urbanization processes in some European large cities, since in these cities international immigrants constitute 10–20 per cent of the population (Zlotnik, 1994: 177). On certain occasions the geographical concentration of international immigrants may have a regional dimension. Thus, for instance, immigrants of Cuban origin tend to cluster in the Southeast area of the United States, immigrants of Mexican origin reside in California and the Southwest, while people of European origin are very heavily concentrated in New England, the Mid-Atlantic state, and the Eastern Midwest. More recently, it has been noted that Mexicans and Asians who immigrate to the United States tend to concentrate in the South and West (Belanger and Rogers, 1992).

Over time, however, as the recent immigrants begin to adapt to the new society, make new contacts and acquire new skills and first hand information and knowledge about the opportunities in the receiving country, they may choose to relocate through a process of internal migration. Trovato (1988) has observed that recent immigrants tend to be very mobile in geographical terms, sometimes even more mobile than the population as a whole. Samuel (1988) has suggested that a high level of migration among recent immigrants might be an aspect of the immigrant adjustment process. The level of internal migration among recent immigrants may vary among sub-groups, reflecting the impact of age structure, life cycle, education and economic mobility. Nogle, for instance, has found that 'human capital characteristics (education, sex, age and marital status) and unemployment ...

have strong effects on migration behavior' (Nogle, 1994: 44). Nogle's findings lend support to the already large body of research that has shown that human capital characteristics and employment opportunities may affect different sociodemographic groups in various ways, and may result in selective patterns of internal migration (Lowry, 1966; White and Woods, 1980). As far as the migration motives are concerned, it has been observed that recent immigrants, who take part in internal migration, do not try to maximize their economic gains but rather to reduce social and psychological costs by locating close to family and friends (Trovato, 1988). As Morrison has suggested there are no significant differences between the motives exhibited at the two stages of migration (Morrison, 1971). Moreover, as several studies have demonstrated, internal immigration of recent immigrants has tended to reinforce the geographical concentration of immigrants (Belanger and Rogers, 1992).

THE IMMIGRANTS' DEMOGRAPHIC AND SOCIOECONOMIC CHARACTERISTICS

Up until 1989 the United States was the preferred destination for Jewish immigrants who left the Soviet Union. In Autumn 1989, however, the US government changed its immigration policy; Soviet Jews were no longer considered as refugees, and the annual number of Soviet immigrants, including Jews allowed to enter the United States, was reduced to 50 000. The change in the American policy had a direct effect on Israel. In 1988 only 2250 Jews arrived in Israel from the Soviet Union; in 1989 this figure rose to 13 000, in 1990 it reached an unprecedented record of 189 000, in 1991 it slightly decreased to a level of 145 000, and in 1992 it reached the 64 000 mark. Thus, between 1989 and 1992 about 460 000 immigrants entered Israel from the former Soviet Union, leading to an increase of about 10 per cent in the country's population.

The immigrants now arriving in Israel from the former Soviet Union are an elite professional group with few parallels anywhere in the world. According to the September, 1992 survey, most of the immigrants (82.3 per cent) come from the large cities of the European republics of the Commonwealth of Independent States (CIS). Most of them are professionals in the applied sciences (about 40 per cent) and in the social sciences and humanities (about 25 per cent). The proportion of those with university educations is 60 per cent, that is four times larger than that of the Jewish population in Israel. Studies of professional groups of immigrants in the United States have shown that the main motive for immigration was the gap between the socioeconomic expectations of members of the group and the available means for realizing those expectations. Evidently, members of such a group develop a range of expectations that they cannot realize in their countries of origin because of a paucity of opportunities. For this reason, they tend to emigrate to another country. In other words, it is the relative gap, rather than the absolute gap, that determines migration.

The situation is, apparently, different in the present case. The reasons for the renewal of immigration from the CIS are the political uncertainty and lack of general security there. All these were felt especially intensely among Jewish professionals and induced them to leave. It may well be that if the gates to other developed countries are opened, the stream of immigrants to Israel will taper off, and the relative socioeconomic gap will channel the immigrants to areas in which it is more possible to realize the immigrants' socioeconomic expectations.

The absorption of professional groups is generally accompanied by a certain decline in their level of employment. From this point of view, the fate of the immigrants in Israel is no different than of those in other countries. In the short run, only a small portion of the immigrants have found employment in their own fields, while the majority has experienced a decline in professional status. About 70 per cent of the immigrants belong in the labor force, and about one quarter of those who are in the labor force are unemployed. Among those who are employed, only a quarter are working in their professions. The rest (75 per cent) work in lower-status jobs, mostly of a blue-collar type.

Two central factors that assisted immigrant accommodation have been the existence of a large private housing market and the crowding of several immigrant families into one apartment. Some 71 per cent of the immigrants rented their apartments from private home-owners, and in each apartment about 20 per cent of the tenants do not belong to the nuclear family. Thus, the size of a nuclear family is 3.2 people and the average number of tenants in an apartment is 4.0. About a third of those interviewed live with older parents, about a quarter with other relatives, and about 7 per cent with other immigrants who are not relatives. Some 38.3 per cent of the families surveyed in September 1992 rent an apartment together with others.

THE GEOGRAPHICAL PATTERN OF SETTLEMENT

To study the geographical patterns of the immmigrant settlement, Israel was divided into three major areas: core, periphery and semi-periphery.

From International Immigration to Internal Migration 171

The core contains the city of Tel Aviv, the Northern, Eastern and Southern sections of the Dan conurbation. The semi-periphery includes the regions of Jerusalem and Haifa. The periphery includes the Southern and Northern regions (see Map).

A study over time shows that the immigrants dispersed gradually from the core to the periphery. In the first stage, represented by the survey taken in June 1990, most of the immigrants still lived in the core area of the country (the Dan conurbation between Netanya and Ashdod) and in the Haifa region. In the May 1991 survey, a tendency toward dispersion to the periphery was already noticeable. The survey of September 1992, the most recent, detected a continuation of this trend. Accordingly, the percentage of immigrants in the core area dropped from 53.7 per cent in June 1990, to 45 per cent in September 1992, as did their share in the Haifa region: from 23.4 per cent to 14.5 per cent. On the other hand, the proportion of immigrants in the Jerusalem region (which includes settlements in Judea and Samaria) increased from 8 per cent to 13.7 per cent, and the proportion in the Northern and Southern regions rose substantially: from 14.9 per cent in June 1990 to 26.7 per cent in September 1992.

As a result, only 45 per cent of the interviewed immigrants lived in the core in September 1992, 28.2 per cent in the semi-periphery, and 26.7 per cent in the periphery. These figures are very close to those of the Central Bureau of Statistics (CBS) for the geographical distribution of the immigrants in 1991: 42.5 per cent in the core, 25.1 per cent in the semi-periphery, and 31.3 per cent in the periphery. (Another 0.8 per cent of the immigrants live in Judea–Samaria and the Gaza District.) There are two reasons for the differences between the CBS figures and those in the sample: the data in the sample are from the end of 1992, whereas the CBS figures are for the end of 1991; and the boundaries of the geographical regions in this study were not defined in precisely the same way as those used by the CBS. A comparison between the spatial distribution of the immigrants with that of old-timers clearly shows that the former group is more widely dispersed than the latter. The core area, which accomodates 45.0 per cent of the immigrants, is home to 53.4 per cent of the old-timers. Conversely, the semi-periphery and the periphery (i.e., the Jerusalem and Haifa regions and the Northern and Southern regions), which accomodate 55 per cent of the immigrants, contain only 44.4 per cent of the old-timers.

One may conclude that the immigrants' first place of residence and the subsequent internal migration processes led to a dispersed pattern of settlement, and that the immigrants are more widely dispersed than the absorbing society. Given that three-fourths of the immigrants rent their homes on the private market, this means that the market trend has caused an increase

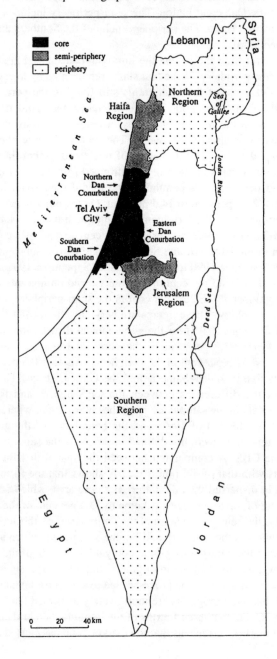

Map Geographical division of Israel

in the immigrants' spatial dispersion and, consequently, in that of the population as a whole. The question which arises at this point is whether this geographical dispersion is temporary and liable to change as a result of internal migration by the immigrants.

THE GEOGRAPHICAL PATTERN OF INTERNAL MIGRATION

The 1991 figures from the Central Bureau of Statistics (CBS) illustrate the internal migration of immigrants who arrived in 1990 and 1991 from an interesting angle. According to the CBS, 75 000 immigrants – 22.6 per cent of the 1990–1 immigrant population – moved within Israel in 1991. The preferred regions for the immigrants who moved were the peripheral ones – the Southern and Northern regions, where migration balances were positive, and to a lesser extent Judea and Samaria. The other regions, Haifa in particular, had negative migration balances. Table 9.1 compares the migration patterns of the immigrants with those of the old-timers. The immigrants' internal migration patterns match those of the old-timers in some aspects and differ in others. The migration balances in the Jerusalem, Haifa, and Tel Aviv regions were negative for both groups; while the balances in Judea–Samaria and the Gaza District were positive for both. The primary differences were the immigrants' preference for the Southern and Northern regions and their tendency to move out of the core area (the Dan conurbation). The pattern for the old-timers was almost the opposite: an equal number moved in and out of the Northern and Southern regions and the migration balance in the center was positive. It is evident, then, that old-timers' migration tends to increase the concentration of the population, whereas that of the immigrants leads to its decrease.

The findings of the September 1992 survey (for the 1989–92 period) correspond to the CBS figures to a large extent. About 25 per cent of the subjects moved from their first place of residence (compared with 22.6 per cent according to the 1991 CBS figures). (The first place of residence was defined in the 1992 survey as the first settlement in which an immigrant lived for two months or more. An internal migrant was defined as anyone who, at the time of the survey, did not live in his or her first settlement. This definition excludes persons who moved within the same settlement.) About four-fifths of the internal migrants (about 20 per cent of the immigrants) moved twice. This may attest to the existence of a hypermobile group that tends to move fairly frequently. Overall, most of the immigrants (about 75 per cent) are staying, for now, in their first place of residence. Much like the CBS's figures, the September 1992 survey shows

Table 9.1 Internal migration of old-timers and immigrants, by region, 1991 (thousands)

Region	\multicolumn{6}{c}{Internal migration}					
	Old-timers			Immigrants		
	In-Mig.	Out-Mig	Balance	In-Mig.	Out-Mig	Balance
All regions	128.9	128.9	0.0	75.5	75.5	0.0
Jerusalem region	8.4	11.6	−3.2	3.0	4.3	−1.4
Tel Aviv city	34.6	38.0	−3.4	17.2	19.8	−2.6
Dan conurbation (excluding Tel Aviv)*	31.0	28.9	2.1	13.9	16.2	−2.3
Haifa region	13.6	16.2	−2.6	13.0	19.1	−6.0
Northern region	13.8	13.0	0.8	13.2	8.4	4.8
Southern region	17.3	17.7	−0.4	13.1	7.0	6.1
Judea, Samaria and the Gaza Strip	10.2	3.5	6.7	2.1	0.7	1.4

* This region corresponds to a large extent to the central district as defined by the CBS. In the survey this area was expanded northward and southward to include the cities of Netanya and Ashdod.
Source: Central Bureau of Statistics, 1992.

positive migration balances in the peripheral regions and negative migration balances in the core. A high percentage (about 40 per cent) of the immigrants who now live in the Northern region used to live in other regions; this attests to attractiveness of this region for recent immigrants who chose to move.

CHOICE OF PLACE OF RESIDENCE AND CHARACTERISTICS OF MOVERS AND STAYERS

How do the immigrants choose their place of residence? Are their motives different in the stages of immigration and internal migration? If so, how can this difference be explained? To answer these questions, the stayers (immigrants living in their first place of residence) and the movers (those who had already moved from their first place of residence) were asked to indicate their main reason for having chosen the locality in which they currently reside.

Looking at the two groups together (Table 9.2), one can see that 47.1 per cent of the immigrants chose their current place of residence because they wanted to live near friends and relatives. As in the previous surveys (June 1990 and May 1991), there was a noticeable tendency to choose the first place of residence for psychological–social reasons, that is, because of closeness to social networks that could provide social assurance in the initial stage of absorption. However, there was a significant drop in the importance of psychological–social factors over time: from 58 per cent in June 1990 to 54 per cent in May 1991, and to 47 per cent in September 1992.

This general picture conceals significant differences in the behavior of the stayers and movers (see Table 9.2). Over half of the stayers (55.9 per cent) said that they chose their settlement because of closeness to friends and relatives; only 19.5 per cent of the movers did so. This means that psychological–social motives are less prominent in internal migration. Employment and housing, however, become more important: they were the primary reasons for 48.5 per cent of the movers as opposed to 13.9 per cent of the stayers. Specifically, housing was the main motive in the decision of 25 per cent of the movers and 5.5 per cent of the stayers; employment was paramount for 23.5 per cent of the movers and 8.4 per cent of the stayers.

As Table 9.3 clearly indicates, the longer the immigrant has been in Israel, the less important closeness to friends and relatives becomes in choosing a place to live. In light of the existing theory, the observed sequence of immigrants' decision making in Israel seems to proceed as follows. Immigrants tend to decide on an initial place of residence based on a desire to minimize the social and psychological difficulties involved in moving to a new country. Living near friends and relatives, especially in the large cities, provides a protected niche where an immigrant understands

Table 9.2 Movers and stayers, by main reason for choosing the present settlement (percentages)

	Total numbers	Per cent	Friends and relations	Employment	Housing	Site character and other
All immigrants	822	100.0	47.1	12.0	10.2	30.6
Movers	200	100.0	19.5	23.5	25.0	32.0
Stayers	622	100.0	55.9	8.4	5.5	30.2

Table 9.3 Choice of settlement because of nearness to friends and relatives, by length of residence in the country (percentages)

Length of residence	Per cent
All immigrants	47.1
September–December 1989	30.4
January–June 1990	32.4
July–December 1990	44.9
January–June 1991	53.0
July–December 1991	54.0
January–September 1992	55.1

the language and can get help from people he or she feels close to. Over time, the need for such proximity decreases. The immigrant learns the language, becomes more independent, gains familiarity with the country and with the nature of different places, discovers housing and job opportunities, and tends to choose a new place to live based on the opportunities available. Once dispersed over the country, the movers create new, peripheral enclaves that may serve as absorbing niches for the newly arrived immigrants. From a geographical perspective, the interesting question is what opportunities movers and stayers tend to stress in various parts of the country. As Table 9.4 shows, in all regions the stayers' main motivation in choosing a place to live was closeness to friends and relatives. For movers, however, a different reason for in-migration was dominant in each region. In the Jerusalem and the Northern regions, the main reason cited by the movers was housing. In the center and the city of Tel Aviv, it was employment. In the Southern region, no one factor was dominant; a combination of several considerations explained the attraction. To conclude, the primacy of housing considerations, which appears at the national level, conceals a more subtle geographical pattern of internal migration. Migrants who moved to the core areas did so mainly because of employment opportunities, whereas migrants who moved to the periphery did so mainly for housing reasons. Disparities in rent and mortgages can explain why those who moved to the Northern region cited housing as their primary reason.

Characteristics of Movers and Stayers

Do the movers differ sociodemographically from the stayers? With the exception of length of residence and to a lesser extent age structure, the answer is no. A comparison of the movers and stayers by a variety of

Table 9.4 Movers and stayers, by the most frequent reason for choosing their present settlement and by region

Region	Movers	Stayers
Jerusalem region	Housing	Friends and relatives
Tel Aviv city	Employment	Friends and relatives
Eastern Dan conurbation	Employment	Friends and relatives
Southern Dan conurbation	Employment	Friends and relatives
Northern Dan conurbation	Employment	Friends and relatives
Haifa region	Several reasons	Friends and relatives
Northern region	Housing	Friends and relatives
Southern region	Several reasons	Friends and relatives

sociodemographic and economic variables, shows that the two groups do not differ significantly. No significant difference was found in terms of the migrant's gender, marital status, level of education, employment (working/not working) or the number of breadwinners in the family. The percentages of employed and unemployed persons were identical, as were those of one-income and two-income families. No significant difference was found in Hebrew fluency and the percentage of purchasing homes either. The main distinguishing variable between movers and stayers was

Table 9.5 Movers and stayers by selected socio-demographic characteristics

	Movers	Stayers	Significance*
Males	45.3	44.8	Not significant
Females	54.7	55.2	Not significant
Unmarried	13.3	12.1	Not significant
Married	69.5	69.8	Not significant
Age below 44	68.8	58.8	Significant
Academic education	56.6	62.5	Not significant
Hebrew fluency-intermediate	76.3	73.6	Not significant
Unemployed	25.1	23.4	Not significant
One bread winner	43.3	40.4	Not significant
Two bread winners	32.0	32.0	Not significant
Home purchasing	8.4	8.9	Not significant

* Significant at 0.05 level.

length of residence in the country. The longer a person has been in Israel, the more likely he or she is to move (see Table 9.6). These differences corroborate the findings about the influence of the stage of migration on the choice of place of residence.

Long-Term Preferences

What will happen to the distribution pattern, shaped by international immigration and internal migration, in the long term? Examining the immigrants' preferences, it appears that seven-tenths of the subjects intend to remain in their current place of residence, and the figure is particularly prominent in the Jerusalem, the Northern and the Southern regions. On the other hand, many residents in the Haifa region and the Southern Dan conurbation – two regions that already have high rates of out-migration – plan to leave. In other words, the long-term preferences are likely to reinforce the actual patterns of geographical dispersion. These findings are encouraging from the standpoint of the periphery, since they seem to suggest that the immigrants who have settled in the Northern, Southern, and Jerusalem regions will continue to live in these areas. One, however, should approach the migrants' declared preferences with caution, since they may represent an attempt to rationalize past decisions. It may well be that the employment opportunities at the center would lead in the long run to a counter-migration from the periphery to the core. Indeed the beginning of such a trend has been noted in the case of Haifa and the Northern regions.

The immigrants who have expressed a preference for remaining where they live cite the following reasons, in descending order: the characteristics of the locality, job opportunities, housing conditions, and the presence of friends and relatives. The regions differ remarkably in the motives that make people decide to stay. In the city of Tel-Aviv and the Eastern Dan conurbation, the main reason is employment. In the Northern and in the

Table 9.6 Movers and stayers, by length of residence in the country (percentages)

	Total	1989	Beg. 1990	End 1990	Beg. 1991	End 1991	1992
All immigrants	100.0	100.0	100.0	100.0	100.0	100.0	100.0
Movers	24.4	47.8	35.5	22.8	20.4	24.4	15.0
Stayers	75.6	52.2	64.5	77.2	79.6	75.6	85.0

Jerusalem regions the major motives are the characteristics of the locality and housing opportunities. Housing opportunities are also a primary motive in the Southern region.

SPATIAL POLICY

For 45 years every Israeli Government has declared its commitment to population dispersion. Under this policy, most of the new towns, built in the 1950s and 1960s to accommodate new immigrants, were located in the Northern and Southern regions. The Northern and Southern regions were also targeted as priority areas for economic development, and special allowances (subsidies, grants, tax exemptions) were made to encourage private entreprenuers to move into these areas.

During the present wave of immigration, however, the previous Likud government refrained from directly intervening to send the newcomers to the Northern and Southern periphery. The mistakes of the past and a commitment to a free-market economic policy kept the Likud Government from assigning immigrants to certain geographical regions. Instead, a 'direct absorption' policy was adopted that made available resources for renting apartments and special loans for purchasing homes, thus allowing the immigrants the freedom to choose their location (Doron and Kargar, 1993).

However, the government did not remain passive, and tended to support the dispersion of immigrants throughout the country. The government's dispersion policy was expressed in the activities of two ministries: Housing, which is in charge of public housing, and Interior, which is responsible for national planning. Each ministry presented a different policy for spatial dispersion of the immigrants. The Housing Ministry did not prepare a detailed plan for where to build new housing, and construction, which was carried out hurriedly, was determined on in accordance with the constraints and interests of the politicians who dealt with the issue. Priority was given to building in the periphery at the expense of the center.

The following figures, based on data provided by the Ministry of Housing, illustrate the Housing Ministry's priorities during the term of the previous Likud government. Between April 1990, and November 1991 (the main period of housing starts), the Housing Ministry began to build 62 000 dwelling units, most of them in the Southern, Northern, and the Jerusalem regions, and only a small per centage in the center. As a result, a wide discrepancy developed between the spatial preferences of the immigrants and the building policy of the Housing Ministry. Only 26.2 per cent of the new dwelling units were built in the central region, where

45 per cent of the immigrants settled. In contrast, 25.4 per cent of the dwelling units were built in the Southern region, where 13.4 per cent of the immigrants settled. Similarly, 23.5 per cent of housing starts were located in the Jerusalem area (including some communities over the Green Line), even though only 13 per cent of the immigrants settled there. Only in the the Haifa and the Northern regions did housing starts match settlement (24.8 per cent and 27.8 per cent, respectively).

While the Housing Ministry was vigorously creating facts on the ground, a detailed, systematic National Outline Scheme (NOS 31) for immigrant absorption and population dispersion was prepared at the initiative of the Interior Ministry. This scheme, which was guided by economic considerations, called for developing the center first, and only afterwards focusing on the periphery. According to NOS 31, the spatial distribution of the immigrant population in 1995 would be more concentrated than under the building pattern followed by the Housing Ministry: 47.1 per cent of the immigrants would live in the core area, 21.1 per cent in the semi-periphery (Jersalem and Haifa Regions), 27.6 per cent in the periphery (Southern and Northern Regions), and 4.2 per cent in Judea, Samaria and the Gaza District.

It is evident that the construction carried out by the Housing Ministry bore no similarity whatsoever to the national outline scheme prepared by the Interior Ministry, and to the actual distribution of the immigrants. On the other hand, the policy of the Interior Ministry closely corresponds to the geographical distribution of the immigrants. NOS 31 thus appears to be more realistic in planning for moderate dispersion of the immigrants, than the radical policy of dispersion assumed by the Ministry of Housing.

However, one should bear in mind that according to NOS 31 about 60 per cent of the old-timers are expected to live in the core area by 1995, but only 47 per cent of the immigrants (NOS 31, 1992). The significance of this policy lies in that it assumes an increase in the proportion of the old-timers at the core area: from 55 per cent at the present to 60 per cent in 1995. On the other hand, it assigns the immigrant group a leading role in advancing population dispersal. Thus in spite of claims to the contrary, NOS 31 continues the traditional policy of pursuing population dispersal through the dispersion of the newcomers.

SUMMARY AND CONCLUSION

Immigrants' decision as to where to settle has been described as an aspect of adjustment behavior. As several studies have suggested the adjustment process may involve several moves in an attempt to reduce social costs (Samuel, 1988; Nogle, 1994).

The study of how Soviet-Jewish immigrants in Israel make decisions about where to settle reveals an interesting pattern, partly similar and partly different from immigration flows in other countries. During the international immigration phase the immigrants arriving in Israel exhibit decisions and patterns of settlement quite similar to those noted in other places; they tend to concentrate in the large cities in the central parts of the country for social and psychological reasons. Moreover, within a short period of time, much like other immigration flows, a large number of Soviet Jew immigrants have migrated internally. Relying on previous studies, one could have expected that the movers (recent immigrants who become involved in internal migration) would differ from the stayers (immigrants who stay in their first place of residence) in their human capital attributes but not in their migration motives. In so far as both groups, movers and stayers, are engaged in adjustment process, one could have expected them, at least in the short run, not to behave as economic maximizers but rather as social optimizers (Trovato, 1988; Nogle, 1994).

These expectations have not been substantiated by the Israeli case. For one thing, the movers and the stayers do not differ in their sociodemographic attributes. The main explanatory variables for internal migration are length of residence in the country and to a lesser extent age structure. For another, a large proportion among the internal migrants in Israel reported that economic considerations, especially housing and employment, were the main reasons for changing their place of residence. Obviously, there is a large body of literature on immigration that shows that sociopsychological factors tend to recede in importance over time and to be replaced by economic considerations. But this change is very slow, and might take a generation or even more. What seems to distinguish the Soviet Jewish immigrants in Israel is the swift pace of change from social optimizers to economic maximizers.

Over a relatively short period of time a large segment of the Soviet Jew immigrants attained information on housing and employment opportunities, and decided to relocate in order to realize these opportunities. It is true that housing and job opportunities represent different spheres of economic activity, namely consumption and production. Nevertheless, both can offer the immigrant short-term, and sometimes even long-term, economic gains in spending and saving. Investing in a low-priced home, which will yield a high return in the long run, may equal or even surpass one's cumulative savings from years of work. Saving on rent is also a major economic consideration. This, it seems, is the reason for the vast importance attributed to housing at the stage of internal migration.

Since cheap housing is available in the new towns built on the periphery during the 1950s and the 1960s, many immigrants tended to move there, subsequently reversing the population concentration tendency caused by the old-timers. The geographical outcome has been a shift of focus from more established localities, where family and friends are concentrated, to new places that offer advantages in terms of accommodation. There has been a counter, though less prominent, flow from the periphery to the center, whose participants emphasized employment opportunities.

It may be suggested that the emphasis placed by Soviet-Jewish immigrants on economic opportunities at the internal migration stage and the concomitant dispersion tendency have to do with the immigrant's human capital characterstics and the government policy. The immigrant group at hand is not one of guest workers or refugees. This is a professional and well-educated group, sensitive to economic opportunities and able to seize them swiftly. As a result, the immigrants do not encounter serious sociogeographical constraints while considering the preferred place of residence, and can easily explore the economic opportunities latent in different places. Moreover, immigrants to Israel enjoy a supportive government policy. Unlike other countries, immigrant absorption is an essential part of Israel's ethos of nation building. Whereas other countries in Western Europe and North America display a reluctant policy towards immigrant absorption, Israel exhibits an open-door policy towards Jewish immigrants. According to the Law of Return every Jew is entitled to full citizenship rights upon immigration to Israel. Under the current policy of direct absorption, the immigrants are entitled to economic support and housing loans, and thus can realize the available housing opportunities.

The Likud government policy of creating a large supply of housing in the peripheral regions may have further affected the dispersion process. It did so directly by making available a pool of low-cost public housing. In fact, there is evidence of a relatively high purchase rate particularly in the peripheral areas. The indirect effect is that the reserve of housing in the periphery, expressed in large stocks of empty houses, pushed rental prices down. This trend will probably continue even if recent immigrants do not purchase the dwelling units, since some homeowners are keen on acquiring a second apartment to rent out as a steady source of income. In all, the policy of the previous Likud government, wasteful as it was in terms of public resources allocation, has apparently led to a greater spatial dispersion of the population, at least in the short term.

The crucial question, however, is whether governmental efforts to counter market forces and disperse the population will succeed in the long run. From a geographical point of view, the question is whether the peripheral and semiperipheral regions will be able to retain the immigrant population for a long period of time. I think the answer to both questions is 'no'. Spontaneous market forces are bound to lead to immigrant concentration in the center. The beginning of such a wave is already indicated by the migrants moving from the Northern and Haifa regions to the center. The lesson for policy-makers is clear: unless suitable sources of employment are directed to peripheral regions, a wave of migration toward the center of the country will be inevitable. Policy-makers have to grapple with an uneasy dilemma: whether to support the immigrants' dispersion trends and divert some economic resources to the periphery, to areas traditionally characterized by large social gaps, or to give priority for economic reasons to investment in the center, where the return on capital is higher.

References

Central Bureau of Statistics (1992) *Statistical Yearbook* (Jerusalem: Hamadpis Hamemshalti).
Belanger, A. and A. Rogers (1992) 'The Internal Migration and Spatial Redistribution of the Foreign-born Population in the United States: 1965–70 and 1975–80', *International Migration Review*, Winter, 26, no. 4, pp. 1342–69.
Chiswick, B.R. (1994) 'Soviet Jews in the United States: An Analysis of Their Linguistic and Economic Adjustment', *International Migration Review*, 23, no. 2, pp. 260–85.
Doron, A. and H.J. Kargar (1993) 'The Politics of Immigration Policy in Israel', *International Migration*, 31, no. 4, pp. 497–512.
Glazer, N. and P. Moynihan (1970) *Beyond the Melting Pot* (Cambridge: MIT Press).
Gurak, T. Douglas and F. Caces (1992) 'Migration Networks and the Shaping of Migration Systems', in M.M. Kritz, L.L. Lim and H. Zlotnik (eds), *International Migration Systems: A Global Approach* (Oxford: Clarendon Press).
Kritz, M.M., C.B. Keely and S.M. Tumasi (eds) (1981) *Global Trends in Migration: Theory and Research on International Population Movements* (New York: Center for Migration Studies).
Lowry, S.I. (1996) *Migration and Metropolitan Growth: Two Analytic Models* (San Francisco: Chandler).
Martin, P.L. (1994) 'Comparative Migration Policies', *International Migration Review*, 23, no. 1, pp. 164–70.
Morrison, P.A. (1971) 'Chronic Movers and the Future Redistribution of Population: A Longitudinal Analysis', *Demography*, 8, no. 2, pp. 171–84.

Nogle, J.M. (1994) 'Internal Migration for Recent Immigrants to Canada', *International Migration Review*, 28, no. 1, pp. 31–48

NOS 31 (1992) *National Outline Scheme for Construction, Development and Immigrant Absorption*, vol. 4 (Tel-Aviv).

Samuel, T.G. (1988) 'Family Class Immigrants to Canada, 1981–4: Some Aspects of Social Adaptation', *International Migration*, 26, no. 3, pp. 287–99.

Trovato, F. (1988) 'The Interurban Mobility of the Foreign Born in Canada, 1976–81', *International Migration Review*, 22, no. 3, pp. 59–86.

Ward, D. (1974) 'The Emergence of Central Immigrant Ghettoes in American Cities: 1840–1920', *Annals of the Association of American Geographers*, p. 58.

Ward, D. (1988) 'Settlement Patterns and Spatial Distribution', in R.A. Easterlin, D. Ward, W.S. Bernard and R. Ueda (eds), *Immigration* (Cambridge, Mass: Harvard University Press), pp. 35–74.

White, P. and R. Woods (eds) (1980) *The Geographical Impact of Migration* (New York: Longman).

Zlotnik, H. (1994) 'Expert Group Meeting on Population Distribution and Migration', *International Migration Review*, 23, no. 1, pp. 171–204.

Part IV

Immigrant Integration: USA, Australia, Britain and France

10 Earlier Immigration to the United States: Historical Clues for Current Issues of Integration[1]
Stanley Lieberson

The historic experience of the United States with respect to immigration from Europe is strikingly positive. The number of immigrants was extraordinarily large relative to the size of the existing population. These immigrants came from diverse sources – often from sources that the earlier settlers looked down on. The process was remarkably successful, leading to substantial acculturation in a relatively short span of time, in such critical dimensions as loyalty to the new nation, linguistic assimilation, productive participation in the economy, and cultural and organizational adaptations. Over the years, discrimination declined, gaps between the groups diminished, and intermarriage increased. Indeed, the ethnic labels and categories themselves have changed and, although hardly gone, are less rigid than they once were. There is evidence that ethnic ties are declining, with the categories and ties in flux. The high levels of intermarriage between various white groups (and also including several of the non-European groups as well) suggests that this process is likely to continue in the years ahead and include as well other ethnic/racial subsets of the population (Lieberson and Waters, 1988, chapters 6 and 7). As an example of the successful incorporation of diverse European groups into the nation, consider that the United States participated in two world wars with Germany, without serious opposition, despite the fact that a substantial proportion of the American population are of German origin (Lieberson, 1992, p. 301).

In addressing issues of contemporary immigration in developed nations, can we learn by considering conditions during the heyday of European immigration to the United States earlier in this century and during much of the nineteenth century? One may be inclined to answer in the negative. After all, these are different eras and even the same nations have undergone changes. Likewise, the motivations for immigration are not the same, the numerical impact is of a different magnitude, the economic opportunities are not comparable, and even the people are different. Jews leaving Russia at present for Israel are dissimilar in their educational and occupational attainment, for example, from Jews who migrated to the United States many decades ago. Yet, it is an interesting question because the outcome of this massive European migration to the United States is so successful. Even though the current situation differs on many important dimensions from this earlier period, one should not emphasize these without also determining if the earlier set of conditions offer any lessons that could be valuable for contemporary issues of immigration.

Following the usual academic form, two caveats are in order before we move ahead. First, the United States is by no means the only country with such an extraordinary history of assimilation. Whether the experiences of other successful nations (such as Canada, Australia, Brazil, and Argentina) would teach us different lessons – or modify these conclusions – is not known. Second, there are those who would declare that ethnic assimilation is an undesirable outcome. So it is a normative matter whether one should view the experience in the United States as a lesson of what should be done or what should be avoided. To be sure, there are those who maintain that the melting pot is something of a myth – that the nation is a salad bowl consisting of different leaves that are still separate. From that perspective, discussion of assimilation is nothing more than an old-fashioned and out-of-date perspective which did not accurately portray earlier events, let alone help us understand present-day reality.

PROCESS *VS* STATUS: LENGTH OF RESIDENCE, GENERATION, AND AGE

Consider two simple and fundamental facts. The first is that each new wave of immigration was received without enthusiasm by earlier white groups. Americans were dubious about new groups, attributing many undesirable characteristics to them. They questioned the newcomers' potential for assimilation, citizenship, values, innate ability, and their cultural characteristics. Questions arose about the danger of the newcomers destroying the quality of life in the United States. The second fact is that with regard to many attributes, the European groups' positions at the time of arrival was essentially uncorrelated with their descendants' current rank on the same characteristics. This means that one would not have predicted the present-day outcome if it was simply based on the initial situation at the time of arrival in the United States. For example, there is essentially no correlation between the relative educational and occupational skills of these groups at the time of their arrival and their positions now (Lieberson and Waters, 1988, Chapters 4 and 5).

What went wrong such that everyone was so 'off' in their evaluations of the new groups? In part this simply reflects the prejudices of the earlier settlers towards new and different peoples. It leads to underestimating the potential of these new peoples. There was a propensity – hopefully less common now – to attribute cultural differences to biological roots. In so far as these different white groups were labeled as *racial*, then there is a conclusion that they arrive with fixed genetic disadvantages that leave them with inescapable handicaps (see, for example, E.A. Ross, 1914). Also the meaning of the lowly positions occupied by immigrant groups was misunderstood – a confusion that I think operates now in many settings as well. If we ignore *desperate* situations such as famine, threats of death, oppression, and the like, groups move because the receiving country offers potential economic advantages over their current circumstances. For those living under massively inferior conditions, they will be *willing* to migrate to a country such as the United States even if the working conditions, wages, and the like are exceptionally unattractive by the standards of residents of the United States. This is because there is still a relative improvement over conditions in the homeland. All of this makes sense, but there is what I would call the *willingness–aspiration confusion*. A willingness to accept something that others would not accept does not mean absence of aspiration for more – rather it means that it is still an improvement. Since migrant groups differ in their homeland circumstances (as well as the aggregate skills that they have), the minimum jobs they will accept vary between groups, but are often unattractive by the standards of the United States. Visualize what kind of wages at present it would take to persuade a Mexican laborer to migrate to the United States as opposed to, say, a Dutch or Japanese laborer (see the discussion of the theory of intrinsic differences, Lieberson, 1980, pp. 370–4).

Beyond all of these factors, the initial view of the newcomers did not take into consideration some fundamental variables that are mandatory in any analysis of immigration. I refer specifically to the distinction between process and status. Terms such as assimilation, absorption, or acculturation refer to both a state of affairs and a process of change. This is reasonable since an unassimilated or disadvantaged group may, over a period of time move towards assimilation or the reduction of their specific disadvantages. Conclusions based on simply looking at a new group, particularly when many members are immigrants of recent origin, cannot tell us much about the processes likely to go on and the eventual trajectory of the group's position. To avoid erroneous conclusions from the observed situation of a group, it is necessary to determine trends over time. Are there shifts occurring (and, if so, what is their magnitude) when members of the group are analyzed by generation in the receiving country? (To be sure, this generational factor becomes progressively less important as one moves away from the early generations; one would hardly care to distinguish between, say, eighth versus ninth generation Americans of German origin.) Likewise, the behavior of the immigrant component should consider length of residence in the new country. Similarly, age must be considered within later generations in order to determine whether shifts are occurring over time within the same generation. (An additional issue which I will not discuss here is whether immigrants arriving from a given source are themselves changing over time.) In short, the generational and length of residence concerns are particularly important when there is a concentration of immigrants at one point in time, with there being a relatively small number of second-, third-, fourth-generation offspring present in the country. Unless the analysis is by generation, length of residence, and age, the behavior of the newcomers can overshadow important shifts that are occurring within the group. Otherwise description of an immigrant group will fail to provide the information necessary for a reasonably informed guess about the eventual outcome many years later.

The historical experience of the United States is significant because it demonstrates that these factors play a major role. They are not merely *possible* influences or minor considerations that academics enjoy making a stir about. There are many examples of the influence of either generation or length of residence. I will cite only a few here to make the point.

- Shifts in educational attainment among Japanese in the United States provides an excellent example of generational considerations. Among Americans of Japanese origin, there was a big jump between 1940 and 1960 in their median educational attainment (from 8.8 to 12.5 years of schooling for adult males; and about the same for women, 8.6 to 12.4). What could have caused this striking upward movement over such a short span? Before you exercise your imagination, consider a simple fact: just about all of the shift was to be expected back in 1940. In point of fact, in 1940 the median for Japanese origin men of American birth was 12.2 and the median for the foreign born living in the United States was 8.3. However, about 80 per cent of the Japanese origin adult men were of foreign birth in 1940 as compared with 27 per cent in 1960. There was virtually no change in the educational levels within the foreign born or within the American born components of the Japanese population during these twenty years. The foreign born went from 8.3 to 8.8, the American born went from 12.2 to 12.4, *but the total population of Japanese males rose from 8.8 to 12.5* (Lieberson, 1973, pp. 562–3). The main source of this change then was a shift in the relative size of the generations.

- Likewise, even within the immigrant group itself, the influence of length of residence is relevant but often hidden without appropriate tabulations – this is particularly the case when large numbers of new immigrants arrive and thereby overshadow changes among their predecessors of a decade or two earlier. The attainment of citizenship among immigrants is a function of length of residence in the United States. As it turns out the newer groups migrating from South-Central-Eastern Europe early in the twentieth century had lower crude rates of naturalization than the immigrants from older sources, but when length of residence is taken into account, actually it is the former who are more disposed to obtain citizenship in the United States (Lieberson, 1963, pp. 141–6). Again the patterns are concealed without considering length of residence.
- Shifts from a non-English mother tongue to an English mother tongue is essentially a generational matter – by definition adult immigrants cannot change their mother tongue after arrival. Likewise, length of residence influences the acquisition of English among immigrants, and there is a strong generational effect such that virtually all the second generation could speak English and virtually all the third generation reported English as their mother tongue.

To be sure, these changes reflect more than shifts in either the lifespan or between generations. Indeed, it is hard to ascertain the impact of major societal shifts, to say nothing of developments that pertain specifically to race and ethnic relations. Still this only supports the main contention of this section: the presence of many unassimilated immigrants *per se* tells us nothing about the future course of events even if they are: spatially segregated; distinctive in occupation, language, values, cultural orientation, religion; perhaps with low incomes and low education; looked down upon by the dominant groups; and viewed as groups that are culturally (if not genetically) inferior.

In short, although many external factors can themselves change over time and in turn impact on the positions of ethnic and racial groups, it is essential, under any circumstances, to observe groups in terms of generation, length of residence among immigrants, and age among much later generations. Issues of absorption, adaptation, political conflict, loyalties, economic contribution and the like entail two meanings that must never be confused: a status and a process.

PREDICTING THE FUTURE FROM CURRENT PROBLEMS AT THE TIME OF ARRIVAL: SOME LESSONS FROM THE UNITED STATES

This view has important implications for thinking about contemporary patterns. It is misleading to compare a country early in the immigration cycle (and thus currently or recently receiving a large stream of newcomers) with the end product in a nation that received sizable immigration at a much earlier time. Such comparisons are not analogous to comparing apples with oranges – rather they are analogous to comparing newly planted apple trees with ones that were planted many years earlier. Using the terminology described previously, we are in danger of comparing the initial immigrant generation in one country with behavior occurring in another country among those who are many generations removed from their immigrant ancestors.

However, there is much to be learned from the successful European migration to the United States that occurred many decades ago. By considering conditions at the outset, we realize that the initial outlook as well as the initial conflicts were not particularly good predictors of what occurred later. Could the same be the case for the prognosis made in other countries that is based solely on the early period of immigration? In this sense, in light of the successful absorption of European immigrants in the United States, consider what the new apple trees looked like when they were first planted.

Large-scale immigration to the United States was fraught with problems; there was antipathy towards each of the new groups and many were pessimistic about the long-term consequences for the nation. In the outstanding review of immigration to the United States, Jones (1960, p. 44) observes, 'At one time or another, immigrants of practically every non-English stock incurred the open hostility of earlier comers'. Consider, for example, the reception early in the eighteenth century towards the Scotch-Irish and German immigrants. Jones goes on to document the suspicions, the prejudices, and the many cultural features of these groups that earlier settlers found offensive (pp. 44ff), and cites the alarm expressed by Benjamin Franklin towards the growing number and influence of Germans in Pennsylvania (p. 48). The mid-nineteenth century is marked by the arrival of many Roman Catholics in a nation that had hitherto been largely (but by no means exclusively) populated by Protestants. This was particularly frightening to many who feared at that time that America would thereby contain within it a population taking orders from the Pope and seeking to overthrow the fundamental political and social tenets which separated the United States from much of Europe (see, for example, the reception towards the Irish described in Handlin, 1959). The response was no less virulent to the arrival of extraordinary numbers of non-English speaking immigrants from South, Central, and Eastern Europe beginning late in the nineteenth century and on through the first few decades of the twentieth. Indeed, the latter eventually led nativists to succeed in both restricting the numbers of immigrants allowed into the United States as well as setting quotas on their origins, which favored Northwestern European origins (see Higham, 1955; Handlin, 1957; Lieberson, 1980).

I have not mentioned the labor strife, the employment handicaps, the pain and suffering, the social disorganization, the prejudice and discrimination, the intergenerational anguishes, the difficulties of adaptation, and the like. You can be sure they were substantial, occurring as they did in periods when there was relatively little in the way of government programs to provide medical care, housing, relief, and so on. Considering how the United States at present is so far behind Western Europe in social programs, just imagine what it must have been like in this earlier period. Keep in mind that Blacks faced a massively more difficult situation (see Lieberson, 1970 for a comparison). However, we should not ignore the conflict, hardships, and uncertainties existing with regard to the long-term impact of the migrations from European sources.

In effect, the situation among descendants of immigrants need not represent conditions at the time of immigration. To assume that what *is*, always *was*, I would call the *fallacy of historical circularity*. One must independently measure conditions in each period, rather than use current patterns to incorrectly infer historical conditions. In the United States, for example, blacks are more segregated residentially than are the European groups from South-Central-Eastern Europe. This was not always the case; in an earlier period many of the European groups were more segregated than blacks (see Lieberson, 1963, tables 42 and 43; 1980, Chapter 9). Likewise, the amount of wealth and the educational levels of Jews at the time of arrival are remarkably different from their current situation (Lieberson, 1963, table 16); and the disposition of blacks towards schooling in the postbellum period is not to be inferred from contemporary patterns in America's central cities (Lieberson, 1980, Chapters 6–8). Indeed, even the thinking about these groups changed through the years; earlier in the twentieth century what we now call 'ethnic groups' were viewed as distinctive races operating under unalterable biological disadvantages (see Ross, 1914; Handlin, 1957, Chapter 5). Immigration history in the United States provides an important lesson. Namely, there was little justification for using the initial problems faced by the immigrants to draw pessimistic long-term conclusions about either the group or American society. Among immigrant groups coming earlier in this century, there is often no correlation between the past and present for such important features as: education, occupation, income, and some cultural attributes (Lieberson and Waters, 1988, Chapters 4 and 5; Waters and Lieberson, 1992). Again the point is that initial conditions need not be a particularly good predictor of the 'final' outcome, that is, the outcome some decades and generations later. Moreover, it also follows that there is an error in looking at the present state of ethnic relations and assuming it always was that way.

WHAT CAUSED THIS SUCCESS?: THE ROLE OF GOVERNMENT

Why did assimilation work so well for European immigrants in the United States whereas other countries have difficulty in absorbing various ethnic and racial populations? Given the importance presently attached to governmental policies in most nations with significant immigration, the relatively passive and inactive role of the Federal Government during the heyday of European immigration provides a striking contrast. This was the case even though there was considerable conflict and agitation among the existing population.

I can only think of a few major governmental policies that were primarily (or largely) directed at the immigrant groups or their offspring. Free public education was viewed in the United States as a highly admired social good for all whites. Beyond this, it had special functions for the immigrants and their children. Education was a means for providing some minimal steps in helping the immigrants to help themselves (through night school where they could learn English and acquire the knowledge necessary to become citizens). Particularly important was the role of education in thoroughly Americanizing the offspring of the immigrants. Through education they would: become loyal to the nation ('loyalty' is always of concern in multiethnic nations); acquire English; become informed citizens and voters by learning the history and political principles of the nation; learn appropriate forms of behavior, ranging from cleanliness, to manners, to honesty, to hard work and appreciation of finer things; and they would prepare to become productive members of the society and be good parents. Although the value of a good education was seen as appropriate for all white Americans, the minimal legislation for mandatory school attendance suggests a special concern with keeping the children of immigrants in school (see Lieberson, 1980, pp. 136–7). To be sure these state and local laws were not always rigorously enforced (see, for example, Perlmann, 1988, pp. 15–17, 24).

Unlike virtually all nations, for a long time there were minimal governmental regulations about the admission of European immigrants in the United States. Before 1882, the federal government played essentially no role, except taking a count of the number of entrants and setting certain minimal standards for living conditions on ships carrying immigrants (see Higham, 1955, pp. 42–4). That was all! In the years following, there were some efforts to be moderately selective about the immigrants, with minimal health restrictions, moral requirements, and eventually a literacy test. It was not until the 1920s that serious restrictions were introduced in both the numbers and sources from within Europe (see Lieberson, 1970, pp. 28–30). A virtual open-admission policy for Europeans existed throughout this period. Unlike many nations, there was no consideration of: wealth, potential work skills, destination in the United States, relatives in the nation, and the like. (The situation for Asians and Blacks was radically different.)

There is one last governmental matter to consider, and it is really more of a constitutional matter than a question of policy or administration. Citizenship in the United States, with all rights and privileges, is automatically given to all persons born in the country, regardless of origin. In addition, it is relatively easy for immigrants themselves to become citizens. Indeed, even without becoming a naturalized citizen, an immigrant upon setting foot in the United States (assuming it was a legal entry and documents were truthful) has at that moment all rights and privileges afforded descendants of the Mayflower – other than running for the Presidency or voting (and the latter is easily possible with the attainment of naturalized citizenship). To be sure, we could devote more than one book citing examples of situations where the theory of full equality did not apply in practice. (Even the theory did not hold for Asian immigrants who faced special obstacles in becoming a naturalized citizen, owning land, and so forth. The deviations are even more extreme for Blacks in the United States.). Returning to the Europeans, however, obtaining citizenship is significantly unhampered – a constitutional provision that is not unique to the United States, but is hardly universal now, let alone in this earlier period (see, for example, Brubaker, 1992). Beyond this, immigrants themselves enjoy an exceptional range of rights at the outset, with some additional ones obtained after becoming naturalized (for excellent reviews, see Schuck, 1992; Liebman, 1992).

How important are these governmental factors for understanding the exceptional outcome in the United States? It is not easy to answer – at least if the standards of rigorous social research are applied one would need data on many nations (see Lieberson, 1991). We can consider the educational factor shortly when social mobility is discussed. Even more difficult is deciding about the lack of *official* distinctions between the groups and the ease of citizenship and equality (in theory, at least) before the law. I speculate that the constitutional equality is particularly significant. In theory, and to a large degree in practice, the government of the United States was a friend of immigrants and their children – not an enemy. At any rate, when we contrast these conditions with those faced in the highly oppressive societies that many emigrated from, the attraction of the new nation must have been enormous. There was enough discrimination to go around for the Europeans, but at least it was not official in nature. Government was intrinsically a *good*; practices may have been disappointing at times, but it was not because of some intrinsic problem with the construction of the government or its official policies. (Incidentally, this is in sharp contrast with the situation for Blacks in the United States where, until the era of civil rights legislation only a few decades ago, governments of all sorts were in varying degrees likely to be enemies rather than friends.)

There is another side to the government issue, one which is even more important: we do see that absorption took place at a very satisfactory pace *without* the benefit of many governmental actions. The historical pattern provides a model which suggests minimum governmental policies are necessary to carry out a goal of settlement and absorption. This contrasts with many contemporary settings that are at present saturated with governmental programs to accomplish the very same end. What are the implications when large-scale immigration is presently accompanied by disruption and conflict? Should one say that absorption took place without the benefit of government policies *or* because there were minimal government policies? If the latter is the case, is the model appropriate since we now live in a period where the role of government has expanded and hence there are demands for policies that were unimaginable earlier? Of course, the second point is more complex because there is the question of *which* policies: policies which include the immigrant groups and their offspring by virtue of their being in the nation; or policies directed specifically at the immigrants and their offspring (granted that the distinction is sometimes arbitrary since a universalistic policy will differentially impact on immigrants if they are concentrated in certain domains). To use a contemporary American example, consider how a policy about farm workers or domestic help would disproportionately affect certain immigrant groups. In any case, there are serious questions raised about the necessity and purpose of policies geared to specific groups, as contrasted with the society as a whole. Put in a broad terms, there are *four* major issues all nations face in dealing with immigrant groups and their children: (1) how to influence the response of the groups to the new nation, including a variety of dimensions here such as political loyalty, assimilation, economic participation, and language behavior; (2) there are the distinctive strains in the initial adjustment after migrating to a different society; (3) there is the impact on the existing population, ranging from questions of competition for jobs, disruption of the existing social, political and economic order, conflicts, and the like; (4) and there are issues of how many immigrants are to be allowed, from what sources, and using what criteria such as family reunions, skills, wealth, education, and even whether they are to be permitted temporary, as opposed to permanent, residence. (The last dimension is not relevant for Israel, since there is a fundamental and unalterable policy regarding the admission of Jews.) In evaluating policies designed to accomplish these goals, one has to consider an issue rarely addressed in social research, although it is commonplace in some domains of research such as work on pharmaceuticals. Namely: in proposing policies about immigrant groups, one has to consider not only the consequences for the problem they address, but also their consequences for other domains of immigrant behavior. Put another way, if a governmental policy is introduced to address a certain social concern or problem, and if there is confidence that the policy will move events in a certain direction that otherwise would not occur or would occur at a significantly slower pace (note that these questions are not so easy to answer), there is still the question of side effects which can be even more damaging to the overall goals. In the drug example, it is easy to visualize a drug which successfully addresses a patient's problem (say severe and frequent headaches) but also over a period of time causes more harm than good by creating exceptionally undesirable side effects (say heart attacks or cancer). Even here we would want to know the risk/reward ratio, that is, the degree of increased risk of heart attack versus the degree of increased benefit from the reduction of headaches. Except for drugs designed to address a certain and immediate death, the side effect issue is a very serious one. Likewise, proposed governmental policies have to consider not only their consequences for the social problem, but also their consequences for other issues of immigrant absorption and societal impact.

The drug analogy has two other implications for government policies. First, are there policies designed to deal with problems that are not problems, that is, conditions which will in their own way change over time? Keep in mind the discussion earlier of change *vs* status, and generational shifts. Second, in analyzing the cause of a problem, we have to keep in mind the possibility of asymmetrical causal processes. If we can determine what factor(s) cause a problem, it does not follow that policies designed to reverse those variables will eradicate the problem. Events have lives of their own such that, once established, they will continue even after elimination of their initial cause. It can take different causal factors to shift it.

Most important of all, is the side-effect question; whether policies designed to address a problem can cause more difficulties than they resolve. Consider the residential segregation of Jewish immigrants to the United States earlier in this century. Jews had high levels of segregation, when compared to other European groups. Is this good or bad from the point of view of the receiving country and their concerns for assimilation and absorption? We have no difficulty recognizing a complicated linkage between segregation and assimilation; on the one hand, high segregation will reduce assimilation and make the group more visible to others; on the other hand, segregation will facilitate a group's adaptation to the stresses and strains of immigrating to a new and different setting. Segregation, for example, will facilitate the adjustment of those unable to speak the new nation's language; at the same time, it will reduce the need to learn the language. On this score, is it necessarily advisable for a government to discourage or reduce residential segregation?

IF NOT GOVERNMENT, THEN WHAT?

If the extraordinary adjustment of European groups occurred in the absence of (or perhaps one should say 'without handicap of') extensive governmental programs, what then are the key factors facilitating this remarkable history? I believe there are six major factors.

First, even if immigrant groups initially enter the country as subordinates – at least in terms of their socioeconomic positions *vis à vis* the earlier immigrants – keep in mind that they are voluntary migrants who *choose* to come to the United States. They are not conquered people and they are not slaves. Usually they migrate because of *economic* motives, either to better their own lives and/or to better the lives of their children. There is strong evidence that these conditions lead to far more rapid forms of assimilation than is the case for conquered peoples (see Lieberson, 1961). Likewise, in Canada, contrast the adoption of English among immigrants arriving after British conquest with the rates of shift among various native groups or the French Canadians who were conquered by the British (Lieberson, Dalto and Johnston, 1975, pp. 56–7).

Second, the mobility potential of the society is a critical feature. The immigrant groups are either initially better off than they were in their homeland or have prospects for improvement. The exceptional socioeconomic mobility potential in the society generates assimilation since there are substantial pecuniary, political, and social rewards available to those change. This rapid intergenerational shift, despite the resistance from parents on at least some dimensions, helps undermine the way of life brought over by the immigrants.

Third, there is *relative* freedom to pursue earlier customs – hence shifts are not *imposed* through authoritarian rules, but to a certain degree are a matter of choice – albeit with many incentives. Hence the maintenance of old customs does not get involved with ethnic–political statements against the oppression of the group. The groups are voluntary participants in the society, and the members are not simply forced to give up their old ways. There are costs in not doing so, but it is an option one can have if willing to pay these costs – it is not a prohibition.

Fourth, there is relative neglect of the groups as groups. For example, such matters as residential segregation within cities or broader forms of spatial concentration within states or subparts of states are not controlled by legislation or formal restrictions. The relative weakness of the central government through much of this period – at least in comparison with many nations – means relative neglect of local political and social developments. There is no national policy, for example, about a given ethnic group attaining voting control of a city or state. It was a matter of conflict *within* a city or state to be resolved through the customary forms of competitive politics and manipulation.

Fifth, since there has never been a restriction on emigration from the United States, it is relatively easy for the disaffected or disappointed to leave. Accordingly, immigrants had an escape valve back to the country of origin or to any other place that would accept them.

Finally, there is the relative absence of repression in the United States – at least compared to many of the nations from which these groups migrated. Dispositions towards differential treatment of the newcomers existed throughout, but never became a broad, long-lasting, formal national policy, as was the case for the differential treatment of Blacks and American Indians.

Approaching the matter from a somewhat different perspective, Greenfeld (1992, p. 435) observes: 'The reasons for the immigrants' loyalty to America and the process in which it was formed [is] ... derived from the uplifting, dignifying effects of liberty and equality, the exhilarating lure of opportunity, and the enjoyment or even the expectation of a greater prosperity'.

ALTERNATIVE INTERPRETATIONS

It could be argued that the aforementioned analysis does not consider a variety of idiosyncratic factors – unique to the United States at that particular place and time – that makes this analysis irrelevant to the United States at present, let alone contemporary immigration issues faced elsewhere (for example, Horowitz, 1992). What are some of these 'idiosyncratic' factors that might *really* explain the earlier experience in the United States? Did the white–black cleavage in the United States play a role in eventually minimizing the distinctions between white groups? Did the shifts in immigration sources impact on assimilation (by reducing the number of newcomers) and likewise make descendants of the earlier immigrants appear relatively less alien? Related to this, did the shutting down of immigration from South-Central-Eastern Europe contribute to the relatively rapid assimilation of the immigrants and their descendants from these sources? Is there something about the looser Federal system in the United States or the political parties of the country being more receptive to the interests of these groups? These are all plausible considerations, but keep in mind that the question is whether they are factors of critical importance in explaining the widely recognized outcome in the United States. Nations differ on a wide variety of attributes, and hence it is always possible to point to some other feature and claim it is the critical one. By *critical*, I mean that without one or more of these factors, the outcome would have been radically different.

The evidence does not appear to support any of these alternative interpretations as being critical in accounting for the patterns observed in the United States. First, there are other nations which have also successfully absorbed – in relatively rapid fashion – immigrants from diverse sources. I will consider the alternative arguments in the order presented above. Because the black population of the United States ranks lower in the queue than these white groups, it is likely that this helped accelerate the gains of immigrants and their children. However, it is unlikely that this is critical for the eventual outcome experienced by these white immigrant groups in the United States. The black–white cleavage can hardly account for the outcome in Canada (where Blacks were a numerically minor population) and really not in Australia where the earlier white settlers from the British

Isles hardly needed the support of later immigrants to deal with Aborigines. Yet the immigrant patterns found in the United States also occur in these countries as well (for a striking empirical analysis of the similarities between the United States and Canada on ethnic outcomes, see Reitz and Breton, 1994). What would be the state of affairs in the United States if immigration from South-Central-Eastern European groups had not been shut down beginning in 1924? This is, of course, a counterfactual question. However, we do know that shifts in sources can hardly account for the outcome in the United States of some other groups: consider that Americans of German origin are one of the largest origin groups in the nation (indeed, one could even make a case that they are the largest). There is no question about their assimilation within the United States or their acceptance (ignoring the periods surrounding the two world wars). Yet there was a sizable flow from this source for much longer than the 40 year period experienced by immigrants from South-Central-Eastern Europe. Likewise, migration from Ireland to the United States occurred for a long span, generating a major component of the population of the United States, without any long-term consequences for assimilation and acceptance (despite difficulties and obstacles initially faced by the group). The economic, political, educational and social incentives for mastery of English makes it is difficult for me to imagine there would be intergenerational maintenance of the Italian language, say, if larger numbers were still flowing into the United States from Italy. The receptivity of political parties to the interests of these diverse ethnic populations misses the point. If a nation is a democracy and if it is relatively easy for immigrants to become citizens (and, in any case, their children born in the receiving country are automatically citizens), then of course one or more political parties will address the interests and concerns of these voters. This is the same as we would expect in a democracy that responds to the interests of farmers, workers, bankers, physicians, or any other group with many voters and/or able to deliver money and/or generate media support and/or with strong ties to the political world. The arrival of immigrant groups often meets strong political opposition and anxiety and a certain amount of wobbling away from democratic processes, but there are built-in forces that generate more favorable responses to these groups. The United States is not unique on this score; we can expect this from any nation which stays the course as a democracy with an underlying recognition of individual rights that require tolerance – even if begrudging – of each ethnic group's distinctive features.

Briefly, subject to the point where there is sufficient data to permit a rigorous quantitative cross-national historical comparison, there is reason to believe that the United States in this earlier period illustrates the operation of forces which are not inherently unique to that time and place. Consequently, the analysis has analytical and policy implications for thinking about contemporary immigration to any multiethnic setting – a matter considered below.

IMPLICATIONS AND SUGGESTIONS

These observations about earlier immigration from Europe to the United States have important implications for other nations experiencing substantial immigration.

1. The outcome in the United States was extremely successful, benefiting both the migrants and the receiving nation. But this was not foreseeable as the immigrants were arriving in large numbers. Indeed, the potential impact of each new immigrant group generated anxiety and concern in the United States. At the very least, one should not confuse the initial responses to new immigrant movements with a sound prediction of the outcome. For many important socioeconomic characteristics, there are minimal correlations between the initial positions of each group and the outcome some generations later.
2. Furthermore, in evaluating the current situation, one has to deal with issues of generation, length of residence, and age. Nothing can be said about the long-term outlook unless these influences are taken into account. Such factors can suggest a trajectory quite different from the initial gross comparisons between immigrants and older residents from other sources.
3. To an exceptional degree, there was a laissez-faire system in the United States. This had its benefits and its liabilities. There was relatively little sense in the state imposing its will on the immigrants and their children in improper ways that might create ethnic consciousness. Ironically, a more aggressive set of policies could even backfire. In the case of residential segregation, for example, governmental passivity served to maintain segregation which, in turn, no doubt affected ethnic consciousness. Nevertheless, segregation and ethnic consciousness does decline over time. It is at least conceivable that governmental efforts to eliminate voluntary forms of immigrant self-segregation could have created more of a long-term problem than this more passive policy (this is separate from segregation imposed by the dominant group itself, as is the case for the segregation of blacks).

4. Conflict is not necessarily a sign of failure. It does not mean that the society is failing if there are conflicts between different ethnic interests within the society. Why should there not be conflict between these interest groups any differently than those between other interest groups? (Obviously, I exclude physical terror, harassment, or danger.) In turn, there can be over-reactions to conflicts that do more harm than good. This is a great dilemma in any multinational country seeking to maintain stability and loyalty. There is a danger in doing nothing, but there is also a danger in policies which do more harm than good by actually arousing ethnic–political feelings (see the classic analysis by the Royal Institute, 1939).
5. The question is raised as to whether any array of government policies directed towards the adjustment of immigrants is all that beneficial. Of course, a government cannot ignore contemporary standards of a modern society, for example, health, sufficient food, unemployment, housing standards, availability of education for those not able to pay, and minimizing other disadvantages of that nature. Beyond dealing with these minimal living standards operating in the society, is there anything to be said for neglect? Are there government policies intended to affect immigrant groups and their children that do more harm than good? If the mobility potential of the United States was a critical feature in generating the adaptation of immigrants and their descendants, then societies may be better off worrying about general issues of the economy and mobility rather than specific issues of assimilation and the like.

Note

1. Several of the problems discussed in this chapter benefited from helpful discussions with Joel Perlmann.

References

Brubaker, Rogers (1992) *Citizenship and Nationhood in France and Germany* (Cambridge, Massachusetts: Harvard University Press).
Greenfeld, Liah (1992) *Nationalism: Five Roads to Modernity* (Cambridge, Mass: Harvard University Press).

Handlin, Oscar (1957) *Race and Nationality in American Life* (Garden City, New York: Doubleday Anchor Books).
—— (1959) *Boston's Immigrants: A Study in Acculturation*, revised edn (Cambridge, Massachusetts: Belknap Press of Harvard University Press).
Higham, John (1955) *Strangers in the Land: Patterns of American Nativism, 1860–1925* (New Brunswick, New Jersey: Rutgers University Press).
Horowitz, Donald L. (1992) 'Immigration and Group Relations in France and America', in Donald L. Horowitz and Gérard Noiriel (eds), *Immigrants in Two Democracies: French and American Experience* (New York: New York University Press).
Jones, Maldwyn Allen (1960) *American Immigration* (Chicago: University of Chicago Press).
Lieberson, Stanley (1961) 'A Societal Theory of Race and Ethnic Relations', *American Sociological Review*, 26: pp. 902–10.
—— (1963) *Ethnic Patterns in American Cities* (New York: The Free Press of Glencoe).
—— (1973) 'Generational Differences Among Blacks in the North', *American Journal of Sociology*, 79: pp. 550–65.
—— (1980) *A Piece of the Pie: Blacks and White Immigrants Since 1880* (Berkeley and Los Angeles: University of California Press).
—— (1985) *Making It Count: The Improvement of Social Research and Theory* (Berkeley and Los Angeles: University of California Press).
—— (1991) 'Small N's and Big Conclusions: An Examination of the Reasoning in Comparative Studies Based on a Small Number of Cases' *Social Forces*, 70: pp. 307–20. Reprinted in Charles C. Ragin and Howard S. Becker (eds) (1992), *What is a Case?: Exploring the Foundations of Social Inquiry* (New York: Cambridge University Press).
—— (1992) 'Socioeconomic Attainment', in Donald L. Horowitz and Gérard Noiriel (eds), *Immigrants in Two Democracies: French and American Experience* (New York: New York University Press).
——, Guy Dalto, and Mary Ellen Johnston (1975) 'The Course of Mother Tongue Diversity in Nations', *American Journal of Sociology*, 81: pp. 34–61.
——, and Mary C. Waters (1988) *From Many Strands: Ethnic and Racial Groups in Contemporary America* (New York: Russell Sage Foundation).
Liebman, Lance (1992) 'Immigration Status and American Law: The Several Versions of Antidiscrimination Doctrine', in Donald L. Horowitz and Gérard Noiriel (eds), *Immigrants in Two Democracies: French and American Experience* (New York: New York University Press).
Perlmann, Joel (1988) *Ethnic Differences: Schooling and Social Structure Among the Irish, Italians, Jews, and Blacks in an American City, 1880–1935* (New York: Cambridge University Press).
Reitz, Jeffrey G. and Raymond Breton (1994) *The Illusion of Difference: Realities of Ethnicity in Canada and the United States* (Toronto: C.D. Howe Institute).
Ross, Edward Alsworth (1914) *The Old World in the New* (New York: Century).
Royal Institute of International Affairs (1939) *Nationalism* (Oxford: Oxford University Press).
Schuck, Peter H. (1992) 'Immigration, Refugee, and Citizenship Law in the United States', in Donald L. Horowitz and Gérard Noiriel (eds), *Immigrants in Two*

Democracies: French and American Experience (New York: New York University Press).

Waters, Mary C. and Stanley Lieberson (1992) 'Ethnic Differences in Education: Current Patterns and Historical Roots', in Abraham Yogev (ed.), *International Perspectives on Education and Society*, 2: 171–187 (Greenwich, Conn.: JAI Press).

11 Immigration and Settlement in Australia: An Overview and Critique of Multiculturalism

Laksiri Jayasuriya

INTRODUCTION

Australia, being a settler society, an immigrant-receiving country from its inception, was until recently, firmly committed to an ideology of settlement which ensured racial and cultural homogeneity. The firm belief in 'one country, one nation', was achieved by a strong insistence on 'anglo-conformity', embodying the cultural mores and national characteristics of the early settlers, the charter groups. This close link between immigration and settlement has become problematic with the influx of waves of immigrants from non-traditional source-countries and the accompanying new philosophy of settlement, based on cultural pluralism and commonly labelled 'multiculturalism'. The ongoing public debate and controversy in Australia[1] about immigration has drawn attention to the problematic nature of the disjunction between policies of recruitment and settlement, and equally to the dilemmas confronting multiculturalism as a philosophy of settlement, and a 'policy regime' (Rein, 1976). In a world increasingly engulfed in ethnic conflicts and tensions arising from migration, the way in which this new policy of 'multiculturalism' developed in the short space of less than two decades represents a success story of migrant settlement worth recounting (see Jayasuriya, 1987; Castles et al., 1990; Foster and Stockley, 1988)).

Following a brief historical account of immigration policy and attitudes to migrants, the chapter focuses on the strengths and limitations of multiculturalism as an experiment in social engineering. It argues that Australian multiculturalism as a form of cultural pluralism may have outlived its utility and significance as a marshalling ideology of settlement, and brought to the fore the inherent contradictions and limitations in its theory and practice. Australian multiculturalism, it is suggested, is in need of a fresh statement of its rationale to be more consistent with the emerging social and political realities confronting Australia as a pluralistic society exposed to the globalization of the world economy.

EARLY ATTITUDES TO MIGRANTS

Immigration has been, as Jupp (1984, p. 3) rightly observes, 'a constant theme in Australian history since 1788 but has often been curiously overlooked or understressed by historians'. Immigrants make up over 20 per cent of the population, and, of these, more than half are of non-British origin. But, more importantly, immigrants and their offspring, be they second or third generations of migrant origin, constitute nearly 40 per cent of the Australian population, and account for just over half the population growth since 1945.

Since the earliest days, the economic factors, particularly the labour and human resource needs of a developing society, have been overriding, though not the only, determinants of this carefully orchestrated policy of immigration. During the early period of settlement, Australia was a 'vast half-occupied country overrun by invaders of British stock' (Hancock, 1940) seeking economic gain and material prosperity for themselves in a new and alien environment. Until the mass immigration of the post-World War II period, there was in force a strict policy of controlled and selective immigration which gave preference to those of British stock, and excluded non-European settlers, mainly Asian immigrants. The racist 'white Australia' policy and the philosophy of 'total assimilation' or 'anglo' conformity, was intended to preserve Australia as a strong cohesive white settlement.[2]

In the 1950s, because of acute labour shortages and other external pressures (e.g., influx of refugees from war-torn Europe), Australia departed from its traditional preference for British migrants by including a programme of assisted immigration from Europe. There was, however, no relaxation of the philosophy of settlement based on hardline assimilationism. The overriding concern was to match these new European migrants with the traditional ethos of 'anglo-conformity' to ensure that they would, within a short space of time, integrate easily into an anglo-celtic environment.

It is clear that, as a result of the mass migration of the 1950s, Australia has become a more cosmopolitan, polyethnic society in which immigrants and their offspring have been the main contributors to population growth.

Immigration accounts for approximately 60 per cent of the growth of the work force. Furthermore, while in 1947 only a tenth of the population was born overseas and less than 3 per cent were of non-British origin, by the 1990s nearly a fifth was born overseas and more than half of the overseas-born were of non-British origin. The number of persons born in the UK and Ireland, as a percentage of all persons born overseas, fell from 73.0 per cent in 1947 to 29.5 per cent in 1991. This demographic shift highlights a marked decline in the dominance of the Australian or British-born 'anglo' element, which has been reduced from just over 97 per cent in 1947 to 85 per cent in 1991; and, this all the more significant because the Australian-born include second/third generations of ethnic origin who account for approximately 20 per cent of the population. For this reason, a significant feature of the 1990s is the increasing presence of second- and third-generation Australians of 'ethnic' origin.[3]

In this radical demographic transformation what is more noticeable is the fact that the 'Asian' element has continued to grow (see Jayasuriya and Sang, 1990). The nature and extent of the so-called 'asianisation' of the Australian population depends on whether one adopts a broad or narrow characterization of what is understood by the label 'Asian'. The broad definition of 'Asian', as used by the Australian Bureau of Statistics (ABS) includes settlers from West Asia and the Middle East. Thus migrants from Cyprus, Turkey, Lebanon and Israel are included in the 'Asian' intake. The narrower definition, the one adopted by the Department of Immigration excludes West Asia and Middle East. The 'Asian' element now ranges from 6 per cent (broadly) to 3 per cent (narrowly) of the total Australian population, and it is estimated that Asian-born residents have increased in absolute numbers by 70 per cent between 1986 and 1991 (ABS, 1991).

By careful government regulation, and skilful management of policies, Australia has been able to settle these new migrants with the least amount of disruption. During the early waves of European migration in the 1950s and 1960s, the state employed two major policy strategies, *viz* dispersal and non-confrontation, to achieve the objectives of total assimilation. The former, the policy of dispersal, was intended to ensure the growth of ethnic or migrant enclaves; and, the latter strategy, to gain community and social support for new settlers (cf. the establishment of Good Neighbour Councils to assist in the settlement of migrants). The success of these policies was also greatly facilitated by the favourable economic climate that prevailed during the 1960s and well into the 1970s, permitting high levels of growth and near full employment.

However, it soon became apparent that the hardline assimilationist policy, that is, one of total assimilation into the ethos and practices of the host society was impractical and unrealistic. There was growing evidence (see Martin, 1978) of the adverse social effects of these policies (e.g., increased alienation, high return rates, mental illness, etc.). The social costs incurred by this mode of incorporation of migrants clearly showed that these policies were highly dysfunctional and ill-suited to the needs of the migrants and society as a whole (Castles *et al.*, 1990). With a sense of realism and pragmatism characteristic of Australian public life, official policy relating to migrant settlement was modified such that assimilation was now regarded as a two-stage process. In the first stage, there was to be a modest relaxation of attitudes towards members from other cultures, 'races' and ethnic groups in the hope that at a later point in time they, or their offspring, would be 'assimilated'. The accommodation of difference afforded in these early stages was conditional in that some degree of assimilation was inevitable in this process of adaptation (e.g., acceptance of the core institutions of society such as the constitution, legal system and English as the official language). In this two-stage view of assimilation, the expectation was that eventually, within the same generation or at least by the next generation, these newcomers would become 'integrated' or 'assimilated' into the institutions and practices of the new society through some 'melting pot' process.

MULTICULTURALISM AS CULTURAL PLURALISM

This modest but significant shift in settlement policy, first initiated in the late 1960s by a conservative Liberal government, was consolidated by the reformist Whitlam's Labor Government of 1972 which introduced a policy of 'multiculturalism'. The notion of multiculturalism in its normative sense, as it evolved in the 1970s and 1980s, sought to replace the rigid, monocultural assimilationism of the 1950s and 1960s with a more tolerant and permissive attitude to the cultural origins of new settlers. The term 'multicultural', itself was borrowed from Canada, and employed as a shorthand way of characterising the doctrine of cultural pluralism.[4] In essence, it meant that 'variant cultures can flourish peacefully side by side' (Wirth 1945), provided there was an acceptance of the commonalities of society, such as those embodied in the political and legal system. It was also of considerable significance that this policy shift coincided with a radical change in recruitment policy. The new Labor government in 1972 rescinded the 'White Australia' policy which had hitherto excluded the entry of non-Europeans as permanent settlers, and established a non-discriminatory policy of migrant recruitment.

The adoption of multiculturalism as a form of cultural pluralism which imposes limits on the degree of acceptable differentiations, draws pointed attention to the veritable paradox of pluralism, namely, that 'differences' cannot flourish without some degree of structural differentiation. With the acceptance of cultural differences, the concepts of *culture* – and more significantly – *ethnicity*, were introduced for the first time into the language of political discourse as public policy was modified to incorporate aspects of 'differences' (e.g., by teaching migrant languages, introducing interpreter services for migrants, etc.). At the same time, ethnic groups and organizations were recognized as having a legitimate role to play in facilitating the adaptation of immigrants within a new environment. Thus, not surprisingly, the tensions created by the paradox of pluralism, especially that ethnic 'structures' may compete with mainstream institutions, were regarded as a potential threat to social cohesion and stability (Jayasuriya, 1984; 1990c).

From the outset, multiculturalism, as a form of cultural pluralism, employed the concept of 'culture' and the related notions of 'ethnic groups' and 'ethnicity' (Jakubowicz, 1981; Bottomley, 1988) to capture the diversity of Australian society (de Lepervanche, 1984). Thus, *ethnicity* – as socially constructed by the definers of public policy – and its cognate notion of *ethnic identity* became central elements in the language of public discourse relating to multiculturalism. However, a distinctive feature of Australian multiculturalism was that ethnicity was employed more in its *expressive* rather than its *instrumental* sense. Whereas the expressive dimension of ethnicity highlights 'life styles', and the affective aspects of ethnicity such as the need for emotional security, a sense of self-esteem and self-confidence, the more instrumental dimensions focus on the material aspects of living, such as the need for economic and social security, power and resources to determine one's 'life-chances'. Concurrently, with this approach, the term 'culture', intrinsic to the notion of ethnicity and often treated as the unproblematic centrepiece of this mode of analysis, was also interpreted in idealist terms. This approach to culture as a pre-given 'informing spirit' is in sharp contrast to the materialist view of culture advocated by Williams (1983), Jakubowicz (1981), de Lepervanche and Bottomley (1988) and others. These theorists stress the shared meanings and experience of individuals as part of 'lived experience' which serves to provide a more flexible and dynamic view of culture, as constituted social experiences capable of adjusting to new and changing circumstances.

In policy terms, the effect of this theorizing has been the adoption of a 'culturalist' approach to multiculturalism most clearly evident in policy initiatives in the field of multicultural education, media and communication. This 'culturalist multiculturalism' was given formal endorsement by the Fraser government which replaced the Labor administration of 1972, when it introduced its new policies of migrant settlement based on an important report, the Galbally Report (Dept of Labour and Immigration, 1978). Consequently policy initiatives in the domain of language maintenance through ethnic (community) languages, media and communication (e.g., the establishment of multicultural television and ethnic radio) were accorded high priority.

Despite the obvious attraction of cultural pluralism as a means of generating greater tolerance and acceptance of 'difference', the difficulties surrounding cultural pluralism were recognized from the outset by social-policy analysts and policy-makers alike (see Lippman Report, Department of Labour and Immigration, 1975; Martin, 1978). Its inherent contradictions and tensions, are chiefly two-fold: the first surrounds the characterization of the notions of *culture, ethnicity* and *identity*, and in particular, the polarization around the expressive and instrumental dimensions of ethnicity; the second concerns the degree of particularist differentiation (structural pluralism) that is permissible without damaging social cohesion, or the integrity and moral order of society (Martin, 1978; Bullivant, 1983; Encel, 1986). The seeds of the contradictions and tensions inherent in the philosophy of cultural pluralism reside in the ethnicity/identity model of multiculturalism. It is these shortcomings which have come to the fore in the face of various critiques (see Foster and Stockley, 1988, for documentation) of multiculturalism; and, it is clear that the fate of multiculturalism will be judged to a large extent by the responses to these two problematic issues (see Jayasuriya, 1990c).

There is no doubt however, that the 'ethnic/identity' model of multiculturalism, promoted and legitimized by the State, has proved eminently functional to newcomers as well as to the dominant groups. For the former, it was a first generation strategy which facilitated the processes of migrant adaptation by providing much needed social support, self-respect and dignity for the culturally different (Jayasuriya, 1984). Above all, it provided a 'psychic shelter' which facilitated the processes of migrant adaptation. Additionally this model as a policy regime, while giving legitimacy to the strivings of these new groups for equality of status, and of respect, was also attractive and functional to the dominant groups by containing the strivings of members of ethnic groups to the private rather than the public domain. By adopting a policy which focused on privatized 'lifestyles', promoting linguistic pluralism and communication as the key to wellbeing and adaptation, the competitive strivings of these groups were effectively diminished. This proved to be an effective means of curtailing their social and political participation, mediating class antagonisms, and in maintaining the dominance and the hegemonic influence of the dominant groups in society (see Castles *et al.*, 1990; Collins, 1988; Lever Tracy and Quinlan, 1988).

Although the migrant contribution to economic growth and capital accumulation was of critical importance to the development of Australian capitalism, policy-makers tended to interpret the problems of migrants, their structural disadvantages and inequalities in a highly segmented labour market, largely in terms of a 'blaming the victim' strategy (Ryan, 1971). As a result, 'migrant problems' were identified as matters of cultural dissonance and problems of communication difficulties for which appropriate remedial strategies were devised through multiculturalist social policies, such as those dealing with language and media.

Cultural multiculturalism, as a form of 'identity politics' (Rex and Tomlinson, 1969), serves to demonstrate how, as in the United States and elsewhere, liberal political philosophy has responded to the ethnic revival movement of the 1960s. Australian multiculturalism being decidedly 'individualistic', was strategically absorbed into the liberal political philosophy of individualism, voluntarism and self-help, characteristic of the conservative Australian government of the 1970s (Fraser Government of 1975–82), in much the same way as in the United States. In brief, as in the United States, the social accommodation afforded ethnic minorities through cultural pluralism was effected within a framework of political liberalism (see Walzer *et al.*, 1982; Kymlicka, 1989). Thus, the potential of social conflict and disharmony was to a large extent avoided by channelling the social and economic strivings of migrants into the private domain of their cultural needs without politicizing ethnicity, that is, by giving formal political recognition to ethnic groups.

As Kymlicka (1989) has rightly observed, liberals – despite their readiness in granting citizenship rights to new settlers – were hopelessly torn between granting public recognition to ethnicity and ethnic groups and the need to respond to their special demands for equality and rights. Consequently, we find the liberal orthodoxy of conservative parties, and equally, social democratic parties such as the Australian Labor Party, undecided and sometimes decidedly antagonistic to giving *formal* recognition to ethnic minority groups. For this reason, to avoid segmental divisions, the rhetoric of multicultural social policies has always been expressed in the language of 'universalism' (e.g., 'multiculturalism for all' ideology in Zubryzcki, 1987) and 'integration' (the need to maintain social cohesion) as opposed to a 'particularist' or a 'conflict-prone approach (e.g., minority groups rights approach advocated by Jayasuriya, 1984). The latter, it was argued, by drawing attention to the special interests and needs of ethnic groups *per se*, was prone to encourage divisiveness, competition and conflict.

Reinforcing this strong emphasis on universalism was the emphasis on social cohesion (see Zubryzcki, 1982). As noted, this paradigm of cultural pluralism, which was accommodated within an inclusionary model of citizenship (Castles, 1992), permitted differentiations only in so far as there was an acceptance of commonalities in the political and legal system (e.g., democratic practices, rule of law etc.), and above all, the acceptance of English as a unifying common language. This insistence on the common and universal aspects of the wider society, as parts of a common citizenship, was linked to a mastery of the English language as an implied requirement of citizenship. Underlying all this was the uncertainty about 'difference' and the fear that a 'particularist' approach (e.g., minority rights approach) highlighting the special interests of groups would threaten the dominance of powerful groups and imperil harmony and cohesion.

Regrettably major policy documents since 1983 (e.g., National Population Council, 1985; DILGEA, 1986) of the Hawke Labor government, which replaced the conservative Liberal Fraser government, have all failed to resolve the ambiguity and uncertainty surrounding multicultural social policies. At best, they have tinkered on the fringes of this paradigm without addressing the critical philosophical and practical social issues. For example, the Jupp Report (DILGEA 1986) endeavours to move in the direction of the instrumental dimension of ethnicity (e.g., by reference to issues of access and equity) but fails to grapple with the complex issues of 'universalism' and 'particularism' in service delivery, or with questions of equality and justice such as the need for affirmative action strategies or the need to confront racism and discrimination (see Jayasuriya, 1987; and Foster and Stockley, 1988a, for a critical examination of these documents).

The Hawke Labor government (1983–93), as well as the Keating government (1993–96) continued to implement the old model of multiculturalism of the Fraser era (1975–82), and was lukewarm to charting a new course for multiculturalism. The Labor government's three principles of multiculturalism, *viz social justice, tolerance of diversity,* and *economic efficiency*, and the eight goals of multicultural public policy enumerated in the *National Agenda* (OMA, 1989), are, barring the rhetoric, not significantly different from those promoted by the Fraser government. At best, they seem to elaborate in greater detail, and give a different emphasis to, the principles of multiculturalism propounded by Zubryzcki (1982), one of the chief architects of the Fraser government's policy paradigm. These refer to *social cohesion, cultural identity, equal opportunity* and *access,* and *equal responsibility for,* and *commitment to,* participation in society. This, incidentally, demonstrates the extent of bipartisan political consensus that evolved in the 1970s and 1980s, but has lately become less so.

However, the multicultural policies of the Hawke Labor government, in comparison with those of the Fraser era, differ importantly on two main points. One concerns a lessening of emphasis on cultural difference and ethnic identity paralleled by an increased attention to aspects of macro-public policy relating to social justice issues. These pertain to delivery of service to ethnic minority groups, and is expressed in terms of an 'access and equity' policy (National Population Council, 1985; OMA, 1992) which is defined as 'a policy to ensure that equitable access to government programs and services by *all* members of the Australian community is not impeded by barriers related to language, culture, race or religion' (OMA, 1992). These initiatives are focussed mainly on examining policy strategies in employment, education, health and welfare, relating to *access* (issues of entry) and *equity* or fairness (issues of utilisation and outcome). What is advocated by these strategies is the softer version of equality (horizontal equity) and not equality as justice or substantive equality (vertical equity) requiring affirmative action type initiatives. This point of view is exemplified by the repeated references to 'equitable multiculturalism' in major policy documents (e.g., Jupp Report, DILGEA 1986) of the Labor government. The other distinctive feature of recent policy discourse is the reference to 'economic efficiency' as a principle of multiculturalism. Foster and Stockley (1988a) correctly observe that this emphasis on 'economic efficiency' fits in well with the avowed intention of the Hawke Labor Government to mould social justice policies, including multiculturalism, into 'the logic of corporate management ... and the rhetoric of economic rationalization and productive culture' (Foster and Stockley, 1988a, p. 11), widely recognized as the philosophy of 'economic rationalism' (Pusey, 1992).

What these policy initiatives of the 1980s have revealed pointedly are the dilemmas, contradictions and tensions inherent in the paradigm of cultural pluralism (see Jayasuriya 1990c). Thus, while on the one hand, the polarization of *expressive* and *instrumental* dimensions of ethnicity, reveals an emphasis on the former; the latter is clearly manifested by the increased particularist differentiation of groups. This is evident in diverse aspects of social life – religious, sporting, artistic and educational activities. Paradoxically, the expressive dimension of ethnicity and its manifestation in 'identity politics' awkwardly confronts the universalistic and homogenizing influences, characteristic of the inclusionary model of citizenship (see Castles, 1992; Jayasuriya, 1993) based on the 'multiculturalism for all' type of public policies. This contradiction throws into sharp public focus the status and legitimacy of the orthodox model of multiculturalism as a form of cultural pluralism.

MULTICULTURALISM IN CRISIS – DILEMMAS AND TENSIONS

The present crisis of multiculturalism relates to the inherent limitations of the ethnicity/identity model of multiculturalism as well as the changing social reality which places a heavy strain on the existing approach. The former concerns the problematic nature of cultural pluralism as a 'policy regime', and its shortcomings – arising from what has been described as the paradox of pluralism (Bullivant, 1983). This is evident by the fact that multiculturalism has had varying degrees of meaning and importance for different groups in society. While it has been attractive to migrant groups, mainstream Australian society has been, for the most part, indifferent towards multiculturalism as a social ideal. This is chiefly because of the continuing belief in some form of hidden assimilationism, a kind of 'melting pot'. There are some who tend to view it as being divisive and threatening social stability, even national security, on the grounds that multiculturalism promotes conflict and endangers social cohesion by institutionalizing differences and reifying ethnic group identity.

These apparent shortcomings are revealed in the way in which *difference* and diversity have been conceptualized and understood, especially in public policy formulation. Here, the language of public discourse is most revealing. For example, the reference is always to persons of non-English speaking background (NESB), not to 'ethnic minorities'; and to 'community relations', not 'race relations'. From a policy perspective, some would argue that, Australian multiculturalism, because of its preoccupation with a 'life styles' approach, in particular, with aspects of 'culture and social stability', has failed to respond to issues of social inequality, discrimination, issues of justice and equality; and, above all, in combatting racism (see Jakubowicz, 1981; Jayasuriya, 1987; 1990c). For these critics (e.g., see Foster and Stockley 1988), multiculturalism as a form of *identity politics* has been largely tokenistic and symbolic; and regarded essentially as an effective form of managing and controlling diversity.

A more far-reaching consideration in understanding the crisis of multiculturalism is the lack of fit between orthodox multiculturalism as a policy regime, and contemporary social and political conditions. All in all, there are *two* major considerations – economic and social – which make the existing model of multiculturalism ill-suited and often irrelevant as an effective policy strategy for dealing with emerging social and political issues. In this regard perhaps the most important, are the economic considerations relating to the impact of the ongoing structural readjustment of the Australian economy. Following changes in global economic relations, the Australian economy, like many other similar economies in Western advanced industrialized societies, has had to engage in extensive restructuring.[5] As far as multiculturalist social policies are concerned, these ongoing structural readjustments of the economy have had a noticeable impact in two respects: one relates to the ramifications of the changing nature of immigration intake policy and its social demographic effects; and the other is more structural and involves social and economic consequences.

A noteworthy consequence of economic restructuring has been the need to align immigration policy more closely to future economic growth. As a result, intake policies have become more skills oriented with precedence being given to recruiting those with high and medium skill levels to cater to the needs of a knowledge-based economy dominated by technology. The logic of this argument has been to locate the main source countries for these types of migrants, primarily in the Asian Region (see DILGEA, 1988). Consequently, the relatively high level of non-Caucasian intake in recent years, especially settlers of Asian origin, has thrown into sharper focus the disjunction between the historically closely linked aspects of recruitment and settlement in immigration policy. The shift in thinking from 'racial' homogeneity to 'cultural' homogeneity, which occurred as a consequence of the massive programme of post-war immigration from Europe, has been severely strained as a result of the increased Asian intake in the 1980s.

There is strong evidence that settlement policy as a mode of incorporation has historically been closely tied to recruitment policy. The time-worn policy of assimilationism, which was consistent with the traditional immigration policy of recruitment of predominantly British migrants, proved inappropriate and ill-suited as a mode of incorporation to deal with the high level of European migration. In this context, as previously noted, the doctrine of cultural pluralism proved to be an effective way of incorporating these new migrant groups, mainly of European origin, by replacing *racial* homogeneity with *cultural* homogeneity provided that the latter was understood as referring to British and European culture. However, the underlying philosophy of these principles of settlement, evolved in the 1970s and 1980s, may not be as attractive and suited to the needs of the new wave of migrants who are largely non-Caucasian (predominantly

Indo-Chinese refugees, Middle Eastern and Asian settlers). This is because Asian migrants are likely to be more 'racially' and culturally different from the early waves of European migrants.

Furthermore, these new settlers, consistent with overseas experience in Canada, Britain and the USA are, from a public policy perspective, more likely to be operating in the public realm rather than wanting to protect their cultural interests, that is, opting for policies in the private domain (see Jayasuriya and Sang, 1990). This perceived disjunction between recruitment and settlement policies, originating with the post-World War II changes in the philosophy of migrant settlement, would seem to lie at the heart of the crisis of multiculturalism. This probably constitutes one of the main reasons for the increasing opposition (see HREOC, 1991; Jayasuriya, 1990b) to multiculturalism as a social ideal, and organizing principle of public policy. The increased intake of non-European migrants who are not only culturally different, but also perceived to be 'racially' distinct, (as phenotypical variation is the basis of the folk understanding of the term 'race') has been seen as a threat to the racial homogeneity and cultural dominance of the dominant groups.

For the first time since the advent of mass migration in the post-World War II period, 'racial' factors have entered into the determination of ethnicity and differentiation of ethnic groups and revealed the extent to which old racist attitudes continue to persist in Australian society. Inevitably, this raises the delicate question of 'racial' as opposed to 'cultural' or ethnic factors in inter-group relations, and opens the door to reactivating latent fears and anxieties about race and 'colour' differences, reminiscent of the days of rampant anti-Chinese feelings and blatant racism in the 1880s and 1890s. The demographic changes, resulting from new patterns of immigration have also increased the potential for inter-ethnic rivalries, ethnic competition and conflicts which have hitherto been kept at a minimum, partly because the ethnic identity model of multiculturalism was more consonant with the early waves of European migration flourished during a period of relatively high economic growth, affluence and stability.

Turning to the social considerations (see Holton, 1990), there is no doubt that migrants who came in the early days of mass immigration enjoyed material benefits of the Australian welfare state and the outcomes of favourable economic climate of the 1960s and 1970s such that 'the membership of the civil society [was] a membership ticket to the nation' (Castles, 1990, p. 13). But, with the downturn in the economy in the 1980s, coupled with the changes in the welfare system and the social composition of Australian society due to new 'waves' of immigration, minority groups generally have become more vulnerable to economic misfortune. There is mounting evidence that, in a depressed labour market, the ongoing restructuring of the Australian economy has had a differential impact on some ethnic groups. On a variety of indicators such as rates of unemployment, retrenchment and industrial accidents, home ownership, educational participation, and compensation, migrants and persons of ethnic origin have, relative to others, had to bear a disproportionate burden of these adverse social effects of economic restructuring. This is particularly the case with subgroups such as youth, women and the new arrivals who are especially prone to economic misfortune, racism and social adversity (see HREOC, 1993, for documentation). These social and economic effects have been further exacerbated by the increasing evidence of structural discrimination in the labour market against ethnic groups,[6] and decreasing opportunities for occupational mobility. The potential of an 'ethnic underclass' has been well documented in the recent HREOC (1993) Report, and raises the dire prospect of marked occupational ethnic stratification. Thus, contrary to the proponents of the 'myth of inequality' (e.g., Birrell and Seitz, 1986), questions relating to the economic wellbeing of ethnic minority groups and their performance in the labour market will increasingly be a key issue of public policy relating to ethnic minority groups (see Collins, 1988; DILGEA, 1988; Lever-Tracy and Quinlan, 1988).

The justification of multiculturalism in terms of an *ethnic identity* model no longer appears to be valid as it becomes increasingly irrelevant to new 'clients' and actors such as second/third generations of migrant origin and non-Caucasian migrants who are more concerned with 'life chances' than 'life styles' (i.e., their personal and social circumstances in a difficult economic environment). Furthermore, the increasing incidence of inter-ethnic marriage (see Price, 1993) among second and third generations (this refers to later generations of ethnic offspring marrying outside their communities), may have transformed the meaning and significance of ethnicity and ethnic identity for these groups. As people inherit many different cultures and mix the cultural elements in their own way, ethnic boundaries become more fluid and permeable. In these circumstances, it is not that ethnicity disappears but that 'primordial' ethnicity, more characteristic of first-generation migrants, is likely to give way to a more 'symbolic' kind of ethnicity (see Gans, 1979), a loose nostalgia for one's historic origins but with no compelling sense of identification or group loyalty.[7] These individuals, offspring of migrants, as Castles (1992) notes, are less likely to articulate their needs in cultural terms and only 'makes use of cultural markers, in order to maintain links with their constituency' (1992, p. 21). The net result is that these groups are likely to make different and more compelling demands on public policy than their parents and grandparents. It will therefore be necessary to redraw the established boundaries between the public and private, rejecting by implication any form of 'benign neutrality' as a policy prescription for dealing with ethnic minorities (see Kymlicka 1990; also Jayasuriya 1991).[8]

In short, in an uncertain and changing, if not declining, economy, multicultural social policies, despite the rhetoric of 'access and equity' strategies (OMA 1992), have failed to respond adequately to the economic, social and political wellbeing of these groups. Orthodox multiculturalism, as a 'policy regime', based not only on certain types of recruitment policies, but also certain patterns of post-war economic growth, has become less attractive and functional. Briefly, then, multiculturalism, as a policy regime has become increasingly problematic on economic grounds, as well as for social and demographic reasons; and furthermore, the perceived disjunction between settlement and recruitment, has lessened its effectiveness in policy terms, and generated adverse public perceptions.

The crisis of Australian multiculturalism and its adverse perception by the public at large, is nowhere better revealed than in the reluctance of Australian mainstream society to accept the growth of 'ethnic structures' and collectivities, themselves often a product of multicultural social policies promoted by the state (see Castles, 1990). Whatever the reasons for disavowing multiculturalism, the reality of ethnic group differentiations and the plurality of Australian society remains an inescapable fact. Ethnic minority groups, as relatively permanent collectivities, need to be accepted and recognized as minority interest groups, that is, as status-devalued groups singled out for differential and pejorative treatment. By conceptualizing ethnic groups as 'minority groups' (Martin, 1978; Dworkin et al., 1982; Callan, 1989), we are able to see these groups as being dynamic, flexible and responsive to varying sociopolitical circumstances. It is only in this manner that they are able to represent the interests of these groups and mobilize their resources in the public domain to gain redress for their powerlessness. In short, what we encounter in reality is an evolving model of interest group politics (see Jayasuriya, 1991; 1994) based on ethnicity, and operating in the public domain.

This formulation of multiculturalism as a policy regime – based on an interest group model – is at variance with the existing model of cultural/individualistic multiculturalism, because it brings to the fore the question of instrumental ethnicity pertaining to conflict, competition and power hierarchies in intergroup relations. In adjusting to this process of change in groups' formations it will be necessary to reconceptualize the notion of ethnic identity as a more complex phenomenon, as something which is not necessarily restricted to a primordial condition of subjective and affective significance. What we are witnessing therefore, is the emergence of a more situationally determined notion of ethnic identity, functioning more as a politico-economic resource than a primordial affective condition. While this new expression of identity may co-exist with a primordial sense of identity, the processes of identity formation itself will depend on historical and specific sociopolitical circumstances. Indeed, identity may be only of symbolic value, but nonetheless real and socially significant (see Jayasuriya, 1990a).

CONCLUSION

The functional value of the conventional multiculturalism as a conservative first-generation strategy (see Castles, 1992, pp. 17–18), of accommodation and appeasement (see Jayasuriya, 1984; 1990c) may have little relevance for the emerging social and political reality we have sketched. Groups with new needs and different 'clients' or 'actors' such as the ethnic youth, militant woman workers, unemployed migrant workers, and non-Caucasian settlers, make quite different demands and have aspirations which cannot easily be accommodated within the framework of orthodox multiculturalism without the politicization of ethnicity.[9]

The Australian experiment of multiculturalism is in danger of total rejection unless the new social reality we have sketched, is confronted sensibly and meaningfully. Though multiculturalism has been accorded political legitimacy over the years, as a state regulated policy of immigrant settlement, it has not gained a high degree of public acceptance and endorsement as a normative ideology. At best, in a period of relative economic growth and stability, multiculturalism enjoyed a measure of success and a modicum of public support. But with changed economic and political conditions in the 1980s, the theory and practice of multiculturalism has become controversial (see Markus and Rickfels, 1985; Lewins, 1987; DILGEA, 1988; Sawer, 1990) These controversies and the vehemence of the conservative backlash against multiculturalism which has put at risk the bipartisan political consensus of earlier years, clearly point to the essentially problematic nature of cultural pluralism as a policy paradigm.

A disquieting feature of this conservative trend is the emergence of a new ideology of racism. This 'new racism' is gaining intellectual acceptance and exists alongside vestiges of the old racism of the nineteenth century 'scientific racism' confined to fringe groups. The new ideology of racism is framed in the language of the inevitability of cultural difference, suggesting that differences between groups are *normal* and *natural*, and seeks to exploit to its own advantage, the liberal attitudes of multiculturalism towards cultural difference by exaggerating the intrinsic worth of these differences (see Castles, 1990; Jayasuriya, 1990b; Husband 1994). But more central to this new ideology of racism is the construction of the concept of the 'nation' as a means of demarcating the boundaries of acceptance and rejection of group membership. This was vividly and poignantly expressed by the former leader of the Australian Liberal Party, John Howard in 1989, in his notion of a *One Australia*.

In essence, for Mr Howard and other conservative critics, the nation, as the 'imagined community' was to be characterized by the group norms, group attitudes and the core values of the dominant groups, echoing the nineteenth century slogan of 'one nation, one identity', with scant recognition of the pluralistic nature of the political community. The plea for social harmony expressed by these conservative critics becomes in effect, a *crie de coeur* of a strident nationalism. It is simply the means for affirming the traditional values of the 'nation' as an anglo-hegemony, what today has come to mean *Australian* and not British. What this in effect represents is the very denial of pluralism, and the reality of the immigrant experience. This conflation of *race, nation* and *culture* is central to the crisis of Australian multiculturalism and warrants careful systematic analysis and critiquing (see Jayasuriya 1991a).

There are *four* key themes that need to be underscored in reconceptualizing Australian multiculturalism. First and foremost is the stark reality of the pluralism in society and the existence of a pluralistic community which is both 'racial' and 'ethnic' in composition. However defined, ethnic groups are now established minority interest groups competing with others in the public domain to satisfy their material needs and aspirations. Hence, the challenge of the 1990s must be to accommodate the genuine political aspirations of these groups in the public domain through appropriate political and institutional changes such as legislative safeguards of minority rights. Second, in a period of economic downturn and compounded by a changing social reality, issues of equality and social rights have come more to the fore and need to be addressed more directly. The multiculturalism of the future will have to address more directly the rights and entitlements of these minority groups who are clearly a markedly differentiated segment of society, with new actors and claimants seeking fair shares.

Third, it is imperative that the next stage of multiculturalism must proceed on a sound theoretical basis and an acceptable political rationale, derived from reconceptualizing the notion of citizenship (see Jayasuriya, 1991; 1994), to go beyond conventional theorizing. A radical view of citizenship will not only enshrine the principle of equality, both as an *equality of status* and respect as well as an *equality of rights*, but at the same time, strive for a substantive equality which departs from a rigid universalism (see Jayasuriya, 1994). Such a view of citizenship goes beyond a liberal individualist model, and espouses a democratic and pluralistic citizenship, based on full and equal membership in a pluralistic community (see Andrews, 1991; Jayasuriya, 1991, 1994). Fourth, in a pluralistic and radical view of citizenship, *participation* becomes a key and central element of a new philosophy of settlement. It is participation which enhances the status of citizenship and enables one to exercise one's rights *qua* citizenship for a broad range of rights. Furthermore, by allowing minority groups to participate fully and exercise their rights in the broad civic domain, citizenship facilitates a social integration creating a civic religion.

Within the domain of the political nation, by strengthening the common bond of citizenship located in a common material culture, individuals in a state are cemented into a sociocultural whole. It is by enhancing the conditions of effective citizenship that one can achieve social integration and facilitate the processes of nation-building through a shared sense of a common destiny. Nationalism, within such a liberal-rationalist paradigm, goes hand in hand with liberty, reason and progress; and to remain a force must gain its substance and meaning from the processes of state formation. The language of public discourse will need to change from that of 'identity politics' (the private domain) to 'minority rights' (the public domain). Instead of a nation-state based on a culturally defined community, what we are likely to see is the emergence of a nation-state as an essentially *political* rather than a *cultural* concept (see Jayasuriya, 1994).

The logic and morality of pluralism, dictated by the demands of civil society enmeshed in a global economy, needs to be informed and infused by the tenets and philosophy of a democratic citizenship (see Jayasuriya, 1994) in order to strengthen social bonds and identifications. To achieve these ends, the social and political landscape will need to incorporate the pluralism of society, especially within the whole spectrum of its institutions, with a range of new and different social forms, images and styles of conduct. In such a context, there will be new social identifications and political legitimacy with a focus on the politics of state formation and nation building. As Australia moves towards 100 years of Federation, clearly as Mouffe (1988, p. 31) rightly notes, 'only a pluralistic conception of citizenship can take account of the current proliferation of new political aspirations ... and accommodate the specificity and multiplicity of democratic demands' of the evolving Australian society.

Notes

1. For a detailed and informative documentation on this see Sawer (1990).
2. See Jupp (1991, pp. 122–4) for a chronology of migration and settlement in Australia.
3. See Rowland (1982) for an excellent account of the ethnic composition of the population and also Hugo (1986) for a comprehensive review of trends in Australian demography.
4. Unlike Canadian multiculturalism which writers such as Gordon (1981) see as a move towards 'corporate pluralism' because of the formal recognition accorded to 'groups' as racial and ethnic entities, Australian multiculturalism was decidedly 'individualistic' as there was no formal standing given to these 'groups' in the national polity (see Lambert and Taylor, 1990).
5. See Dwyer (1989).
6. See Centre for Working Women (1989); Coughlan (1989); AIMA (1986); McAllister and Jones (1990); and, Niland and Champion (1990), for detailed documentation of the evidence of employment discrimination.
7. However, Lambert and Taylor (1990) caution us about assuming that mixed ethnic marriages invariable eradicates one or both ethnic heritages. They argue that in some instances, we encounter 'double breeds' rather than 'half breeds' or 'no breeds'.
8. Kymlicka (1990) provides a useful discussion of the public/private distinction in liberal political philosophy. As in feminist theory, it is suggested that cultural features associated with ethnicity (e.g., cultural rights) should no longer be confined to the 'private' domain.
9. It is worthwhile recalling that Jean Martin (1978) observed very early that the cultural pluralism advocated in Australia by Zubryzcki and others was encouraged and welcomed only to the extent that it was not political.

References

ABS (Australian Bureau of Statistics) (1991) *Census of Population and Housing*, Cat. No. 2922.0 (Canberra: AGPS).
AIMA (Australian Institute of Multicultural Affairs) (1986) *Reducing the Risk* (Canberra: Australian Government Publishing Service) (AGPS).
Andrews, G. (ed.) (1991) *Citizenship* (London: Lawrence & Wishart).
Birrell, R. and A. Seitz (1986) 'The Myth of Inequality in Australian Education', *Australian Journal of Population* 12 (1), pp. 52–74.
Bottomley, G. (1988) 'Ethnicity, Race and Nationalism in Australia', *Australian Journal of Social Issues* 23 (3), pp. 169–83.
Bullivant, B.M. (1983) 'Australia's Pluralist Dilemma', *Australian Quarterly*, 55 (2), pp. 136–48.
Callam, V.J. (1989) *Australian Minority Groups* (Sydney: Harcourt Brace Jovanovich).
Castles, S. (1990) 'Global Workforce, New Racism and the Declining Nation-State', *Occasional Paper No. 23* (Wollongong: Centre for Multicultural Studies, University of Wollongong).

Castles, S. (1992) *The Challenge of Multiculturalism: Global Changes and Australian Experience* (Wollongong: Centre for Multicultural Studies, University of Wollongong).
Castles, S., B. Cope, M. Kalantzes and M. Morrissey (1990) *Mistaken Identity*, 2nd edn (Sydney: Pluto Press).
Centre for Working Women (1986) 'Women Outworkers'. *Migration Action*, 8 (2), pp. 8–13.
Collins, J. (1988) *Migrant Hands in Distant Lands* (Sydney: Pluto Press).
Committee of Inquiry into Labour Market Programs (1985) *Report of the Committee of Inquiry into Labour Market Programs* (Canberra: AGPS).
Coughlan, J.E. (1989) 'A Comparative Study of the Labour Force Performance of Indochinese born Immigrants in Australia: a Preliminary Analysis of the 1986 Data', *Asia Papers* (No 48, Centre for the Study of Australian-Asian Relations. Brisbane: Griffith University).
de Lepervanche, M. (1984) 'Immigration and Ethnic Groups', in S. Encel and L. Bryson (eds), *Australian Society*, 4th edn (Sydney: Longmans).
de Lepervanche, M. and G. Bottomley (eds) (1988) *The Cultural Construction of Race* (Sydney: Association for Studies in Society and History).
Department of Labour and Immigration (1975) *Interim and Final Report of Committee on Community Relations* (Lippman Report) (Canberra: AGPS).
Department of Labour and Immigration (1978) *Report on the Review of Post-Arrival Programs and Services for Migrants* (Galbally Report) (Canberra: AGPS).
DILGEA (1986) *Dont Settle for Less* (Jupp Report) Review of Migrant and Multicultural Programs and Services (Canberra: AGPS).
DILGEA (Department of Immigration, Local Government and Ethnic Affairs) (1988) *Immigration: A Commitment to Australia* (FitzGerald Report) vol. 1 (Canberra: AGPS).
Dworkin, A., G. Anthony and J. Rosalind (1982) *The Minority Report* (New York: Holt)
Dwyer, P. (1989) *Public and Private Life* (Melbourne: Longmans Cheshire).
Encel, S. (1986) 'The Concept of Ethnicity and its Application to Australian Society', Melbourne: Australian Institute of Multicultural Affairs (unpub).
Foster, L. and D. Stockley (1988) *Australian Multiculturalism: A Documentary History and Critique* (Clevedon: Multilingual Matters).
Foster, L. and D. Stockley (1988a). 'The Politics of Ethnicity: Multicultural Policy in Australia', *Journal of Intercultural Studies*, 10 (2), pp. 16–31.
Gans, H. (1979) 'Symbolic Ethnicity', *Ethnic and Racial Studies*, 2, pp. 1–20.
Gordon, M. (1981) 'Models of Pluralism', *The Annals. American Academy of Political and Social Sciences*, 454, pp. 178–88.
Hancock, W.K. (1940) *Survey of British Commonwealth Affairs*, vol. 2, part 2. (Oxford).
Holton, R. (1990) 'The Social Impact of Immigration', in M. Wooden, R. Holton, G. Hugo and J. Sloan, (eds), *Australian Immigration: A Survey of the Issues*. (Melbourne: Bureau of Immigration Research).
HREOC (1991) *Report of the National Inquiry into Racist Violence* (Canberra: AGPS).
HREOC (Human Rights and Equal Opportunities Commission) (1993) *State of the Nation* (Canberra: AGPS).

Hugo, G. (1986) *Australia's Changing Population. Trends and Implications* (Oxford: Oxford University Press).
Husband, C. (1994) *'Race' and Nation: the British Experience* (Perth, Curtin University: Paradigm Press).
Jakubowicz, A. (1981). 'State and Ethnicity: Multiculturalism as an Ideology', *Australia and New Zealand Journal of Sociology*, 17 (3), pp. 4–13.
Jayasuriya, L. (1984). 'Whither Multiculturalism?', *10th Annual Lalor Address* (Canberra: Human Rights Commission).
Jayasuriya, L. (1987) 'Immigration Policies and Ethnic Relations in Australia', *Occasional Paper*, No. 2, Department of Social Work and Social Administration (Perth: University of Western Australia).
Jayasuriya, L. (1990) 'Language and Culture in Australian Public Policy', *International Migration Review* 24 (1), pp. 149–60.
Jayasuriya, L. (1990a) 'The Problematic of Culture: and Identity in Cross-Cultural Theorising', in M. Clare and L. Jayasuriya (ed.), *Issues of Cross-Cultural Practice* (Department of Social Work and Social Administration. Perth: University of Western Australia).
Jayasuriya L. (1990b) 'Racism and Immigration in Australia: From Old to New Racism', in Proceedings of Conference, Australian Society for Human Biology, entitled: *Human Biology: An Integrative Science* (ed.) P.O. Higgins (Perth: University of Western Australia).
Jayasuriya, L. (1990c) 'Rethinking Australian Multiculturalism', *Australian Quarterly*, 62 (1).
Jayasuriya, L. (1991) 'Citizenship, Democratic Pluralism and Ethnic Minorities in Australia', in R. Nile (ed.), *Immigration, Multiculturalism and Politics of Ethnicity and Race in Australia and Britain* (University of London: Centre for Australian Studies).
Jayasuriya, L. (1993) 'Australian Multiculturalism and Citizenship', Occasional Paper No. 1, Ethnic Communities Council, Perth.
Jayasuriya, L. (1994) 'The Political Foundations of Australia's Pluralist Society', *Australian Journal of Social Issues*, 24 (4), pp. 319–33.
Jayasuriya, L. and D. Sang (1990) 'Asian Immigration: Past and Current Trends', *Current Affairs Bulletin*, 66 (11), pp. 4–14.
Jupp, J. (1984) 'Waves of Immigration: Terra Australis to Australia', *Bulletin*, no. 3. (Canberra: Australian Academy of Humanities).
Jupp, J. (1989) *The Political Participation of Ethnic Minorities in Australia* (Centre for Multicultural Studies, Canberra: Australian National University).
Jupp, J. (1990) *Ghettoes, Tribes and Prophets* (Canberra: Office of Multicultural Affairs).
Jupp, J. (1991) *Immigration* (Sydney: Sydney University Press).
Kymlicka, W. (1989) *Liberalism, Community and Culture* (Oxford University Press).
Kymlicka, W. (1990) *Contemporary Political Philosophy* (Oxford: Clarendon Press).
Lambert, W.E. and D. Taylor (1990) *Coping with Cultural and Racial Diversity in Urban America* (New York: Praeger).
Lever-Tracy, C. and M. Quinlan (1988). *The Divided Working Class* (London: Routledge & Kegan Paul).
Lewins, F. (1987) 'The Blainey Debate' in Hindsight', *Australia and New Zealand Journal of Sociology*, 23.

Markus, A. and M.C. Rickfels (eds) (1985) *Surrender Australia? Essays in the Study and Uses of History: Blainey and Asian Immigration* (Sydney: Allen & Unwin).
Martin, J. (1978) *The Migrant Presence* (Sydney: Allen & Unwin).
McAllister, I. and R. Jones (1990) 'Immigration, Unemployment and Labour Market Programs' (paper), *National Immigration Outlook Conference* (Melbourne: Bureau of Immigration Research).
Mouffe, C. (1988) 'The Civic Lesson', *New Statesman and Society* (Oct).
National Population Council (1985) *Access and Equity* (Canberra: AGPS).
Niland, C. and R. Champion (1990) 'EEO Experience for Immigrants' (paper), *National Immigration Outlook Conference* (Melbourne: Bureau of Immigration Research).
OMA (1988) 'Towards a National Agenda for Multiculturalism', *Discussion Paper* (Canberra: AGPS).
OMA (Office of Multicultural Affairs) (1989) *National Agenda for Multicultural Australia* (Canberra: AGPS).
OMA (1992) *Report on Access and Equity*, vols 1 & 2 (Canberra: AGPS).
Price, C. (1993) 'Ethnic Mixture in Australia', *People and Places*, 1(1), pp. 6–9.
Pusey, M. (1992) *Economic Rationalism in Canberra: A Nation-Building State Changes its Mind* (Sydney: Cambridge University Press).
Rein, M. (1976) *Social Science in Public Policy* (New York: Penguin).
Rex, J. and S. Tomlinson (1967) *Coloured Immigrants in a British City* (London: Oxford University Press).
Rowland, J.J. (1982) 'Ethnic Composition of the Population', in *Population of Australia*, vol. 1 (New York: ESCAP/UN) chap. 5.
Ryan, W. (1971) *Blaming the Victim* (New York: Pantheon).
Sawer, M. (1990) *Public Perceptions of Multiculturalism* (Canberra: Centre for Multicultural Studies, Australian National University).
Smith, S.J. (1988) *The Politics of Race and Residence* (Cambridge: Polity Press).
Walzer, M., M. Kantowicz, J. Higham and M. Harrington (1982) *The Politics of Ethnicity* (Cambridge: Belknap Press).
Williams, R. (1983) *Culture* (Cambridge: Fontana).
Wirth, C. (1945) 'The Problem of Minority Groups', in R. Linton (ed.), *The Science of Man in World Crisis* (New York: Columbia University Press).
Zubryzcki, J. (1982) *Multiculturalism for All Australians* (Canberra: AGPS).
Zubryzcki, J. (1987) 'Multiculturalism and the Search for Roots', *First Annual Lecture* (Centre for Multicultural Studies. Adelaide: Flinders University).

12 The Theory and Practice of Immigration and 'Race-Relations' Policy: Some Thoughts on British and French Experience

John Crowley

Immigration has in recent years acquired unusual prominence in European political debate, fuelled by fears about a rising tide of asylum-seekers and demographic disparities North and South of the Mediterranean. One important strand is the perception that a process of 'integration', which worked reasonably well in the past, has got stuck. It is frequently assumed that the problem is due to something specific about recent migrants; more plausibly, fear of immigration may be seen as a symptom of a wider social *malaise*. Whichever view one subscribes to, however, the failure of integration is undoubtedly associated with severe problems of discrimination, racism and unequal opportunities for both immigrants and European-born minority groups, and suggests that Europe may now be incapable of absorbing migrants within a genuinely democratic framework.

Immigration is of concern to policy-makers for several reasons. The legal and administrative regulation of migration, residence and access to citizenship – the control of the territorial and symbolic boundaries of the state – is invariably regarded as the cornerstone of sovereignty. The issue is of vital macroeconomic concern. Finally the politicization of xenophobia may unleash forces that are destructive not just of social peace but also of the constitutive assumptions of policy as an attempt rationally to pursue the public interest.

The perception of integration[1] as problematic adds a particularly complex strand to such concern. The instruments of immigration policy are fairly well defined, and their implementation is subject to considerations of practicability, expediency, efficacy and (occasionally) justice rather than to any profound uncertainty about what precisely is being done. Integration, on the other hand, is elusive. The formulation of 'the' policy problem is from the outset theory-laden, and contentious in a far more profound way than where debate focuses primarily on conflicting judgments of fact and value with respect to commonly recognized problems. As the French and British cases show, policy is essentially problem-defining rather than problem-solving. In practice, however, definition is inscribed within attempts to solve a problem that is itself ostensibly not problematized. Breaking this circularity, rather than specific policy prescription, is the major challenge to policy-relevant research.

Nonetheless, social 'reality' is not an infinitely plastic artefact, and the efficacy of policy depends on its compatibility with the nature of the social reality it is designed to modify. While understanding of social reality is, even in principle, incomplete and indeterminate, and is inherently incapable of dictating 'the' correct policy approach, certain things may be excluded. For example, any policy designed to deter illegal migration and any form of multiculturalism necessarily embody assumptions about, respectively, the causality of migration and the relation of people to culture. An *analytical* view of migrants as rootless short-term utility maximisers, or of culture as a static, well-defined 'inheritance', is unlikely to be conducive to effective policy, regardless of its additional normative presuppositions.

The policy relevance of this kind of analysis does not lie in its ability to produce recipes susceptible of general application. Rather it provides some indications about the relations between (analytical and normative) ways of *thinking* about the issues deriving from immigrant absorption and the forms of *action* deriving from policy. Section I sketches a general framework, useful in comparative terms, that focuses on the ways in which politics mediates between policy and research. Section II uses material from French and British experience to illustrate the historically important 'liberal' agenda, premised on depoliticization of the policy–research interface. Section III shows one important way in which politics may be reintroduced: the 'radical' process of appropriation by the 'objects' of policy of the discourse directed at them. Finally, section IV concludes that the formal structure of *effective* policy must incorporate the essence of 'radicalism': the legitimacy of such appropriation and its inherently conflictual nature. Much that is of pressing concern to policy-makers cannot be dealt with at this level, yet helping to avoid mistakes remains of immediate significance and value.

I THE POLICY–RESEARCH INTERFACE: SOME GENERAL COMMENTS

Policy is a theory-laden concept devoid of unambiguous empirical content. A convenient definition for the purposes of this chapter is that policy is a *self-conscious framework for authoritative action* (not therefore reducible to action). Furthermore, immigration and race relations belong to the subclass of *state* policy, which introduces additional complications. To speak of a 'self-conscious framework for authoritative *state* action' implies that the state is an identifiable and autonomous sociological entity rather than, say, a management committee of the bourgeoisie or a clearing-house for pluralist interest-group interaction. Whether this is true in any general sense is both arguable and beyond the scope of this chapter. I shall assume, however, that it holds as an empirical generalization for France and the UK in the post-war period. In addition – still as an empirical working hypothesis – the state that makes and implements policy is accorded a fairly high degree of cohesion and centralization: a 'state elite' comprising high-level professional politicians and permanent civil servants has a large measure of control over the 'self-consciousness' that defines policy. This in no way conflicts with the existence of narrow practical limits on state *action*, including those imposed by powerful social groups (e.g. trade unions or employers' organizations) exerting control over vital policy-implementation resources such as information and compliance.

Policy and research are the concrete activities of people, organized into more or less cohesive groups expressing interests that cannot be reduced to the content of their output. In particular, research communities have natural objectives of influence and autonomy that, where the policy elite has significant control over funding (as in both Britain and France), may conflict. The relation between research and policy may take two very different forms, depending on the cohesiveness of the policy elite and the exclusiveness of the policy–research interface. Firstly, research may provide empirical material to facilitate the formulation of state policy, for example statistics on such things as residential segregation or school results. The demand for such facts arises within a policy agenda that has already been defined, and the role of research is thus subordinate support or back-up. A related form of back-up is designing detailed policy 'recipes' aimed at meeting certain objectives specified by the policy-makers. On the other hand, research may sometimes be able to set the agenda, contributing to the definition of both the means *and* ends of policy. In practice, both processes are likely to coexist and to interact dynamically, and the same is true of the relation between policy and politics. Finally, except in the very peculiar case where research neither responds to any political agenda nor impacts on political mobilization, a similar dynamic equilibrium characterizes relations between research and politics, the core process being attempts within each field to set the agenda for the other. Neither of these two-way interfaces can be seen in isolation: in the specific case addressed in this volume, politics is at one apex of a complex triangular policy–research interface.

Relevance and influence are themselves far more complex, and politically contested, than any simplistic technocratic approach to policy can capture. They can, in particular, be conceived with reference either to state policy-makers or to society (or some section of it, e.g. the working-class). The first, state-centred, model may be thought of as *liberal* because of its (usually tacit) assumption that the state is the locus of rationality as opposed to the often unenlightened demands expressed by civil society. State relevance and influence thus capture a commitment to abstract, universalizable values rather than 'narrow' social interests. Conversely I shall describe the competing model as *radical* because of its implicit scepticism about state rationality. If the state merely represents one dominant interest, possibly an undesirable or oppressive one, research relevance should be evaluated by reference to desirable (e.g. progressive) social interests and the proper focus of influence should be political debate and mobilisation. The state will of course, for its own reasons, have a vested interest in defending the first model against the encroachments of the second.[2]

II FIRST MODEL: THE LIBERAL AGENDA

Like several other European countries, France and the UK received considerable economic migration in the three decades after the Second World War.[3] However, although the logic (particularly the economic logic) of migration was politically contentious, it did not become an object of public debate and party competition until the late 1950s in the UK, and until the mid-1970s in France, because the state elite was concerned (and able) to depoliticize the issue. This illustrates a technocratic variant of the liberal model, in which the policy–politics interface is highly attenuated and the policy–research interface is structured by the logic of autonomous state activity so that research that is not oriented towards the development of effective tools for the implementation of autonomously defined state objectives is marginalized.[4] In practice a small group of politicians and civil servants are in a position to define immigration policy, without reference to public opinion – still less to the opinions of the migrants themselves – in order to derive maximum economic benefit from immigration, given the constraint of likely public hostility. This is particularly congenial to a conception of immigration in terms of temporary migrant labour. Recent European experience shows, however, that the technocratic agenda based on the migrant-labour principle is unstable, because xenophobia and minority demands cannot be kept out of politics indefinitely.

The UK faced the implications of this earlier than elsewhere because of its unique lack of a clear conception of citizenship. In abstract terms, citizenship comprises both a relation between the individual and the state and a complex of rights and duties within the state, the degree of overlap being indeterminate in theory and highly variable in practice. The first was historically non-existent in the UK, since the constitutive relation was that of the subject (not the citizen) to the sovereign (not the state). The substantive rights and duties of UK citizenship[5] thus developed without reference to any distinctive national status, and suffrage and other political rights were *de facto* granted to the entire Commonwealth as well as to all the colonies.[6] Consequently, the state had no legal means of regulating the migrant labour-force in response to economic conditions. This removed the hypothetical safety-valve provided by technocratic regulation of migrant labour (compulsory termination of contracts, expulsions, bilateral repatriation agreements). The state was, unlike its French counterpart, unable to pre-empt public expressions of hostility by administrative action and, since any attempt to recover some degree of autonomy required a change in the law, the issue was, from the late 1950s, brought within the compass of political debate. Once this had happened, it was impossible to get the political genie back into the technocratic lamp.

The Commonwealth Immigrants Act of 1962 was intended by the Conservative government elected in 1959 to take the political heat out of immigration,[7] but it was strongly opposed by the Labour Party[8] and was not very successful in meeting the demands of the anti-immigrant lobby for restriction *per se* rather than simply for control: immigration was actually higher after 1962 than before 1960. This unstable situation was the origin of the alternative liberal agenda that crystalized in the 1960s, as the Labour Party became increasingly worried about its electoral vulnerability to the politicization of xenophobia.[9] Whereas the technocratic agenda was predicated on the non-existence or irrelevance of the policy–politics interface, at the heart of the new liberal agenda was the idea that an autonomous sphere for policy must be preserved in order to guard against the potentially deleterious effect of popular pressure, particularly cynically promoted anti-immigrant hostility. While liberal establishments are invariably far more sensitive than the general public to both the utilitarian economic defence of immigration and moral obligations towards migrants, they may nonetheless be led to a restrictive stance on immigration (incorporating xenophobia) in order to contain anti-immigrant hostility (making the expression of xenophobia illegitimate). In principle, this is both hypocritical and self-contradictory. In practice, however, detailed comparison of the contrasting electoral fortunes of the French and British far right,[10] suggests that, on balance, the strategy of depoliticization has worked (Crowley, 1993).

Xenophobia is but one aspect of the possible intrusion of politics into policy. Although it is numerically the more pressing (there are usually far more potential racists than migrants), it cannot remain indefinitely the sole concern of state policy. Closing the borders, unless accompanied by a deliberate policy of (compulsory) repatriation, tends to stabilize the foreign population as temporary workers leave and are not replaced and as the children of migrants who have settled as families make up a steadily increasing share of the 'foreign' population. Therefore, while migrants may maintain links with home-country politics, they will also gradually acquire concerns and interests characteristic of their country of residence and come to formulate these as political demands. Their ability to do so effectively will depend on their access to political resources, particularly formal citizenship, but the underlying movement is sociological.

On grounds both of autonomy and of substantive judgment, the liberal logic is to treat these demands in the same way as politicized xenophobia: declaring them illegitimate while meeting them, if necessary, half way. Because the rejection of racism implies the rejection of any idea that migrants and their descendants are either incapable of assimilation or should be prevented from assimilating, assimilation is at the heart of the liberal agenda rather than peripheral to it.[11] Whether desirable *per se*, or simply inevitable in the absence of any state intervention to halt it, it effectively removes (in theory) both of the threats to the liberal state (racism and minority particularism) created by immigration. It does however raise two difficult questions: (a) is assimilationism actually conducive to assimilation? and (b) if so, is it compatible with other democratic values? Answering 'no' to both, which is the current policy consensus in the UK, leads naturally to the decline of the liberal agenda and its replacement by the 'radical' agenda analyzed in section III. The French example, on the other hand, is of interest precisely because both research and policy are generally predicated on the principle that assimilation remains both possible and desirable.

Current debates about the place of the descendants of post-war migrants in French society draw on two historical traditions: the myth of the universalistic nation-state, and the successful assimilation of the European migrants that helped France to compensate for a falling birth-rate and the exactions of war between the 1850s and the Second World War. Until the mid-1970s, these traditions remained largely implicit. French borders were open[12] on grounds of economic efficiency, and migrants (some 200 000 each year in the late 1960s and early 1970s) were largely invisible, both literally (because of residential concentration in shanty-towns or *bidonvilles* at the periphery of large cities) and metaphorically (because of their almost complete absence from national political debate). In 1974–5, this shifted very sharply (Weil, 1991, pp. 77–106; de Wenden, 1988, pp. 189–219). Slum clearance brought immigrants into the residential mainstream, the evidence of family migration (which grew rapidly from the late 1960s) showed the migrant-labour paradigm to be inapplicable, and the oil crisis of 1973 and subsequent recession turned the balance of economic argument against unskilled migration. Labour migration was officially halted in 1974 (administratively, for the legal reasons already mentioned) and concerns about assimilation (or integration), particularly of North African immigrants, began to be expressed. During the following ten years, the largely unarticulated French tradition was challenged from both sides by rejection of the desirability of assimilation: the mainstream right[13] (and later, and more virulently, the *Front National*) on grounds of immigrants' cultural or 'racial' difference; and the left,[14] defending immigrants' right to cultural autonomy.

This unnatural alliance broke down in the mid-1980s, as minority political movements,[15] and the left-wing parties that supported them, came to see right-wing rejection of assimilation (embodied in proposals for compulsory repatriation) as a serious threat to the position in France of immigrants and their children (Weil and Crowley, 1994, pp. 113–116). The traditional French 'model'[16] was reappropriated by anti-racist discourse, and reconstructed explicitly. The turning point came with the Chirac government's plan to reform nationality law in 1986 (so as to end the automatic acquisition of citizenship at the age of 18 by foreigners born and permanently resident in France). A rhetoric of suspicion about the loyalties of French citizens by birth (disparagingly called *'Français de papier'*) surrounded the proposal, which was withdrawn following a wave of popular protest (Wayland, 1993). As a compromise, the government set up a commission of inquiry, which recommended less radical reform, although still making acquisition of citizenship by French-born foreigners conditional on a declaration of intent (*Commission de la nationalité*, 1988). This was presented as exemplifying rather than negating the French tradition, and indeed the eventual implementation of the Commission's recommendations in 1993 encountered little serious resistance.

More significant than the policy outcome was however, the fact that the debate took place. It showed that the model continues to exert a powerful influence over both policy and research, and considerably clarified its content. Its essential features can be summarised as follows.

(a) The absorption of migrants is a process of nation-(re)building, analogous to the construction of modern France under the 3rd Republic.
(b) The nation is a political or spiritual principle based on shared norms and values.
(c) These are not culturally specific but universal, namely those of the Enlightenment and Revolution as implemented by the 3rd Republic.
(d) Sub-national loyalties, norms or values may exist, but any formal recognition of them is both dangerous (b) and unnecessary (c).

The principal debate within France arises with those writers who would reject the simplistic reduction of (a) to (b) (of nation-building to the ideology of the nation) as a distortion of history, and would stress the role of historically situated struggle – political, social and economic – in the actual process of assimilation.[17] Such criticism leaves (c) and (d) largely unaffected, and it is therefore broadly true to say that the rejection of any form of recognition of minorities, communities, cultural particularities, ethnic groups, and so on, is the distinctive feature of current French debate. This rejection is why criticism of the (often poorly understood) politics of 'race' in the UK and the US looms so large in France: the integration model in its ideological form could not survive the introduction of an explicitly relaxed attitude towards cultural heterogeneity, but no alternative model is available within the liberal agenda, and even to attempt to formulate one is generally seen as illegitimate.[18]

This underlines the position of research with regard to the policy–politics interface in the 'liberal' agenda (section I). The objective of the state being to minimize direct political pressure on policy, it will seek to promote work conducive to this objective, typically producing bias towards research into the concrete mechanisms of assimilation in the short-term sense favoured by the liberal agenda (paradigmatically education) and into the consequences of failed assimilation (e.g. the preoccupation with 'youth' and with the inner cities – in French terms the *banlieues*), with a view to facilitating social control. Conversely, research based on a longer-term view of, or indifferent to, assimilation will be unwelcome. Similarly, the symbolic gratification of proximity to power, notably the availability of formal or informal positions as policy advisers (the only real option, in the absence of any active research–politics interface, for research that has a claim to relevance) has its own peculiar rules. Policy-makers may not be prepared to listen to challenges to their preconceptions, which makes the balance between the quest for relevance and self-censorship very fine. In particular, research that rejects positivistic objectification and problematization – the view that definitions of 'problems' are independent of the social 'reality' they claim to 'describe' – will be marginalized.

III SECOND MODEL: THE RADICAL AGENDA

As defined here, liberalism has two major weaknesses that together explain the possibility of movement towards a radical agenda (see also Saggar, 1993). The first is epistemological. To combine the quest for state autonomy with methods of social control based on positivistic scientific inquiry leads to the naive and ultimately untenable view that social 'objects' are unaffected by the social analysis applied to them. But to use social analysis in a self-conscious attempt to influence social reality – for example the promotion of the assimilationist ideology deliberately in order to crowd theories of democratic heterogeneity out of public discourse — is to activate the inter-penetration of policy, research and politics that the liberal agenda was intent on avoiding. Assuming the crowding out to be determined, thorough and successful, this strategy may reach an equilibrium in which its contradictions remain latent, but this (which roughly describes the current French situation) is highly precarious.

The second weakness is that liberal depoliticization assumes (implicitly) that state control of the policy–politics and policy–research interfaces is decisive, forgetting that the research–politics interface may be significant and partly autonomous. Anyone wishing to challenge assimilationism has an obvious interest in developing and articulating an alternative agenda, based on a critique of liberalism both on its own terms (how does the practice fit the theory?) and externally (are the implicit assimilationist assumptions valid?). Such an agenda need not be drawn up in academic language, but the ability to draw on the rhetoric of both sophistication and common-sense is an important political resource. The radical challenge to liberalism also provides an alternative strategy of relevance and influence for researchers who would otherwise have to choose between 'officialization' and marginalization. The combination promotes the various interactions that were downplayed in the liberal model: the autonomous influence of research on policy, reciprocal links between research and politics, and effective political pressure on policy.

The development of the radical agenda in Britain from the late 1960s illustrates this. In parallel with the growing restrictions on immigration starting in 1962, laws were enacted banning certain forms of racial discrimination and creating specialised quasi-administrative bodies to implement them.[19] The legislation was however set within the liberal agenda, and concerned less with immigrants' rights for their own sake than with mechanisms of social control designed to further 'good race relations'. It therefore led to cooptation of moderate 'responsible' community leaders rather than to genuine representation. The gradual erosion of the liberal model may be seen as an attempt to reverse this, on the minority's own terms rather than on those (responsibility, respectability, etc.) specified by the establishment. The actual political processes draw together a number of distinct strands.

The first (non-existent in France) is the development of a genuinely radical research agenda, based on an explicit rejection of liberal assumptions about the appropriate relations between policy, politics and research. An early influence was American black nationalism which, although it failed to achieve a distinctively British intellectual formulation,[20] contributed significantly to a new climate of self-affirmation. The major source of intellectual input was however class-based analysis of 'race relations', as developed most influentially in the early work of John Rex (1970, 1973; Rex and Moore, 1967). The resulting mainstream sociological paradigm may be summarized as follows:

(a) The most fundamental relations in modern society are those of economic class.
(b) Immigration is determined by the economic requirements of advanced metropolitan capitalism.
(c) Migrants are objectively part of the working class.
(d) Metropolitan society is divided not just into classes but also into status groups defined by differential access to non-market (particularly welfare-state) resources.
(e) The social position of migrants reflects the interplay of class, status, and the ideologies (particularly racism) that cut across them.
(f) The core of racism is the stigmatization of skin colour.

This model has two major political implications. First, the specific position (if any) of ethnic minorities is determined by the consequences of immigration and racism, neither of which is significantly affected by cultural particularities. West Indians, Indians, Pakistanis and others thus share a common status as 'black'[21] that is far more important than differences of culture (language, religion, family structure, etc.) and directly replicates the phenotypical emphasis, and indifference to distinctions between immigrants, of racist discourse. Second, the natural core of 'black' (as just defined) politics is relations with the 'white' (i.e. non-'black', with the same *political* connotations) working class: in practice with the trades unions and the Labour Party.[22]

This political model has proved remarkably durable, and remains common to most participants in the debate.[23] Thus, notwithstanding major differences of emphasis, Marxist writers accept the basic principle of (non-anthropological) blackness as intimately related to the working-class struggle.[24] The intellectual challenge from sociologists who consider the mainstream concern with class to be excessively structuralist, and insufficiently attentive to the diverse situations, motivations and objectives of social actors (notably Banton, 1967, 1983), is politically marginal. In France, on the other hand, while class-based analysis played an important role in the early strategy of the left-wing parties towards migrant workers (Freeman, 1979), it is entirely alien to current mainstream discussion.

The second feature of recent developments is the appropriation, by people who would describe themselves as black, of the analytical tools of radicalism – originally forged by white radicals much as liberalism was formulated by white liberals. Over the past 20 years the process has gathered momentum as a direct result of disillusionment with the politics of class-based analysis. Political action has not, as it should have in the class-based paradigm, prevented (racial, national and cultural) 'false consciousness' from disguising supposedly common class interests. As increasing social complexity[25] (particularly the post-industrial heterogeneity of the working class) has made status groups of central significance in political identity and mobilization, black people can no longer rely on traditional left-wing politics to further their interests. The black appropriation of radicalism is, on this view, a condition for the black voice to be heard at all.

The anti-racist movement of the 1980s summarizes these tendencies. Its impetus was emphatically black and its core assumption was the inability of the Labour Party to speak for black people. Because, however, leading black politicians are fully aware of the constraints on minority organization in the British political system, their challenge to Labour was delivered from within the Party. Demands for the recognition of black sections, with guaranteed representation on national Party bodies, were a *leitmotiv* of Labour politics in the second half of the 1980s. They were unpopular within the Party and even with the black electorate, and the leadership did its best to neutralize the issue. Despite powerful opposition, however, black activists have, very significantly, been able to keep the problem on the agenda and obtain (a limited degree of) symbolic recognition.

Anti-racism also rejects the liberal attack on discrimination using the civil law as misrepresenting the position of black people in British society by assuming both the perpetrators and the victims to be identifiable persons and, by implication, reducing racism to discrimination. Black radicals contend that British society is *structurally* racist because of deeply entrenched cultural bias. They demand therefore an assault on the exclusionary aspects of mainstream culture, with the ultimate objective of building a new, genuinely non-racist culture. In this view, the liberal concept of colour-blindness serves only to let deep-rooted racism pass unnoticed: the eradication of racism requires heightened colour-sensitivity.[26] Many of the policies conceived to implement this programme – promotion of racially segregated child-adoption, criticism of the standard literary canon as racist, 'racism awareness training' for local-authority employees, ethnic monitoring – have been controversial. While only moderately successful in their own terms, however, they have consistently succeeded in defining a new national agenda.

The third strand in the development of the radical agenda is in some ways the most profound and the most durable. Over the past 15 years, black politicians, activists, academics and intellectuals have acquired a range of political resources. To the rhetorical resource, already discussed, of a coherent, aggressive agenda should be added the electoral resources that have now put six black MPs in the House of Commons. At local level, there are now several hundred black local councillors, who often owe their election to their own machine as much as to party favours (Geddes, 1993). For the same reason, black activists exert considerable influence in the Labour Party through their control of some constituency parties. Many other resources have potential political significance, such as the increased black presence in the media, the professions (notably law) and business which, if nothing else, guarantees that the black population will not in future be left virtually without a voice as in the 1960s.

For comparative and predictive purposes, this analysis requires an important qualification. To the extent that these resources are the natural consequence of citizenship, operating over time in a society with some degree of equality of opportunity, they are irreversible and may be expected to develop in much the same way in France. The whole analysis is however permeated by the radical agenda it seeks to describe. To use the word *black* to designate certain political resources is meaningless unless it is assumed that people actually believe in the relevance of a purely political concept of blackness. There is no *prima facie* reason to think that Indian businessmen contribute to the political clout of the Bangladeshi community, or that a West Indian television personality guarantees British Muslims a voice, precisely because defining people by reference to national origin or religion stresses their divisions. To redefine them as black provides such a reason, but the change is clearly politically highly significant. In this sense there is a close relation between the practical effectiveness of radicalism and the articulation of the research–political agenda that makes it thinkable.

The radical agenda is under increasing challenge in ways that, because of the relation just specified, impact on both politics and research. Anti-racism has been attacked by right-wing Conservatives who have had little difficulty in using its excesses to discredit it. More damagingly, it has been criticized by black radicals who, while accepting its premises in principle, are concerned about its excessive preoccupation with cultural difference, which they see as dangerously similar to that of the racist right (Gilroy, 1990). Interestingly, similar conclusions have been reached, despite the very different ideological context, in connection with the (comparatively anecdotal) French anti-racism of the 1980s (Taguieff, 1987). More generally, there is a growing tendency to reject the radical conception of blackness. The single most important political and theoretical challenge (as a consequence, in particular, of mobilization against Salman Rushdie's *Satanic Verses*) is the new insistence of many British Muslims on being designated by reference to religion and/or national origin (Modood, 1992). It appears to disprove the radical paradigm's analysis of common economic positions as the major determinant of identity or, more accurately, shows its failure to provide, on the basis of this analysis, an effective framework for political mobilization. Yet far from solving the theoretical problems of anti-racism, the competing multicultural agenda that has developed in the past ten years (a variant of the radical paradigm, in the terms of this chapter) has actually aggravated the reification of 'race', 'culture' and 'ethnicity' (Anthias, 1994). To retrieve radicalism requires a reappraisal of its underlying values, its political aims and its analytical content.

IV DOES IT MATTER? SOME CONCLUDING COMMENTS

It is tempting to conclude from this discussion that both the liberal (French) and the radical (British) models are in the process of collapse because of accumulated internal contradictions, that neither provides a solution to any relevant problem, but that the best features of each may be desirable components for a new model. However the two models are not on an equal competitive footing: radicalism developed precisely out of certain major inadequacies of liberalism. In addition, to think of choosing between models, or of designing a model, is to forget that politics cannot in general be evacuated from the policy–research interface. Finally, the crisis of 'integration' takes quite different forms in France and in the UK, and neither is simply related to a cohesive model. There is no way to avoid choosing criteria of judgment (which, inevitably, depend intimately on one's theoretical model) and applying them, empirically, to both cases.

Concern for equality and non-discrimination is common to liberalism and radicalism, and indeed to all attempts to set immigration within a democratic framework. With respect to *formal* rights, France and the UK are essentially similar. It is however now widely accepted in the UK,[27] but overwhelmingly denied in France, that formal rights are not sufficient (Crowley, 1994a). Rejection by French policy-makers and researchers is ostensibly due to incompatibility with the 'French republican model' of integration, but the real reason is that it is almost impossible to take race-related problems seriously within the liberal agenda because of the essentially contested nature of the idea of 'real' equality. This points to one clear advantage for radicalism.

It is more difficult to formulate an overall comparative judgment on politics and the general tone of debate because of the fundamental differences in values that are superimposed on the opposition between liberalism and radicalism. A major French criticism of the British 'model' is that it places excessive emphasis on the preservation of minority culture, to the point of cultural separateness. The French republican model, on the other hand, is far more concerned with the construction of a coherent political community. The argument cannot be dismissed lightly, and the uncertain status of cultural difference is indeed a theoretical weakness of the multicultural variant of radicalism. To deal with the issue in detail is beyond the scope of this chapter, but I would suggest that the exploration of the relations between the fundamental democratic premiss of the radical agenda and the competing conceptions of community as primarily political or cultural is the single most important theoretical task in this field (see further Crowley, 1994b, 1995).

Abstract theoretical analysis cannot, however, provide detailed policy prescriptions. A 'self-conscious framework for authoritative action' cannot be value-free, nor indeed is it desirable that it *should* be. But values take us from the domain of technical expertise into that of political argument. Liberalism and radicalism are not simply analytical concepts, but also reflect value systems. Liberalism is closely tied to a specific end-state principle – assimilation – that in itself is both plausible and in many ways attractive. Liberal assimilationism is however flawed because of its uncertain effectiveness in achieving its own objectives. Conversely, the only alternative to assimilation within liberalism is a depoliticized form of communitarian multiculturalism, no less problematic than its radical counterpart. Radicalism, on the other hand, is compatible with a wide range of end-state principles because its focus is on the political process. Its core is simply that the democratic values taken for granted among 'nationals' should be applied to all. There are no grounds for accepting confiscation of the minority voice by either the state elite (technocracy) or a coopted minority elite (liberalism), still less its outright exclusion. Minority demands, however unorthodox, should be part of the every-day stuff of political debate, framed by the democratic values that legitimize their inclusion.

Whether any straightforward policy prescriptions can be derived from this framework is unclear. The whole point of the plea for democratic 'radicalism' is to highlight the dangers of policy imperialism and to make a case for the indispensability of politics. This requires a shift in thinking more than any particular policy initiative. Some conclusions, often highlighting past mistakes, do however suggest themselves.

Immigration has traditionally been removed from democratic control, raising sometimes acute legitimation issues. The implementation of democracy is however a complex matter. The people who have a legitimate interest in the issue, and therefore a *prima facie* right to participate in controlling it, include both migrants *and* non-migrants. Yet migrants cannot exercise such a right until they have migrated, unless their status is contractual, and thus agreed individually in the context of a system designed to protect migrants' interests in general. In a world too interconnected for its gross inequalities to be sustainable, such a scheme seems wildly unrealistic, and underlines the impossibility of an autonomous, self-contained immigration policy. Paying due attention to the rights, interests and aspirations of migrants themselves means recognizing that, whatever the economic advantages for us, it is not desirable that oppression, fear or hunger should force people to migrate. Conversely, there is ample evidence that, between countries with roughly similar living standards, migration is self-regulating, economically efficient and politically non-problematic.

The absorption of migrants lends itself far better to the application of democracy. I assume, without being able to discuss the issue in detail here, that, over a long period, the natural outcome of social intercourse between people belonging to initially distinct groups is assimilation, in the sense of a blurring of both the boundaries (through intermarriage) and the defining characteristics (through cultural hybridization) of the groups involved. Conversely, where such a process fails to occur, the reasons can invariably be traced to coercive boundary 'policing', which both implements and reinforces reflexively constructed antagonisms that are potential sources of conflict. The responsibility of policy in this respect is primarily negative: neither itself enforcing boundary controls (possibly reflecting, for instance, elite concerns about racial, national or cultural 'purity') nor over-reacting to the inevitable slowness of the process: *de facto* cultural diversity is largely unproblematic and the democratic presumption precludes any form of coercive assimilationism. Even where, because of prior boundary policing or the internal dynamics of migration, long-term spontaneous self-segregation appears to occur, the likelihood that such a process should be genuinely non-coercive is very small, and the state has a straightforward responsibility to protect democracy against crude majoritarianism that does not rely on any value judgment specific to the migratory process.

Thus, paradoxically, policy can achieve both more and less than is commonly recognized. *Less* to the extent that economic interdependence and social complexity prevent technocratic control of the migratory process (as distinct from mere administrative control of physical borders). *More* in the sense that the limits to technocracy open the door of democratic politics to immigration, subject to a basic shift in thinking: the recognition that migrants are human beings and legitimate social actors, rather than simply socioeconomic phenomena.

Notes

1. While contentious, the term remains convenient shorthand for the positive features (as its obvious antonyms *disintegration* and *segregation* suggest) of a process of mutual adaptation within heterogeneous societies. Indeed the underlying issues are articulated in a very similar way in the UK and in France (Weil and Crowley, 1994) – and, in fact, in most of Western Europe.
2. For a more detailed discussion of this distinction, see Crowley (1993).
3. It is impossible within the compass of this paper to summarize all the relevant facts for the two countries. For the historical background, see e.g., on the UK, Layton-Henry (1992), Miles and Phizaclea (1984), Saggar (1992), Solomos (1993); on France, Noiriel (1988), Weil (1991), de Wenden (1988) and, in English, Brubaker (1992), Horowitz and Noiriel (1992).
4. A convenient indicator of the vitality of the liberal model is the relative weight of economics within migration-related research. In the UK or France sociology and political science are dominant (implying that the liberal

Immigration and 'Race Relations' in Britain and France   243

agenda is contested or obsolete), whereas in Germany (Menski, 1994; Spencer, 1994) or Israel (see the chapters in this volume) economists exert a major influence.

5. In British legal usage citizenship differs from nationality (historically the status of a British subject) instead of being, as in France and most other countries, basically a synonym. In addition, to be a British citizen is essentially to be exempt from UK immigration control and confers, contrary to the etymology of the word and to common international usage, no distinctive *political* status.

6. The Commonwealth comprises all former British colonies that recognize the British monarch as 'Head of the Commonwealth' (although many are republics). The colonies that acquired independence after the Second World War (all except Australia, Canada, New Zealand and South Africa) are informally referred to as the 'New Commonwealth'. Until 1983, suffrage rights were enjoyed by all resident British subjects (and since 1983 the law has referred explicitly to Commonwealth citizens, which in practice means exactly the same). Until 1962, the right of free movement and abode (as distinct from merely *de facto* open borders for migrant workers) was also enjoyed by all British subjects.

7. The Act distinguished, for immigration purposes, between citizens of the UK and Colonies, who retained the right of free entry to the UK, and Commonwealth citizens, who were, with certain exceptions, made subject to immigration control.

8. Principally on the grounds that it constituted state sanction for racism, would be detrimental to the UK's relations with the Commonwealth, and was in any case unnecessary since migrant labour flows were self-regulating.

9. The Labour Party won the general election of 1964 with a very narrow majority, and suffered unexpected losses in several seats, attributable apparently to voter resentment of the perceived pro-immigrant stance of the Labour candidates. It was returned to power with an increased majority at the general election of 1966, in which immigration played no significant role.

10. Despite occasional short-lived successes in local elections since the early 1970s, British far-right parties have failed to make any significant national breakthrough. By contrast, the French *Front National*, which has made anti-immigrant sentiment (including calls for compulsory repatriation) a cornerstone of its platform, has, since its initial breakthrough in 1983, consistently attracted between 9 and 15 per cent of the national vote.

11. Even more than 'integration', the term 'assimilation' is contentious, to the point where it is now widely regarded as illegitimate in European political debate. However, on condition that two misunderstandings are dispelled, the concept retains its usefulness. Firstly, the process of assimilation is distinct from the policy designed to promote it. Historically, assimilation has been viewed in coercive terms: as the destruction of minorities' cultural peculiarities by deliberate action premised on the superiority of majority culture (what is here called 'assimilationism'). The construction of modern France proceeded in this fashion, and British responses in the 1960s to New Commonwealth immigration followed a similar pattern. Where, however,

the same process occurs spontaneously, as a consequence of individual migrants' decisions, there seems to be no reason not to use 'assimilation' as a value-neutral description. Secondly, assimilation is often used (and generally argued against) in a narrowly cultural sense. To be assimilated, in this view, is to lose one's language, traditional dress, dietary customs, and so on. That such things may happen (and indeed may be desired by migrants themselves) is not at issue, but the view of culture that they reflect is, paradoxically and misleadingly, both reified and superficial (for the same conclusion from a different perspective, see Gilroy, 1990). Emphasis on external manifestations of culture without reference to family, social and economic structures, and to the physical environment, misses the essence of the problem that assimilation highlights, namely the 'exportability' of culture and the conditions required for the maintenance of community closure (Crowley, 1995). As shown convincingly by Emmanuel Todd (1994), the process of intermarriage (or of persistent endogamy) is the theoretical and empirical core of assimilation.

12. *De facto*. The vast majority of migrants arrived (technically) illegally, and were indeed encouraged to do so on the grounds of enhanced economic flexibility. In legal terms, the state retained tight control over immigration.
13. The two main parties are the christian-democratic UDF (which held the presidency under Giscard d'Estaing from 1974 to 1981) and the Gaullist RPR (which held the prime ministership under Mitterrand's socialist presidency in 1986–8 and 1993–5, and currently holds both the presidency and the prime ministership).
14. The socialists governed France in 1981–4 (in coalition with the communists and the centre-left), and in 1984–6 and 1988–93 (in coalition with the centre-left). President Mitterrand faced right-wing majorities after the legislative elections of 1986 and 1993.
15. The early 1980s saw a high level of political mobilization within the so-called 'second generation' of North African origin (i.e. children born in France of immigrant parents). Within the context of protest against discrimination and inequality, the anti-assimilationist theme of the 'right to be different' (*droit à la différence*) acquired great prominence. Its most visible promoter was *SOS-Racisme*, which had close links with the Socialist Party.
16. The word 'model' itself plays a major role in French discourse, as illustrated by the title of the relevant report of the *Haut Conseil à l'intégration* (1991). It conveniently summarizes the characteristic assumption that there is a single, coherent set of principles that (a) effectively explains historical processes, (b) furnishes directly relevant policy prescriptions, and (c) reflects widely shared norms. Put more simply, *was*, *is* and *ought* are essentially fused. By contrast, Anglo-American debate is predicated on a contradiction between 'is' and 'ought' (Crowley, 1994a).
17. Among references given here, see particularly Horowitz and Noiriel (1992), Noiriel (1988) and Weil (1991).
18. Despite theoretical suspicion of diversity, France is in fact an unusually *heterogeneous* country, particularly if judged by anthropological criteria such as family structure rather than more visible manifestations of cultural practice. The durable combination of diversity and its ideological negation (stretching back to the *ancien régime* monarchy) leads Emmanuel Todd to

the hypothesis that a degree of ostensible denial of diversity is actually a functional requirement for the efficient working of a diverse society (Todd, 1994, esp. pp. 194–382). A similar argument is advanced for the US by Arthur Schlesinger (1992), but it should be stressed that, in Todd's anthropological terms, the US is not in fact diverse, but unusually *homogeneous* (Todd, 1994, pp. 39–107).

19. The Race Relations Acts of 1965 and 1968, which respectively created the Race Relations Board and the Community Relations Commission.
20. For the argument that black nationalism in *both* the US and the UK is inscribed within a broader and deeper-rooted 'black Atlantic' synthesis, see however Gilroy (1993).
21. This peculiarly British usage differs sharply from current US usage. The 'political' concept of 'blackness' is however at the heart of recent British debate, and the vocabulary cannot be modified without betraying the reality of that debate.
22. The quotation marks around the now defined black/white (and their derivatives) will henceforth be dropped. The terms should however always be read with the peculiarly British political definition in mind.
23. It is impossible to prove this within the scope of this paper. As an illustration of how the model described here has permeated common sense, take the following statement (from the introduction to the souvenir booklet of an exhibition on the black presence in Liverpool at the Merseyside Museum of Labour History in 1991): 'Used in its political sense, the word Black applies to all people who have experienced and have a common history of imperialism, colonialism, slavery and racism and may be African, Caribbean, Chinese or Asian'. What is striking here is the straightforward statement, the absence of any qualification of what is clearly regarded as an indisputable *fact* about current British usage.
24. Among references given here, see Miles and Phizaclea (1984) and Solomos (1993).
25. For an attempt to operationalize this notoriously vague concept, see Crowley (1994c).
26. By contrast, the idea that obsessive concern with racism is the best way to eliminate it is universally rejected in France.
27. Acceptance is institutionalized, particularly by the provisions of the 1976 Race Relations Act providing remedies against indirect (non-racially motivated) discrimination.

References

Anthias, Floya (1994) 'Rethinking "Race-Conscious" Policies in Britain', *Innovation – The European Journal of Social Sciences*, 7(3) pp. 249–58.

Banton, Michael (1967) *Race Relations* (London: Tavistock Publications).

—— (1983) *Racial and Ethnic Competition* (Cambridge: Cambridge University Press).

Brubaker, Rogers (1992) *Citizenship and Nationhood in France and Germany* (Cambridge (Mass.): Harvard University Press).

Commission de la nationalité (1988) *Etre français aujourd'hui et demain*, report to the Prime Minister, 2 vols (Paris: La Documentation française).

Crowley, John (1993) 'Paradoxes in the Politicization of Race: A Comparison of the UK and France', *New Community*, 19(4), pp. 627–43.

—— (1994a) 'L'égalité prise au sérieux: le modéle anglo-américain d'intégration dans les débats français', in Bernard Pellegrini (ed.), *Mélanges Vaucresson 1992–4 – Champ et fonction de l'intervention éducative sur décision de justice* (Vaucresson: Centre national de formation et d'études de la protection judiciaire de la jeunesse).

—— (1994b) 'Some problems with multicultural democratization', paper presented at the XVIth World Congress of the International Political Science Association, Berlin: 21–5 August 1994.

—— (1994c) 'Social complexity and strong democracy', *Innovation – The European Journal of the Social Sciences*, 7(3) pp. 309–20.

—— (1995) 'Minorities and Majoritarian Democracy: The Nation-State and Beyond', in Michael Verkuyten and Kebeet von Benda-Backman (eds), *Nationalism, Ethnicity and Cultural Identity in Europe* (Utrecht: ERCOMER).

Freeman, Gary (1979) *Immigrant Labor and Racial Conflict in Industrial Societies – The French and British experience, 1945–1975* (Princeton (NJ): Princeton University Press).

Geddes, Andrew (1993) 'Asian and Afro-Caribbean Representation in Elected Local Government in England and Wales', *New Community*, 20(1) pp. 43–57.

Gilroy, Paul (1990) 'The End of Anti-Racism', in Wendy Ball and John Solomos (eds), *Race and Local Politics* (Basingstoke: Macmillan).

—— (1993) *The Black Atlantic: Modernity and Double Consciousness* (London: Verso).

Haut Conseil a l'intégration (1991) *Pour un modèle français d'intégration*, report to the Prime Minister (Paris: La Documentation française).

Horowitz, Donald and Gérard Noiriel (eds) (1992) *Immigrants in Two Democracies: French and American Experiences* (New York: New York University Press).

Layton-Henry, Zig (1992) *The Politics of Immigration – Immigration, 'Race' and 'Race' Relations in Post-War Britain* (Oxford: Blackwell).

Menski, Werner (1994) *The Impact of Immigration: The German and British Experience* (London: Anglo-German Foundation).

Miles, Robert and Annie Phizaclea (1984) *White Man's Country – Racism in British Politics* (London: Pluto Press).

Modood, Tariq (1992) *Not easy Being British – Colour, Culture and Citizenship* (Stoke-on-Trent: Trentham Books Ltd).

Noiriel, Gérard (1988) *Le creuset français – Histoire de l'immigration XIXe-XXe siècle* (Paris: Seuil).

Rex, John (1970) *Race Relations and Sociological Theory* (London: Weidenfeld & Nicolson).

—— (1973) *Race, Colonialism and the City*. (London: Routledge & Kegan Paul).

Rex, John and Robert Moore (1967) *Race, Community and Conflict: a study of Sparkbrook* (London: Oxford University Press).

Saggar, Shamit (1992) *Race and Politics in Britain* (Hemel Hempstead: Prentice-Hall).

—— (1993) 'Black Participation and the Transformation of the "Race Issue" in British Politics', *New Community*, 20(1) pp. 27–41.

Schlesinger, Arthur (1992) *The Disuniting of America* (New York: W.W. Norton).

Solomos, John (1993) *Race and Racism in Contemporary Britain*, 2nd edn. (Basingstoke: Macmillan).

Spencer, Sarah (ed.) (1994) *Immigration as an Economic Asset: the German Experience* (London: Trentham Books).

Taguieff, Pierre-André (1987) *La force du préjugé – Essai sur le racisme et ses doubles* (Paris: La Découverte).

Todd, Emmanuel (1994) *Le destin des immigrés – Assimilation et ségrégation dans les démocraties occidentales* (Paris: Seuil).

Wayland, Sarah (1993) 'Mobilizing to Defend Nationality Law in France', *New Community*, 20(1) pp. 93–110.

Weil, Patrick (1991) *La France et ses étrangers – L'aventure d'une politique de l'immigration 1938–1991* (Paris: Calmann-Lévy).

Weil, Patrick and John Crowley (1994) 'Integration in Theory and Practice: A Comparison of France and Britain', in Martin Baldwin-Edwards and Martin Schain (eds), *The politics of immigration in Western Europe* (London: Frank Cass).

de Wenden, Catherine (1988) *Les immigrés et la politique* (Paris: Presses de la FNSP).

Index[*]

absorption of immigrants
   direct absorption   108, 162–3, 179, 182
   ex-FSU immigrants in Israeli labor market   5–6, 107–26
   society's willingness   46, 48–52
   Southern California   100–2
   see also integration
academic/scientific occupations   see scientific/academic occupations
'access and equity' policy   214
acculturation   4, 66, 68, 78–81, 83
   bicultural   80, 83
   delayed   79–80
   see also assimilation
age
   immigrant physicians in Israel   130, 136–7, 138, 139–40
   influence on integration   188–92, 202
ageing population   14
aid   101–2
Akbari, A.H.   21
Alba, R.   40
Alonso, W.   1, 15
ambivalence, patterns of   131–2
Americanization   194
Amir, S.   107
'anglo-conformity'   206, 207, 208–9
Anthias, F.   239
anti-immigration policies   2
anti-migrant right-wing parties   51, 58, 59, 232, 243
anti-racist movement   237–9
Arab States   49
Ariav, A.   107
Arslans, Yeliz   49
Asians   49, 55, 56–7
   in Australia   208, 216–17
   in US   41, 56–7, 77, 79, 91–2;
      second generation   69, 73

assimilation   23, 66, 243–4
   Australian policy   206, 207, 08–9
   liberalism and   232–3, 240–1
   'straight-line' theory   19, 66–8, 78, 79
   see also acculturation; integration
attitudinal barriers   132
Australia   8, 46, 200–1, 206–26
   citizenship   50–1, 221–2
   early attitudes to migrants   207–9
   Galbally Report   211
   immigration flows   17
   Jupp Report   213
   multiculturalism   see multiculturalism
Austria   26–7

Baker, S.G.   100
Banton, M.   237
Baron, M.   148
Barsotti, O.   16
Bean, F.   94, 100
Beenstock, M.   107
Belanger, A.   168, 169
Bennett, D.C.   50
Bernstein, J.   127–43
bicultural acculturation   80, 83
blacks   245
   radicalism   236–9
   in US   24, 36–7, 38, 40–1, 193;
      black–white cleavage   200–1
Blau, F.   95
Blau, G.J.   133
Borjas, G.J.   22, 87, 94, 96
Borrie, W.D.   24
Bottomley, G.   210
boundaries   31–2
   'policing'   242
   see also walls
Bouvier, L.   87
Breton, R.   201

---

[*] Prepared by the publisher.

Britain 8–9, 16, 230, 240
  British Nationality Act 1981 47
  citizenship 51, 231, 243
  Commonwealth Immigrants Act
    1962 231, 243
  liberalism 231–2
  Muslims and education 55, 56
  radicalism 236–9
  rights 8–9
Brubaker, W.R. 50
Bullivant, B.M. 215

Caces, F. 167
California 4, 32–3, 86–104
  estimating economic costs and
    contributions 94–6
  global change and local outcomes
    91–100
  immigrants and integration 96–100
  immigration policy 100–2
  resentment of illegal immigration
    52
Canada 17, 18, 21, 46–7, 198–9,
  200–1
capitalism 32
characteristics of immigrants 18, 19
  Israel 111, 150, 168–70, 176–8
Cardenas, G. 95
Carens, J.H. 50
Carmon, N. 1–10, 13–29, 148
Castles, S. 209, 213, 217, 218, 219,
  220
Chassidim 77, 83, 84
children see second generation
Chiswick, B.R. 107
choice: place of residence 174–6
cities
  immigrants and concentration in 6,
    21, 168, 181
  quartered 36–7, 43
  walls 32–3
  see also Tel-Aviv; urban
    restructuring
citizenship
  Australia 50–1, 221–2
  at birth 54
  France 50, 233
  rules as determinant of integration
    48–52, 54

  rights see rights
  UK 51, 231, 243
  US 51, 191, 195–6
Clark, W.A.V. 17, 86–104
class 40, 77–8, 236, 237
  see also social/occupational mobility
Coleman, D. 16
Commission de la nationalité 233
commitment
  determinant of integration 3, 52–6
  immigrant physicians in Israel
    132–3, 133–7, 138, 139–40
Commonwealth 231, 243
communication 211
competition
  for education, jobs and housing
    58–9
  gentrification and housing
    opportunities 161–2
  immigrants as employers 73–4
competition model 147
complementary model 147
concentration, spatial see spatial
  concentration
conflict 23
  between immigrants groups
    99–100, 192–3, 203
  between immigrants and local
    population 51–2, 59
  political power in Los Angeles
    County 98
  see also xenophobia
constitutional equality 195–6
construction industry 74
  Israel 115, 119, 121, 123
costs of immigration 21, 94–6
counter-urbanization 168
Crowley, J. 227–47
Cubans in Miami 40
cultural impact of immigration
  22–5
cultural pluralism 24, 42–3
  contradictions and tensions within
    211
  multiculturalism as 206, 209–15
  valuing migrant community's
    culture 54
  see also multiculturalism
customs, freedom and 199

Dalto, G. 199
De Lepervanche, M. 210
delayed acculturation 79–80
democracy 241–2
demographic changes
  Australia 207–8
  global 90–1
  post-industrial societies 14, 15
determinants of integration 3–4, 46–62
  citizenship rules, rights and benefits 48–52, 54
  labor market 46, 56–60
  migrant preferences 46, 52–6
developing countries 17, 18, 46
development, carriers of 1
direct absorption 108, 162–3, 179, 182
disparities 14–15, 15
dispersion, spatial 7, 168–9, 170–83
dispersion policy 179–80, 182, 208
diversification of lifestyles 14, 25–6
diversity of immigrants 25, 47, 77
doctors *see* physicians
dominating city 36
Donato, K. 100
Doron, A. 179
Dummet, A. 47

economic efficiency 214
economic growth periods 74
economic impact of immigrants 19–22
  estimating costs and contributions 94–6
economic needs, host country's 138–9
economic niches 70–2, 73–4
economic optimization 7, 181–2, 198–9
economic restructuring
  Australia 8, 216–19
  post-industrial societies 14, 16
  urban *see* urban restructuring
economy, ethnicity and 66–81
Edmonston, B. 100
education
  and labor market 57
  multicultural 55–6, 211

  and occupational change 110
  second generation: education-driven upward mobility 68–70, 82; educational failure 72–3
  US 55–6, 194–5
education costs 95–6
Egypt 20, 21, 90
emigration, freedom of 20, 199
employment 15, 19, 87
  absorption in Israel 5–6, 107–26
  choice of place of residence 175–6, 178, 181–2
  decisions in Israeli health-care system 131
  expectations of immigrant physicians 135–6
  opportunities as determinant of integration 3, 56–60
  second generation 4, 65, 66, 68–76
  urban restructuring 144–5, 150–4, 161, 162
  see also labor market; occupations
Enchautegui, M.E. 21, 22, 94
enclaves 3, 30, 38–43, 43, 53
entitlements 87
  see also rights
entrepreneurship 22
Enzensberger, H.M. 22–3
equality 240
  'access and equity' policy 214
  citizenship and multiculturalism 221–2
  constitutional in US 195–6
Espenshade, T.J. 95, 100, 101
ethnic diversity 77, 79, 215
ethnic identity
  and multiculturalism 210, 211–12, 214–15, 215, 217, 218–20
  separate identities 24–5
ethnic succession 70, 73, 82
ethnicity
  changing attitudes to ethnic groups 193–4
  changing ties/labels 187
  economy and 66–81
  interest groups 219–20
  multiculturalism 210, 211–12, 214–15, 218–20
  symbolic 67, 218

Europe 16–17, 46, 50
  see also under individual countries
European Community 17–18
Evans, M.D.R. 51
expectations, immigrants' 20, 135–6, 169–70

Fainstein, N.I. 144
Fainstein, S.S. 144
far right 51, 58, 59, 232, 243
Flug, K. 107–26
former Soviet Union (FSU) immigrants 5, 18, 55, 148
  absorption into labor market 5–6, 107–26
  physicians 6, 129, 132, 134–7, 139, 140
  settlement process in Israel 7, 166–84
  in Tel-Aviv 149, 150–63
Foster, L. 214
Frazier, F. 23
France 8–9, 54, 230, 237, 239, 240
  citizenship 50, 233
  illegal immigrants 17
  immigration flows 16
  liberalism 232–4
  Muslims 55, 56
Franklin, B. 192
Fraser government 211
Freeman, G. 237
Friedberg, R.M. 107
Front National 233, 243
Fuchs, L.H. 24

Galbally Report 211
Gans, H.J. 19, 65–85, 218
Geddes, A. 238
gender
  economic adaptation and 19–20
  immigrant physicians 130, 133–7, 138, 139–40
  see also women
generation 188–92, 202
  see also second generation
gentrification 147, 148, 161–2, 162–3
  gentrified city 36
  Tel Aviv 7, 150, 154–9, 160, 161–2

geographic patterns see spatial concentration; spatial dispersion; spatial separation
Germany 18, 21, 47, 49–50, 52, 53
ghettos 3, 30, 38–43
Gilroy, P. 239
Glazer, N. 23, 24, 24–5
global change 88–91
global orientation 14, 25–6
global responsibility 4–5, 100–2
globalization 146
  social 9, 27
Gold, S.J. 72, 79
Gordon, L.W. 57
government 27
  intervention in housing and public services 162–3
  policy see policy
  role in integration in US 8, 194–200, 202
  support in training 6, 123–4
Graicer, I. 149
Greece 16
Greeley, A.M. 69
Greenfeld, L. 199–200
group egoism 22–3
guest workers 25, 48–9, 168, 231, 233
Gurak, T.D. 167

Hailbronner, K. 49
Haitian immigrants in US 77
Hall, D.T. 137
Hammar, T. 50
Hancock, W.K. 207
Hasson, S. 166–84
Hawke government 213–14
health care system, Israeli 6, 127–43
  gender 132–7
  policy and immigrant physicians 128–30
  structural barriers 131–2
  values 127–8
Herberg, W. 24
Herzlich, C. 136
hi-tech industries 6, 110–11, 123
Higham, J. 195
Hispanics 36–7, 91–2, 97, 98
Hoag, E. 93
Hoefer, M. 93, 102

Hoelter, J.W.   133
Holton, R.   217
home country/homeland/sending
    country   20
    rejection by   53
    second generation and   76–7, 83
home ownership   156–9
host country/receiving country
    disillusionment with   83
    economic gains   22
    economic needs   138–9
housing
    gentrification   147, 148, 161–2,
      162–3; Tel-Aviv   7, 150,
      154–9, 160, 161–2
    Los Angeles   97
    mis-match with jobs   115
    rental   154–6, 170
    policy in Israel   179–80, 182
    settlement patterns in Israel   170,
      175–6, 178–9, 181–2
Howard, J.   221
HREOC Report   218
Huddle, D.   94
human capital   5
    absorption in Israel   5–6, 107–26
    characteristics   *see* immigrants'
      characteristics
    'reconstitution'   119

identity
    ethnic   *see* ethnic identity
    multiple identities   133
    national identity   100–1, 221
illegal immigrants   4–5, 47, 57
    California   93; resentment   52
    children of   74
    growing numbers   17, 93
    measures to reduce   17–18, 100, 101
Ima, K.   73
'immigrant' jobs   4, 65, 66, 70–2
    second-generation decline   74–5
immigration flows
    growing   15–18, 86–7
    Israel   5, 111, 129, 138, 169
    US   17, 46, 88; California   93
immigration sources
    Europe   16
    US   17, 88, 89, 200–1

income disparities   15
individualism   212
informal economy   14, 75
integration   23–5
    Australia   206–26
    British and French experience
      227–47
    determinants of   *see* determinants
      of integration
    economic   19–22
    government role in   8, 194–200,
      202
    models   23–4
    perceived as problem   227–8
    social and cultural   22–25
    urban areas   145–7
    US   96–100; historic experience
      see United States
    see also absorption; acculturation;
      assimilation; policy
interest group politics   219–20, 221
internal migration   168–9, 181–3
    characteristics of internal migrants
      176–8
    choice of place of residence   174–6
    geographical pattern   173–4
    long-term preferences   178–9
investment   20
Iran   90
Israel   5–7, 30
    composition of immigrants in 1990s
      148, 168–9, 169–70, 176–8
    direct absorption   108, 162–3, 179,
      182
    ex-FSU immigrants' absorption in
      labor market   *see* labor market
    government policy   *see* policy
    immigrant physicians   *see* health
      care system; physicians
    immigration flows   5, 111, 129,
      138, 169
    immigration policy   108, 127, 128,
      182, 197
    'Law of Return'   108, 182
    National Outline Scheme (NOS)
      180
    settlement process   *see* settlement
      process
    spatial policy   179–80, 182–3

Israel *continued*
 values and immigration 127–8
 see also Tel-Aviv
Italy 6

Jakubowicz, A. 210
Japan 47
Japanese migrants in US 190–1
Jayasuriya, L. 206–26
Jensen, L. 95
Jewish ghettos 39
Jewish immigrants
 in Israel *see* Israel
 in US 169, 198; Chassidim 77, 83, 84
Johnson, J.H. 99
Johnston, M.E. 199
Jones, M.A. 192
Jordan 20
Jupp, J. 207
Jupp Report 213

Kanungo, R.N. 133, 136
Kargar, H.J. 179
Kasir (Kaliner), N. 107–26
Kejner, M. 133
Kennedy, P. 15
King, R. 16, 95
Korean immigrants in US 71–2
Kymlicka, W. 212

labor market
 American/US 22, 56–7, 75
 Australia 218
 as determinant of integration 46, 56–60
 immigrant physicians in Israel 6, 131–2, 138–9
 impact of immigrants on 21–2, 94
 Israel's absorption of ex-FSU immigrants 5–6, 107–26; comparison with 1979–81 immigrants 121–3; 1990–3 113–15; 1990s 115–21; policy implications 123–4
 post-industrial societies 15–16
 see also employment; occupations
labor migration, temporary 25, 48–9, 168, 231, 233
Labour Party, British 231, 237, 243

language 53–4, 191
Lawrence, J. 97
Layard, R. 101
Lecchini, L. 16
length of residence 177–8, 178, 188–92, 202
Lestschinsky, J. 39
liberalism, political 212
 and integration 230–5, 239–41
licensing, physicians and 128, 129, 131, 131–2
Lieberson, S. 187–205
lifestyles, diversification of 14, 25–6
Lodahl, T.M. 133
Logan, J. 40
Los Angeles County 91–100
Lowell, C. 94
Lynch, L.M. 124

manufacturing sector
 hi-tech industries 6, 110–11, 123
 immigrant employment 115, 116, 117, 118, 119, 122
 Tel-Aviv 149
Marcuse, P. 30–45
Martin, J. 209
Martin, P.L. 168
mass migration 15–18
McCarthy, K. 95
McNulty, T. 40
media 211
medical doctors *see* physicians
melting pot 23–4, 188, 209
Menahem, G. 144–65
Mexico 90, 90–1
 illegal immigrants in US 100
 proposed wall along US–Mexican border 30
minority group rights approach 212–13, 219, 222
mismatch theory 145–6
mobility, social *see* social/occupational mobility
Modood, T. 239
Moreno-Evans, M. 21, 93, 95, 96
Morris, M. 151
Morrison, P.A. 97–8, 98, 169
Mouffe, C. 222
Moynihan, D.P. 24

Index

Mueller, M. 97
Muller, T. 17, 95
multiculturalism 3, 42–3
  Australia 8, 206–26; in crisis
    215–20; as cultural pluralism
    206, 209–15;
    reconceptualization 221–2
  criticisms of 55
  multicultural education 55–6, 211
multiple identities 133
Muslims 55, 56, 239

Nachnias, D. 149
Napoleon Bonaparte 32
nation-state 1, 222
national identity 100–2, 221
naturalization rates 50
  see also citizenship
Netherlands 50
New York City 32–3
Newman, K.S. 71
niches, economic 70–2, 73–4
Nicol, A. 47
Nogle, J.M. 167, 168–9
Noiriel, G. 50
non-confrontation 208

Oberg, S. 16, 16–17, 18
occupational mobility *see*
  social/occupational mobility
occupations
  ex-FSU immigrants in Israel 5–6,
    107–26; absorption by
    occupation 115–23;
    composition 111, 112, 148
  urban restructuring 144–5;
    Tel-Aviv 6–7, 150–4, 155,
    159–61
  see also employment; labor market
Ofer, G. 107, 128, 133
Ogden, P. 16
Oliver, M.L. 99
Ong, P. 97

Pakistan 20, 21
Palestinians 49
Park, R. 23
participation, political 222
particularism 212–13
Passell, J. 93, 100

Peck, J.M. 47
physicians, immigrant in Israel 6,
  127–43
  gender and professional
    commitment 132–7
  occupational absorption 116, 117,
    118, 120
  policy regarding 128–30
  structural barriers 131–2
  place of residence, choice of 174–6
pluralism 221–2
  cultural *see* cultural pluralism
  paradox of 210, 215
polarization, occupational 7, 144–5,
  151–2, 161
policy 203, 227–47
  Australia 207–9; recruitment
    216; *see also* multiculturalism
  determinants of integration 46,
    48–52, 60
  impact on spatial distribution
    168
  Israel 108; admissions policy
    108, 127, 128, 182, 197; direct
    absorption 108, 162–3, 179,
    182; spatial policy 179–80,
    182–3
  liberal agenda 230–5
  multiculturalism *see*
    multiculturalism
  national identity and absorption
    100–2
  policy–research interface 229–30,
    234–5
  radical agenda 235–9
  selectivity 56–7, 111, 195, 207
  US and role in integration 8,
    194–8, 202
  see also government
political change 90–1
political parties 201
political power 87, 98–100
political resources 238–9
politics, policy and 229–42
population dispersion policy 179–80,
  182, 208
  see also spatial dispersion
population growth 90
Portes, A. 40
Portugal 16

post-industrial societies 2, 13–29, 110
  characteristics 13–15
  economic considerations 9–22
  mass migration 15–18
  social and cultural issues 22–5
poverty 14–15, 19, 87
  second-generation decline 75–6, 76–81
Price, C. 218
prison walls 35–6
process, status and 188–92
professional groups 169–70
  downward mobility 109–10, 139, 170
  see also physicians
Pusey, M. 214

quartered city 36–7, 43
quotas 89, 193

Rabinowitz, S. 137
Race Relations Acts 236, 245
racism 245
  anti-racism 237–9
  new ideology in Australia 220–1
radicalism 235–9, 239–41
redistricting 87, 98–100
refugees 51, 52
Rein, M. 206
Reitz, J.G. 201
remittances 20–1
rental housing 154–6, 170
research
  radical agenda 236
  research–policy interface 229–30, 234–5
residence, length of 177–8, 178, 188–92, 202
residential locality, choice of 174–6
residential segregation see separation
resource distribution 101–2
revenues 21, 87, 94–6
Rex, J. 212, 236
right, extreme 51, 58, 232, 243
rights 26–7, 240
  citizenship: as determination of integration 48–52, 54;
  multiculturalism 221–2; US 51, 191, 195–6

Rogers, A. 168, 169
Royal Institute 203
Rumbaut, R.G. 72–3, 79
Russell, S.S. 15, 17, 20
Ryan, W. 212

Samuel, T.G. 168
Sang, D. 208, 217
Sassen, S. 15, 22, 41, 145, 146
Schlesinger, A. 93, 98
Schneider, F. 14
Schnell, I. 149
Schuck, P.H. 51
scientific/academic occupations
  absorption of ex-FSU immigrants in Israel 116, 117, 118, 119, 122
  urban restructuring 151, 152–5, 155
second generation 4, 65–85
  negative scenarios 72–4
  policy and theory questions 76–81
  positive scenarios 68–72
  'second-generation decline' theory 19, 65, 66, 74–6
segregation, residential see separation
selective policy 56–7, 111, 195, 207
separate identity 24–5
separation, spatial 40–3, 97–100, 193, 198, 202
  see also enclaves; ghettos
service sector 14, 70
  absorption of ex-FSU immigrants in Israel 116, 117, 118, 120–1
  urban restructuring 144, 146; Tel-Aviv 149, 154
settlement, ideology of 206–7
  see also Australia
settlement process 7, 166–84
  choice of place of residence 174–6
  geographical pattern of settlement 170–3
  geographical pattern of internal migration 173–4
  immigrants' characteristics 169–70; and internal migration 176–8
  immigrants' preferences 178–9
  Israel's spatial policy 179–80

Index

theoretical and empirical background 167–9
shadow (informal) economy 14, 75
Short, J.R. 145
Shuval, J.T. 127–43
Simon, J. 22, 87, 94
skills
  brain drain 18
  labor market demand 57
  post-industrial economies 16
  relevance for labor market 138–9
  urban restructuring 145–7, 162; Tel-Aviv 152–4, 155
  see also occupations
Smith, N. 35
Smith, R.M. 50
social cohesion 213
social construction of reality 132–7, 138, 139–40
social contracts 3, 46, 47, 48–60
social globalization 9, 27
social impact of immigration 22–5
social networks 78, 167–8, 175–6
social/occupational mobility 19
  downward for professionals 109–10, 139, 170
  ex-FSU immigrants in Israel 5–6, 109–10, 115–23
  immigrant physicians 133, 139
  potential and integration 199
  second generation: decline 65, 66, 74–6; negative scenarios 72–4; positive scenarios 68–72
  urban restructuring 147, 150–1, 159
social optimization 181
Sorenson, E. 94
SOS-Racisme 244
sovereignty 227
Soyal, Y.N. 27
Spain 16
spatial concentration 6, 21, 97, 167–8, 181, 183
  see also enclaves; ghettos
spatial dispersion 7, 168–9, 170–83
spatial policy 179–80, 182–3
spatial restructuring 145, 147, 149–50, 162–3
  immigrants' housing opportunities 154–9, 160, 161–2

spatial separation 40–3, 97–100, 193, 198, 202
  see also enclaves; ghettos
Srole, L. 66–7
state-centred model of policy-making 230, 230–5
Steinberg, S. 69
Steinmann, G. 21
stereotypes 132
Stockley, D. 214
'straight-line' assimilation theory 19, 66–8, 78, 79
suburban city 36
succession, ethnic 70, 73, 82
Sudan 20
Sullivan, M.L. 75
support systems 78, 167–8, 175–6
symbolic ethnicity 67, 218

Taft, R. 23
Taguieff, R.A. 239
tax revenues/contributions 21, 87, 94–6
Taylor, L.J. 94
technology transfers 20
Teitelbaum, M.S. 15, 17, 20
Tel-Aviv 6–7, 148–62
  economic and spatial restructuring 149–50
  housing patterns and preferences 154–9; from rental to ownership 156–9
  immigrants' occupational structure 150–4
temporary migrant labor 25, 48–9, 168, 231, 233
tenement city 2–3, 36
tertiarization of the economy 14
Third World 17, 18, 46
Thoits, P.A. 133
Tienda, M. 87, 95
Tomlinson, S. 212
training/retraining 131, 162
  absorption of immigrants 6, 119, 124
Trejo, S. 96
Trovato, F. 168, 169
Turkish immigrants in Germany 49, 53

258 Index

undocumented immigrants *see* illegal immigrants
unemployment 14, 15
 ex-FSU immigrants in Israel 5–6, 114, 115, 121
UNESCO 24
Union of Soviet Socialist Republics *see* former Soviet Union
United Kingdom *see* Britain
United Nations (UN) 14, 18, 20, 21
United States (US) 32–3, 36–7, 168
 Bracero program 89
 Chinese Exclusion Act 1882 89
 citizenship 51, 191, 195–6
 classification of immigrant status 47
 economic impact of immigration 21–2
 education 55–6, 194–5
 enclaves and ghettos 38, 39, 40–1, 42
 historic experience of integration 7–8, 187–205
 illegal immigrants 17, 100, 101
 Immigration Act 1924 89
 Immigration Act 1965 89–90
 immigration flows 17, 46, 88; California 93
 Immigration Reform Control Act 1986 (IRCA) 17, 93, 100, 101, 102
 Jewish immigrants 169, 198
 labor market 22, 56–7, 75
 melting pot 23–4
 origins of immigrants 17, 88, 89, 200–1
 proposed wall along US–Mexican border 30
 Quota Act 1921 89
 second generation *see* second generation
 separate ethnic identities 24–5
 skilled immigrants 18
 waves of immigrants 102
 see also California
universalism 212–13
unskilled immigrants 57, 116, 117, 118, 121
 see also occupations; skills

urban restructuring 6–7, 144–65
 competing approaches 145–7
 immigrants and urban economics 144–5
 policy implications 162–3
 spatial changes and integration of immigrants 147
 Tel-Aviv *see* Tel-Aviv

Valdez, R. 95
values
 and immigration in Israel 127–8
 liberalism and radicalism 240–1
Vinkoor, A. 107
voice 238–9
von Laue, T.H. 1
voting power 87, 98

wages 87, 94
Waldinger, R. 70, 79
walls 2–3, 30–45
 enclaves and ghettos 38–43
 quartered city 36–7
 types of 34–6
Warner, W.L. 66–7, 81
Warren, R. 93
Waters, M.C. 77, 77–8, 187, 189, 194
Wayland, S. 233
wealth redistribution 101–2
Weil, P. 233
Weiner, M. 46–62
Weintraub, S. 95
West Indians 77–8
White, P. 21
Whitlam government 209
Williams, R. 210
willingness
 society's willingness to absorb immigrants 46, 48–52
 willingness–aspiration confusion 189
Wilson, W.J. 40, 75
Wirth, C. 209
Wirth, L. 23
Woldemikael, T.M. 77
women
 economic adaptation 19–20
 immigrant physicians 133, 134–7, 138, 140

occupational absorption 114, 115
second generation 78, 83
see also gender

xenophobia 22–3
factors affecting 58–9

hostility in US 192–3
politicisation of 227, 231–2
see also conflict

Zlotnik, H. 168
Zubryzcki, J. 213, 214